Jazz
A Century of Change

Jazz:

A Century of Change

Readings and New Essays

Lewis Porter

SCHIRMER BOOKS
An Imprint of
SIMON & SCHUSTER MACMILLAN
NEW YORK

PRENTICE HALL INTERNATIONAL
LONDON • MEXICO CITY • NEW DELHI • SINGAPORE • SYDNEY • TORONTO

Schirmer Books
An Imprint of Simon & Schuster Macmillan
1633 Broadway
New York, New York 10019

Book design by Charles B. Hames

Permissions to reprint works excerpted in this volume may be found on
pages 287–88.

Library of Congress Catalog Number: 97-25600
Printed in the United States of America
Printing number
1   2   3   4   5   6   7   8   9   10

LIBRARY OF CONGRESS CATALOGING-IN-PUBLICATION DATA
Jazz : a century of change / readings and new essays. Lewis Porter.
     p.   cm
Includes index.
  ISBN 0–02–864713–0
  1. Jazz—History and criticism.   I. Porter, Lewis.
ML3507.J42   1997
781.65—dc21   97–25600
                                                   CIP
                                                   MN

This paper meets the requirements of ANSI/NISO Z39.48–1992
(Permanence of Paper).

Contents

Preface   vii
Acknowledgments   xi

1. Where Did the Word *Jazz* Come From?   1

2. Definitions   13

3. Analyzing Jazz   39

4. Where Did the Music Come From?   77

5. Responses to Early Jazz, 1919 to 1934   121

6. African Americans and the Swing Era   159

7. Reactions to Bebop   173

8. The Drug Problem   189

9. Race Politics and Jazz in the 1950s and 1960s   197

10. Avant-garde and Fusion: Two Opposites?
1960 to the Present   219

11. Traditionalism, Revivalism, and
the "Young Lions," 1980 to the Present   245

12. Crossing Boundaries, 1980 to the Present   275

Bibliography   283

Permissions   287

Index   289

Preface

Over the years, while researching my books and articles, I have made a habit of saving any article devoted to jazz that I have come across, in English, French, German, Italian, and a few other languages. I have found many interesting things that were of great value but were not generally known. When Schirmer's senior editor Richard Carlin suggested I compile an anthology specifically devoted to jazz history, I was well prepared.

When jazz began, and each time it changed, there was controversy. And each time, the debate revolved around the question, What is jazz? This book is organized around some key questions regarding jazz—its origins, the word *jazz*, definitions, and analysis of the music—and its important movements, such as 1920s jazz, swing, bebop, "avant-garde," fusion, and the repertory movement. Throughout I focus on these matters. This book is not a collection of profiles of jazz greats, nor of interviews with them. For a reader who wants such profiles there are many places to turn, such as the various anthologies of Whitney Balliett's work. I don't think this book, however, presupposes a deep knowledge of jazz artists. References to specific artists in these pages are generally tied in to a particular discussion, and wherever some further identification is needed I have provided it in my notes. By focusing on the issues rather than on a few individuals, I hope to show that jazz history is a lively, evolving process. I've tried to illustrate in places how the history and problems of the jazz community are connected with and relevant to the larger society.

I've also attempted to approach some of the major issues in jazz history without giving simple answers and pat solutions. Part of the reason jazz historiography, the writing of history, is in a state of flux is that there is not one universally accepted solution for each question. In this compilation I occasionally push a particular point of view, but I think it is obvious when I do, and I have tried to present other points of view for historical balance. So, for example, I have included a number of theories about the origins of the word *jazz*, and both positive and negative, flattering and insulting, responses to the jazz of the 1920s and of the present.

With regard to those insults, I trust the reader will understand that these articles necessarily reflect attitudes held by each author in his or her place and time. I've made no attempt to censor these voices of the past, even when their statements, particularly regarding African Americans, are downright rude. I believe strongly that knowledge is power, and that full disclosure, no matter how it hurts or embarrasses, makes us stronger, more informed, and more prepared to deal with the prejudices that still remain in human society. Of course, neither I nor Schirmer Books shares or condones those prejudices.

The African American press has been much neglected in writings about jazz. Editors usually offer the excuse that there were no African Americans writing about jazz until perhaps the 1960s, but for evidence these skeptics have only looked at what was the mainstream white press of the day. Before the 1960s everything was more segregated, and blacks who were writing about jazz—there were not many, but there were some—were writing primarily in black newspapers and in general-interest, nonmusic magazines for black audiences. I have included a few samples by African Americans from each time period. This volume is also international in scope; a number of British and French publications are represented, and there is one contribution by an Austrian critic.

Each chapter consists of a new essay that outlines some of the key issues and presents excerpts from a variety of sources. Complete bibliographical information is provided for those who want to read further, as well as a few additional references. The essay is followed by a few longer extracts. To keep this collection to a manageable length, there are in some cases only one or two longer articles per topic, in other cases as many as five or six articles. Where I felt it necessary, I have added missing words in brackets to clarify the meanings of the originals. Original spellings have been retained, but obvious errors have been silently corrected.

It is my hope that the reader will finish this book with a real sense of jazz and its history, a vital sense that cannot be obtained through reading a conventional narrative. This book can stand alone to introduce readers to the basic issues in jazz history and will also work well as a complement to a narrative history (such as *Jazz: From Its Origins to the Present,* by myself and Michael Ullman, with Ed Hazell, for Prentice-Hall) or to a selection of profiles. The jazz novice will, I hope, find this selection a stimulating introduction to the historical process of jazz, while the initiated should be fascinated to read materials not generally available. Most of the writings excerpted here have not been reprinted since their original publication dates. Two—Krin Gabbard's piece on Louis Armstrong and Peter Pullman's transcription of the interview with Jelly Roll Morton—appear here in versions that have not been published before.

Acknowledgments

Three colleagues—Carl Woideck, Bill Kirchner, and Steven Strunk— gave me detailed and helpful comments, for which I'm grateful, on the first draft of this collection. Woideck also shared comments about drugs made by Charlie Parker and Cab Calloway, and reminded me of Armstrong's piece on bebop in *Metronome*. Kirchner steered me toward some biographical information about Abbe Niles (via Dick Sudhalter) and showed me Francis Davis's piece "Like Young." Joshua Berrett handed me the Charles Winick study, and Paul Cohen discovered the Julius Korngold item. Dan Morgenstern, director of the Institute of Jazz Studies and my colleague at Rutgers-Newark, provided detailed responses to my list of queries.

My assistant, Steve Bloom (a fine jazz guitarist himself), helped research and obtain permissions for many of the articles. Every attempt has been made to locate the copyright holders of the pieces that are quoted in part or in their entirety.

It has been a pleasure working with Richard Carlin, Jill Lectka, Andrew Libby, and Alicia Williamson at Schirmer Books.

Lewis Porter
RUTGERS UNIVERSITY–NEWARK

Jazz
A Century of Change

1

Where Did the Word *Jazz* Come From?

To start at the beginning, what is this word *jazz*? The problem in tracing the word is that it originated as slang, that is, as a spoken and not a written word. Evidence of this genesis is that its spelling was not standardized in the early days. Looking, for example, at the 1917 ad for the first recording by the Original Dixieland Jass [*sic*] Band, generally considered the first jazz record, it states "Spell it Jass, Jas, Jaz, or Jazz—nothing can spoil a Jass band."

The reader will find herein much interesting discussion about the origins of this word and quotations of the earliest known printed references to it (which are about sports, not music). But be forewarned: not one theory about the origin of the word has been proven true, and many have been proven false. In the 1920s it was often said that *jazz* was a shortened version of the name "Jasbo" and that it was named after the band of Jasbo Brown in Chicago. The bandleader James Reese Europe told a similar story in 1919, except his band was named "Razz's band" and it got changed to "jazz's band." Both stories appear to be fairy tales.

None of the linguistic theories about *jazz* has been proven—not the theories that relate it to African words, or the one that relates it to the French word *jaser* (to chatter), or the one that relates it to the slang word *gism*, which meant "enthusiasm" but also may have meant "semen." All of the derivations from foreign languages are speculative because they are purely based on the sound of the word, and etymologies based on sound alone are notoriously unreliable. Numerous words sound alike that are unrelated. One must show an actual connection, such as the speakers of one language influencing or evolving into speakers of another. Remember that most African Americans were several generations away from African languages by 1900. Further, as we will see, the word *jazz* first appears among whites, not in black society. However, it is certain that individual African words survived in African American culture, and it is possible that whites picked up or adapted the word *jazz* from black speech. In New Orleans, the original center of jazz, many blacks were partly of French ancestry and were known as black Creoles. In addition to English, they spoke a variant of French called "Creole" or "Creole patois" (French for dialect), to which they imported some African words. Here are the linguistic suggestions of Clarence Major, a distinguished novelist and poet and a professor at the University of California at Davis:

> Jazz . . . very likely a modern word for *jaja* (Bantu), which means to dance, to play music . . . possibly a Creole version of the Ki-Kongo word *dinza*, and the early New Orleans variant "jizz"; also, from Creole *patois* ("to speed things up"); another, less likely theory has it that "jazz" is a French word meaning sexy or sensuous. . . . Another theory has it that "jazz" is derived from the African word *jaiza*—the sound of far-off drums. (Clarence Major, *Juba To Jive: A Dictionary of African-American Slang* [New York: Viking, 1994], p. 255)

Major seems to favor the first suggestion, *jaja*, which he elsewhere implies came to the United States with the African slaves as far back as the 1600s.

Major's reference to Creole patois is a little unclear, but I believe he means that the dialect has a word like "jazz" that means "to speed things up." This reference, however, is probably incorrect, as it originally came from a much-quoted but unreliable source, an article written by Walter Kingsley in 1917. Dick Holbrook, a specialist on the word *jazz,* explains that Kingsley was simply a press agent whose assignment was to publicize the famous producer Florenz Ziegfeld's then-current musical show, "Midnight Frolic," which apparently used some jazz songs. Holbrook says that Kingsley's account of the word's origin "is fiction. Kingsley invented it. . . . Savants forgot who said it, where and when—and ended up quoting each other!" ("Our Word JAZZ," in the British periodical *Storyville* 50 [December 1973–January 1974]). (*Storyville* was established in 1965 and published many groundbreaking articles during its thirty-year existence. Jazz writers have yet to discover much of its information. The publication is highly recommended for further reading.) Kingsley's piece is further discussed in Lawrence Gushee's article in chapter 4.

Holbrook favors the idea that *jazz* came from *gism,* as explained in his article "Our Word JAZZ." Holbrook's reasoning is as follows:

> Peter Tamony, the San Francisco etymologist with a long list of credits in this field of American Speech, wrote a most informative critique on the word "jazz" in the first issue of Ralph Gleason's *Jazz*—a quarterly of American music. This was in October 1958. . . .
>
> I was impressed to read in Peter Tamony's 1958 report on *Jazz, The Word* that the early Americanisms "gism" and "jasm" helped launch our word "jazz". I think they did. They date well back into the 1800s—always carrying the meaning of spirit, energy, talent, courage, enterprise, enthusiasm and ability. A second colloquial meaning is "semen", the male sperm.
>
> *Gism* and *Jasm* sound much alike. With the passage of years could not the ear have lost that final soft "m" sound—and left us with *Jazz?*
>
> *Gism* is listed in Bartlett's *Americanisms,* published in 1877. An example was in print as early as 1848, says Tamony. *Jasm* appears in an 1860 book called *Miss Gilbert:* "If you'll take thunder and lightning and a steamboat and a buzz-saw and mix 'em up and put 'em in a woman, that's jasm." Again, in the September 1886 edition of *Harper's Magazine:* "Willin', but hain't no more jas'm than a dead corn-stalk." (Dick Holbrook, "Our Word JAZZ," *Storyville* 50 [December 1973–January 1974])

We must remember, however, that his reasoning, though impressive, is still a theory. The *Oxford English Dictionary* notes under "jazz" that the connection between *jazz* and *jasm* "cannot be demonstrated."

Still, several commentators have reported an early sexual connotation of the word. For example, language professor Robert S. Gold, in his useful reference book *Jazz Talk* (New York: Bobbs-Merrill, 1975), cites *The Journal of Abnormal and Social Psychology* ([April–June 1927]: 14–15) as follows: "Used both as a verb and a noun to denote the sex act, jazz has long been common vulgarity among Negroes in the South, and it is very likely from this usage that the term 'jazz music' was derived."

Holbrook collected some opinions from old-timers about this:

> I canvassed some of the older alumni of my college who had come from the Far West and had graduated (from Dartmouth) before 1912. One replied, "Yes, I recall hearing the word Jazz used as a slang sex word in California, New Mexico, Arizona and New Hampshire since 1904 to now." Another man wrote, "Yes. Circa 1910—in Chicago. When you went out for a little Jazz, you just weren't singing *Dixie*." (Dick Holbrook, "Our Word JAZZ")

Holbrook continues with the first known printed use of the word *jazz*, which appeared in a newspaper story about George McCarl, a promising new member of the San Francisco Seals baseball team! The Seals were holding practice games at Boyes Springs in Sonoma County, California.

> When did our word *jazz* first appear in print? Again, give the credit to Peter Tamony. He found it in the *San Francisco Bulletin,* one of the daily newspapers of that city, in the month of March, 1913. The Tamony article reproduces a story by "Scoop" Gleeson that ran on the sports pages March 6th. Three days earlier, in another story by "Scoop" Gleeson, the word *jazz* first sees the light of day. . . . "McCarl has been heralded all along as a 'busher' but now it develops that this dope is very much to the 'jazz.' He has more boosters right now than any other two players at the Spa."

Sportswriting is a language all its own. . . . A "busher" is a clumsy novice. But that reputation, reported Gleeson, was very much *to the jazz.* Like: a lot of hot air? . . .

In various later uses, the word seemed to fit a good many situations and meanings. Here are quotes from his baseball stories March 6th to 29th:

6th March: "Everybody has come back full of the old 'jazz.' What is the 'jazz'? Why, it's a little of that 'old life,' the 'gin-i-ker,' the 'pep,' otherwise known as the enthusiasalum. The team which speeded into town this morning comes pretty close to representing the pick of the army. Its members have trained on ragtime and 'jazz' and Manager Del Howard says there's no stopping them."

Note: "Jazz" is still in use to imply "pep and enthusiasm," though its coupling with "ragtime" is prophetic of its ultimate musical meaning.

8th March: "Spence the catcher zipped that old pill around the infield. He opened a can of 'jazz' at the tap of the gong. Henley the pitcher put a little more of the old 'jazz' on the pill."

14th March: "A few days has made all the difference in the world up at Boyes Springs—where there's 'jazz' in the morning dew, 'jazz' in the daily hot bath, and "jazz" in the natural spring water. Even if there's one 'jagger' (loafer?) in among the crowd of 'jazzers,' prospects are none the less bright."

24th March: "This is about the time when the first innoculation of the old 'jazz' wears off. This is the last week of the boys at Boyes, and a grand 'jazz' party has been prepared for the last night. At that time the Seals will be wished all kinds of success by the camp followers and farewells will be exchanged until another year."

Note: This was to be a pep rally—not a musical shindig.

29th March: "Now the local players have lost the 'jazz' and don't know where to find it. The San Francisco club of today is made up of 'jazzless' Seals. There is a chance that the old 'jazz' was sent by parcel post—which may account for its failure to arrive yesterday. Manager Del had better send out a hurry call for the 'jazz wagon.' Quick! Quick! Bring on the old 'jazz'!" . . .

. . . In the course of further question-and-answer correspondence with sportswriter Edgar "Scoop" Gleeson, he mentioned that a fellow-reporter on his paper did a feature article on the word *Jazz* not long after the sports stories ran. With the help of several Bay City friends I found the story. . . . (Dick Holbrook, "Our Word JAZZ")

In Praise of "Jazz," a Futurist Word
Which Has Just Joined the Language

ERNEST J. HOPKINS

This column is entitled "What's not in the news," but occasionally a few things that are in the news leak in. We have been trying for some time to keep one of those things out, but hereby acknowledge ourselves powerless and surrender.

This thing is a word. It has recently become current in The Bulletin office, through some means which we cannot discover but would stop up if we could. There should be every precaution taken to avoid the possibility of any more such words leaking in to disturb our vocabularies.

This word is "Jaz." It is also spelt "Jazz," and as they both sound the same and mean the same, there seems to be no way of settling the controversy. The office staff is divided into two sharp factions, one of which upholds the single z and the other the double z. To keep them from coming to blows, much Christianity is required.

"Jazz" (we change the spelling each time so as not to offend either faction) can be defined, but it cannot be synonymized. If there were another word that exactly expressed the meaning of "jaz," "jazz" would never have been born. A new word, like a new muscle, only comes into being when it has been long needed.

This remarkable and satisfactory-sounding word, however, means something like life, vigor, energy, effervescense of spirit, joy, pep, magnetism, verve, virility, ebulliency, courage, happiness—oh, what's the use?—JAZZ.

Nothing else can express it.

When you smile at the office-boy (time, 7:30 a.m.) as though you thought him nice, that is "jaz." When you hit the waiter for serving you cold waffles, that is "jazz." When you work until midnight, then get up and work until midnight again without cursing your boss, that is "jaz." When you look upon a girl and she loves you, that is "jazz."

Some idea of the utter usefulness and power of this wonderful word now begins to appear.

You can go on flinging the new word all over the world, like a boy with a new jack-knife. It is "jazz" when you run for your train; "jaz" when you soak the umpire; "jazz" when you demand a raise; "jaz" when you hike thirty-five miles of a Sunday; "jazz" when you simply sit around and beam so that all who look beam on you. Anything that takes manliness or effort or energy or activity or strength of soul is "jaz."

We would not have you apprehend that this new word is slang. It is merely futurist language, which as everybody knows is more than mere cartooning.

"Jazz" is a nice word, a classic word, easy on the tongue and pleasant to the ears, profoundly expressive of the idea it conveys—as when you say a home-run hitter is "full of the old jaz." (Credit Scoop.) There is, and always has been, an art of genial strength; to this art we now victoriously give the splendid title of "jazz."

The sheer musical quality of the word, that delightful sound like the crackling of a brisk electric spark, commends it. It belongs to the class of onomatopoeia. It was important that this vacancy in our language should have been filled with a word of proper sound, because "jaz" is a [*sic*] quite often celebrated in epic poetry, in prizefight stories, in the tale of action or the meditative sonnet; it is a universal word, and must appear well in all society.

That is why "pep," which tried to mean the same but never could, failed; it was a rough-neck from the first, and could not wear evening clothes. "Jazz" is at home in bar or ballroom; it is a true American.

To conclude, just a few examples of its use.

"Miss Eugenia Jefferson-Lord was clad in a pink pongee creation suitable for a rainy day, and of great jaz." (Society Notes.)

"Our Harry, sighting true for once, swung the willow against the pill with all his jazz." (Baseball account.)

"Though fatally shot, the unfortunate captain still had sufficient jaz to murmur 'He done it' in the ears of the police." (Murder story.)

"All the worl' am done gone crazy, Yassah, sure it has; How mah brain am reeling, dazy, Sighin' for the ol', ol' jazz!" (Plantation melody.)

"And Saturn strode athwart the cedarn grove, Filled with the jaz that makes Creation move!" (Paradise Lost.) (*San Francisco Bulletin*, April 5, 1913)

Holbrook cautions the reader that all the "examples" given at the end of Hopkins's piece are fabricated: "Don't be tempted to go through the 107,542 lines of [John Milton's poem] 'Paradise Lost,' as I did, to find no trace of Hopkins' garbled Milton!"

Some of the original uses of the word jazz still survive. People still use it to mean "lively" or "energetic," as in "That's a real jazzy outfit" or "Let's jazz up this party." Sometimes one still hears it in the sense of "hot air": "Don't give me any of that jazz." (I like saxophonist Jackie McLean's way of turning this phrase around. Back in 1986 he told me that he liked to say "Don't give me any of that classical stuff!") One can reasonably assume that the word *jazz* was in use, at least around San Francisco, a bit before 1913, but it must have been fairly new or the writers would not have needed to explain it to their readers.

Although New Orleans musicians traveled quite a bit (despite the old canard that they stayed home until 1917), the fact that the word *jazz* first came to light in San Francisco, as far as we know, makes one question whether it is a New Orleans word, or even a black American or African-derived word. Lawrence Gushee, music professor at the University of Illinois and probably the leading researcher on early jazz, notes that most New Orleans musicians say they first heard the word *jazz* in the North after the first Original Dixieland Jazz Band recordings in 1917 (see pages 102–3).

Two reported uses of the word *jazz* prior to 1913 turn out to be spurious. One comes from Jasper (or Jaspar) Ridley's biography of Henry Palmerston, prime minister of England in the mid-1800s. As William Safire reported:

In a chapter on the Belgian crisis of 1831, historian Ridley quotes this private letter from Palmerston: "I am writing in the Conference, Matuszevic copying out a note for our signature, old Talley jazzing and telling stories . . ."

Wow. I zipped the evidence off to Robert Burchfield, chief editor of the Oxford Dictionaries, known to wordsmen as "Superlex" . . .

"If Palmerston's word has been read correctly by Jasper Ridley," writes Mr. Burchfield—adding, parenthetically, "(historians can never be trusted in this respect in the end)," and, oh, will he hear from the historians—"it must be an isolated Anglicized spelling of French *jaser*, 'to chatter, to gossip.'" (William Safire, "On Language," *New York Times Magazine*, April 1981)

Ironically, Burchfield himself may have spread the other erroneous attribution, since it is found in the 1989 edition of the *Oxford English Dictionary* and he was editor of the supplement that was incorporated into this edition. The long entries on "jazz" include a marvelous collection of citations showing the word used in a variety of printed sources from 1916 on. The first and earliest citation, however, is not from a printed source:

1909 C. STEWART *Uncle Josh in Society (gramophone record)*, One lady asked me if I danced the jazz.

In his article, Dick Holbrook reported on the origin of this Stewart citation, proving it false:

Peter [Tamony] gave me his reprise on this study—dated December, 1968. Among his addenda is this: "During 1960, while auditing *Uncle Josh In Society*, Victor 16145 (recorded 1906–08?), I was surprised to hear Cal Stewart's monologue, including, 'Well, they had a dance. I think they called it a *cow*tillion. Well, sir, I hopped right out on the floor, and cut more capers than any young fellow there. Just looked as though all the ladies wanted to dance with me. One lady asked me if I danced the jazz, and I told her no. . . . I danced with my feet. Ha ha!'."

This would have been a most important documentation of the earliest proven use of the word jazz. . . . except that the critical sentence, "One lady asked me if I danced the jazz. . . ." is *not* on the record. I have the record myself. All the rest of the quoted monologue is there—but *not* the part about Jazz. I'm afraid Peter Tamony got swindled on that and was reporting what somebody else told him. But I assure you, dear reader, wherever else the word jazz might have been heard before 1910, it was *not* on any gramophone record. (Dick Holbrook, "Our Word J AZZ")

So the 1913 date for the first printed use of the word *jazz* still holds. The next step in the progress of the word was for it to be applied to a type of music, as was only hinted at in the above 1913 reference to training on "ragtime and 'jazz.'" The sports writer E. T. "Scoop" Gleeson recounted in 1938 how he thought the word first became attached to a musical group. His story, reproduced in Peter Tamony's article, is, however, anecdotal and not generally accepted. Gleeson recalled that bandleader Art Hickman performed for dancers at Boyes Springs while the San Francisco Seals were practicing there. He continued:

> [T]he very word "jazz" itself, came into general usage at the same time. We were all seated around the dinner table at Boyes one evening and William ("Spike") Slattery, then sports editor of *The Call,* spoke about something being the "jazz", or the old "gin-iker fizz."
> "Spike" had picked up the expression in a crap game.
> Whenever one of the players rolled the dice he would shout, "Come on, the old jazz."
> For the next week we gave "jazz" a great play in all our stories. And when Hickman's orchestra swung into action for the evening's dances, it was natural to find it included as "the jazziest tune tooters in all the Valley of the Moon." (E. T. "Scoop" Gleeson, "I Remember: The Birth of Jazz," *San Francisco Call-Bulletin,* September 3, 1938, p. 3)

It may be that Hickman's orchestra was described as "the jazziest," but nobody has found this line in any printed story. It seems generally agreed and more reliable that the word spread to Chicago, where the white New Orleans band of Tom Brown was described as *jazz* in 1915, and that the name became applied to that type of music in general. (Gushee confirms Tom Brown's priority.)

In fact, the word *jazz* was applied to a much wider range of music than it is today. In the 1920s, white observers writing about jazz used the term to refer to the written songs of George Gershwin and Irving Berlin just as much as to the recordings of such black artists as Duke Ellington and Louis Armstrong. In fact, black artists are often not mentioned at all in contemporary writings. For instance, Henry O. Osgood's *So This Is Jazz* (originally Boston: Little, Brown and Company), one of several pioneering books on the subject published in 1926, does not refer to any African Americans.

This omission has been taken to indicate that people in the 1920s didn't know what jazz was, as in French critic Hugues Panassié's *The Real Jazz* (published in French, 1940; first English edition, New York: Smith and Durrell, 1942; revised and corrected edition, New York: A. S. Barnes and Co., 1960). This influential volume opened with a chapter entitled "True and False Jazz," wherein Panassié states that "the public has not the least idea of what this music really is" because the word *jazz*, which "originally" referred to music in the "true" Negro style, had become "wrongly" associated with "a commercial counterfeit of jazz" offered by Paul Whiteman and others. The author had made similar distinctions in his earlier book, published in English as *Hot Jazz* (New York: M. Witmark and Sons, 1936), but at that time he had not realized that, "from the point of view of jazz, most white musicians were inferior to black musicians."

Panassié's views were widely accepted among serious jazz fans, but in practice, as we will see in chapter 2, there are not universally accepted criteria by which to sift out false jazz from true. It makes more sense, and it is more respectful to the people of the 1920s, to conclude that "jazz" really meant something different at that time. As Nick Straus, a former graduate student at Rutgers University, suggested, when a majority of people are using a word in a certain way they *cannot* be wrong, because each word is defined precisely by the way the majority employs it. In practice, "jazz" was used to refer to any kind of popular, dance or jazz music with a lively beat.

We must also realize that when the 1920s is called "the Jazz Age" it's in that same spirit. From today's vantage point, we could say the average person in the 1920s was no more a jazz fan than the average person today, and the broader sense of the word that was current at the time applied to much of the popular music that everyone did like.

The name *jazz* stuck, for better or worse, and many musicians—Duke Ellington was among the first—objected to it because of its negative connotations. Some musicians claimed that the use of the word *jazz* was intended to equate the music with sex or semen, but that's not so. For one thing, that use of the word hasn't been proven. Second, it's clear from the early references that the writers only meant that the music was lively. It was the nightclubs that employed the musicians that were associated with liquor and sexuality. Many middle-class blacks opposed jazz for that reason; many whites who disliked jazz held not only a negative view of the music but also a negative, racist view of blacks as people. Thus, jazz musicians found it difficult for their music to gain a stronghold in influential circles and education institutions.

Surely, jazz music's rise to respectability has paralleled and been intertwined with the rise of black people in American society. And it is surely good news on both fronts that the word *jazz*, to the younger generation, no longer has any negative connotation. In my teaching of college students I have seen a change during the past twenty years. Since around 1990, when I talk about historical prejudice against jazz and the music's disrespectable reputation, my students tell me they have never heard of such a thing. For all the work still needed to improve race relations, this lack of stigma marks important progress. Meanwhile, it is no accident that, also since around 1990, jazz has become a regular part of the programming at Lincoln Center, the Kennedy Center, and elsewhere. These important arts centers presented many jazz programs in the past, but as occasional enterprises, not as part of an ongoing series.

Over the years there have been many attempts to rename jazz music, but none has caught on, and each had its problems. Jazz is "African American classical music" (but then what of George Walker, Hale Smith, and T. J. Anderson, who write for chamber groups and orchestras?); it's "black music" (but so are many other kinds of music); it's "improvisational music" (but so are most types to some degree, contrary to common perception); and so on. "Jazz" is surely here to stay, so let's be thankful that the stigma of the past has faded and vanished.

2

Definitions

Now that we've agreed to keep the word *jazz*, let's try to understand how we distinguish it from other types of music. Regardless of whether or not we think it is valuable to categorize things, experience tells us that we do, in fact, make distinctions between jazz and other types of music. Although we may not be able to decide in every specific case whether we consider something jazz—or we may not care to do so—it is useful to examine what general principles we employ in trying to make such distinctions.

Let's begin with the insights of Jelly Roll Morton, a leading early jazz musician and recording artist from New Orleans. Although not really a definition in the formal sense, his words are an invaluable look at what this early stylist thought was important to his art. Born Ferdinand Joseph Lamothe (sometimes incorrectly spelled Lemott; his birth name and date were uncovered by Lawrence Gushee), Morton talked about the musical elements of jazz, or the characteristics that he considered essential. Morton was interviewed by Alan Lomax, a folklorist working for the Library of Congress, during several sessions from May to December 1938. Lomax had recorded the black blues and folk master Huddie "Leadbelly" Ledbetter in 1933 (his first recordings) and documented other kinds of American music, but Morton was his only jazz subject.

Morton turned out to be a terrific choice. An engrossing story-teller and a marvelous musician, he had a vast amount of experience in the business and wasn't afraid to give out his opinions. He sat at the piano throughout the interviews, amply illustrating his points with examples and playing complete pieces as well. At one point he got into a general discussion on the nature of jazz. The recordings were first issued to the public in the late 1940s, but some bits have, to date, never been issued. Much of what Morton said was printed, in edited form, in Lomax's book *Mister Jelly Roll* in 1950 ([Berkeley: University of California Press], pp. 63–66), and the following passage was also transcribed and published by Ralph Gleason. For this book, author and jazz researcher Peter Pullman has transcribed all of Morton's words from the original recordings, issued or not. (I have lightly edited it as well after hearing the issued recordings.) Pullman has effectively rendered not only what Morton says but how he says it.

"A Discourse on Jazz"

JELLY ROLL MORTON

NOTE: *These words are all Morton's, except for the few statements of Alan Lomax (AL).*

That was "The Kansas City Stomp." You may notice that in playing jazz, the breaks are one of the most essential things that you can ever do in jazz. Without breaks and without clean breaks, without beautiful ideas in breaks, you don't need to even think about doin' anything else; if you can't have a decent break, ya haven't got a jazz band or you can't even play jazz.

AL: Show us a good break, Jelly.

(Morton plays a two-bar piano break.)

That's what ya call a pretty good break (not totally satisfied with himself). For instance, I'll play just a little bit of melody of somethin' and show you.

(Morton plays a piano solo with breaks; talks while playing:)

That's what you call a break. Maybe I better play something that you can understand more, for instance "[Darktown] Strutters' Ball."

(Piano solo)

AL: (while Morton plays) You're strutting?

I made those breaks kinda clean because, the fact of it is, everybody knows this tune and they know how it's played and they['ll] know where the break come in.

Without a break, ya have nothin'. Even if a tune have no break in it, it is always necessary to arrange some kind of a spot to make a break. Because without a break, as I said before, you haven't got jazz. And [you wouldn't have] your accurate tempos with your backgrounds of your figures which is called riffs today. Of course, that happens to be a musical term, *riffs*.

AL: What's the difference between a riff and a break? Aren't they about the same thing?

Oh, no, no. There's difference, uh, a riff is a background. A riff is what ya would call the foundation—as like you would walk on, something that's standard. And a break is somethin' that you break; when ya make the break, that means all the band break but [except] maybe one, two, or three instruments. It depends upon how the combination is arranged, and as you, as the band breaks, you have a set given time, possibly two bars, to make a break.

AL: Isn't the break what you, when you, when you make the breaks, isn't that what you mean by swingin'?

No, no, that's not what swingin' is. Swing don't mean that. Swing means somethin' like this.

(Piano solo)

Third speaker (possibly Charles Edward Smith): . . . to have that conception of it, ya know, I mean . . .

Okay, I'll, I'll show you what's the slow thing. Oh, absolutely, [there's] a lot of people have the conception, but the conception is wrong. Uh, naturally, a person's conception is bound to be wrong unless they know what they're talkin' about. Uh, a lot of times you may be right, but that only comes from guess work. The fact of it is, every musician in America had the wrong understanding about jazz music. Somehow or 'nother it got into the dictionary that jazz was considered a lot of blattin' noise and discordant tones, that is something that would be even harmful to the ears.

I know many times that I would be playin' against different orchestras, and I would notice some of the patrons as they would be dancing around. They'd get near to an orchestra—of course, I wouldn't permit mine, so (laughs) I'd, I'd be a little more careful than that—they'd get near to an orchestra and they['d] hold their ears. I heard a very funny fellow said once in a colored dance, "That fellow blows any louder, he'll knock my eardrums down." Of course, you gotta be careful of that.

Jazz music is based on strictly music. You have the finest ideas from the greatest operas, symphonies, and overtures, in jazz music. There's nothing finer than jazz music because it comes from everything of the finest class music.

AL: Well, show us what this discordant type of jazz was like, Jelly.

Well, it's so noisy, it's impossible for me to prove to you because I only have one instrument to show to you, but I guess the world is familiar with it. Even Germany don't want it, but she don't know why she don't want it, because of the noise—that's why. Italy don't want it because of the noise. Jazz music is to be played sweet, soft, plenty rhythm; when you have your plenty rhythm with [your] plenty swing it becomes beautiful. To start with, you can't make your crescendas and diminuendas [*sic*] when one is playing triple forte. You've got to be able to come down in order to go up. If a glass of water is full, you can't fill it any more, but if you have a half a glass, you have an opportunity to put more water in it, and jazz music is based on the same principles.

(Plays piano while he says the following.)

I will play a little number now of the slower type to give you an idea of the slower type of jazz music, which you can apply to any type tune; that depends upon your ability for transformation.

(Plays a very flowery, impressive solo based on a familiar chord sequence.)

There you've got sweet jazz music.

AL: (While Morton plays) [What's the name of it?]

I don't, I don't have any name for it—just a number that I just thought I'd play a while here just to give a person a good idea here.

(Continues to play and performs a brief double-time passage, then comments:)

That's also one of my riffs in, what ya call riffs in jazz, you know, in [the] slow tunes. I've seen this blundered up so many times, it has given me the heart failure.

(Continues playing)

No, I haven't got a drum, that's my foot if you happen to think of something I (laughs) could [say].

More formal definitions of jazz generally bog down in such details as whether all jazz swings, if all jazz is improvised, and so on. At one level, perhaps all this detail is unnecessary. Since when does a definition have to contain such a detailed description of the thing being defined? For example, if we define a chair as "a piece of furniture with a back to it, for sitting on," nobody would suggest we then need to describe its color, its type of wood, or its design. Similarly, we tend to group together under "classical music" everything from Gregorian chant to Philip Glass and so on. Nobody could possibly describe what all of these pieces have in common, for what they share is not a common sound but a common history.

Likewise, in the case of jazz, it may be enough to say that jazz is a type of music developed by African Americans in and around New Orleans in the early years of the twentieth century and since practiced all over the world, and in which improvisation is central, a certain type of "swinging" rhythm (relying heavily on a walking bass) is typical (but not essential), and expressive characteristics of African American music generally (such as "blue notes") are important to the generic sound. But where do we go from there when faced with a particular example of music? That's where Mark Gridley comes in. A psychology professor, Gridley has another career as a jazz historian and has written *Jazz Styles: History and Analysis* (Upper Saddle River, N.J.: Prentice-Hall, 1997, 6th edition), a widely used textbook. He and two colleagues have done an admirable job of re-creating the thought processes we go through when confronted with a new piece of music and when trying to categorize it. (I realize that we could decide not to categorize it at all, but the exercise is useful nonetheless.) Their article begins with a useful sampling of definitions and comments on jazz. It proceeds to discuss three ways in which people have defined jazz in practice. A "strict definition" states that, to be jazz, music must have certain agreed characteristics. A "family resemblances" approach maintains that, like classical styles, jazz styles do not share one thread running through all, but are connected historically; they are members of one family. Finally, one can approach jazz as a dimension; some music is very jazzy (or has a high degree of "jazzness," as the authors prefer), some is slightly jazzy, and some is not jazzy at all. The authors feel that jazz fans tend to use this last approach, while scholars may be more inclined to use the first. (I tend to use the second approach myself, which is more inclusive.)

Three Approaches to Defining Jazz

MARK GRIDLEY, ROBERT MAXHAM, AND ROBERT HOFF

We will examine three approaches to defining jazz. None of them is entirely satisfactory, but each has virtues that the others lack. All specify somewhat different, though overlapping, bodies of music that can be called jazz. Too few speakers and far too few authors take the time or thought to explain what they mean by jazz. When they assume that listeners and readers share their frame of reference, endless problems result. The term "jazz" has always been particularly problematic. Even its origins are in dispute, and it has been used in widely disparate ways. This has caused endless controversy, much of which is probably needless. Numerous books on the subject do not even offer a definition of the term.[1] When a definition has been attempted, the results have often been confusing. Compare, for example, the following definitions that have been offered by various journalists and teachers:

> Sigmund Spaeth: "Jazz is not a musical form; it is a method of treatment. It is possible to take any conventional piece of music, and 'jazz it.' The actual process is one of distorting, of rebellion against normalcy."[2]
>
> *Chambers' Encyclopedia*: "Jazz—dance music, generally syncopated, played by a band eccentrically composed. The jazz drummer, a sort of one-man band, provides the characteristic feature of jazz, which is noise. . . ."
>
> Virgil Thomson: "Jazz, in brief, is a compound of (a) the fox trot rhythm (a four measure, alla breve, with a double accent), and (b) a syncopated melody over this rhythm."[3]
>
> Henry Osgood: "It is the spirit of the music, not the mechanics of its frame or the characteristics of the superstructure built upon that frame, that determines whether or not it is jazz."[4]

---

1. Recent examples include *Jazz: America's Classical Music* by Grover Sales, Prentice-Hall, 1984; *Jazz: A Listener's Guide* by James McCalla, Prentice-Hall, 1982; and *The Origin and Development of Jazz* by Otto Werner, Kendall-Hunt, 1984.
2. "Jazz Is Not Music," *The Forum* (Aug. 1928).
3. *American Mercury* (Aug. 1924).
4. *So This Is Jazz* (Boston, 1926), p. 26.

George Antheil: "The works of Vincent Youmans are clear, and extremely beautiful examples of jazz that is a pure music."[5]

Wilder Hobson: "To some it means the whole cocktail-swilling deportment of the post-War era. To others it suggests loud and rowdy dance music. Many people go so far as to divide all music into 'jazz' and 'classical.' By 'classical,' they mean any music which sounds reasonably serious, be it 'Hearts and Flowers' or Bach's 'B-Minor Mass,' while their use of 'jazz' includes both Duke Ellington's Afric brass and Rudy Vallee crooning 'I'm a Dreamer, Aren't We All?' . . . But Duke Ellington bears just about as much relation to Vallee as the 'B-Minor Mass' to 'Hearts and Flowers.' . . . Ellington's music is jazz."[6]

Willie Ruff: "More than anything else, jazz is a feeling, a way of playing music, a way a musician feels at any given time. It isn't written . . . we want to give musicians room to improvise. . . . Another important ingredient in jazz is syncopation."[7]

Leonard Bernstein: "Jazz is a very big word; it covers a multitude of sounds, all the way from the earliest Blues to Dixieland bands, to Charleston bands, to Swing bands, to Boogie-Woogie, to crazy Bop, to cool Bop, to Mambo—and much more. It is all jazz . . . it is an original kind of emotional expression, in that it is never wholly sad or wholly happy. . . . Rhythm is the first thing you associate with the word 'jazz.' . . . But jazz could not be jazz without its special tonal colors, the actual sound values you hear. . . . A popular song doesn't become jazz until it is improvised on, and there you have the real core of all jazz: improvisation."[8]

Harvard Dictionary of Music (2nd Edition): "A kind of indigenous American music of the 20th century, originally identified with social dancing, featuring rhythmic patterns peculiar to the 'jazz beat.'"[9]

Joachim Berendt: "Jazz differs from European music in three basic elements: 1. a special relationship to time, defined as 'swing' 2. a spontaneity and vitality of musical production in which improvisation plays a role 3. a sonority and manner of phrasing which mirror the individuality of the performing jazz musician. These three basic characteristics create a

---

5. In a letter to the editor of *The Forum,* published Dec. 1928.
6. *Fortune* (Aug. 1933).
7. 1958 Young Audiences lecture/demonstration that was recorded and released as *Jazz For Juniors,* Roulette R5205.
8. "The World of Jazz" from CBS "Omnibus" series, telecast Oct. 16, 1955.
9. Cambridge, Mass., 1972, p. 317.

novel climate of tension, in which the emphasis no longer is on great arcs of tension, as in European music, but on a wealth of tension-creating elements, which continuously rise and fall. The various styles and stages of development through which jazz has passed since its origin around the turn of the century are largely characterized by the fact that the three basic elements of jazz temporarily achieve varying degrees of importance, and that the relationship between them is constantly changing."[10]

Henry Martin: ". . . jazz is a twentieth century music originated in America by black Americans and characterized by improvisation and a strong projection of rhythm."[11]

Max Harrison: "Attempts at a concise—even a coherent definition of jazz have invariably failed. Initial efforts to separate it from related forms of music resulted in a false primacy of certain aspects such as improvisation, which is neither unique nor essential to jazz or swing (the quality of rhythmic momentum resulting from small departures from the regular pulse), which is absent from much jazz, early and late."[12]

Lay uses of the term have been so confused and inconsistent that the following popular issues remain unresolved, pending a clear and consistently applied definition for jazz: Is jazz art music? How can we answer this question unless we have clear definitions of jazz and of art music? And what definition of jazz would apply to the music of Al Jolson from his 1927 film *The Jazz Singer* or the music of Peter, Paul, and Mary, that won first place in the vocal division of "jazz" popularity polls run by *Playboy* in 1964, 1965, and 1966?

Was jazz popular during any given era of twentieth-century music? Can the highly arranged music of certain best-selling records of the 1930s and 1970s be called jazz if it lacks improvisations or if improvisations are so brief that they do not contribute significantly to the overall result?

How should we interpret discographer Brian Rust's statement about Glenn Miller: ". . . the majority of the Bluebird and Victor sides are of little or no jazz interest . . ."?[13]

---

10. *The Story of Jazz* (Englewood Cliffs, NJ, 1978), p. 7.
11. *Enjoying Jazz* (New York, 1986), p. 4.
12. *The New Grove Dictionary of Music and Musicians,* Vol. 9 (London, 1980), p. 561.
13. *Jazz Records,* Vol. 2 (Chigwell, England, 1970), p. 1125.

To attack these questions and dilemmas, we will look at three different kinds of definitions and test their fit on styles that have proved especially difficult to classify. We will examine first a strict definition that requires improvisation and swing feeling. A second and different approach ties styles together only by family resemblances. The third is an "essence approach" in which the relative presence of certain components determines the relative "jazzness" of a performance.

Framing a Strict Definition

Let us first evaluate a strict definition that requires a performance to be improvised and to swing in the jazz sense.[14] For the sake of the preliminary parts of this discussion we shall say that "to improvise" is to compose and perform simultaneously; "to swing" is to project rhythmic qualities that elicit from the listener the perception of a lilting, buoyant feeling peculiar to jazz. (Such circularity in this characterization is unavoidable here.) Traditionally, swing feeling and improvisation have been considered essential to jazz. In fact, these two traits are prominently featured in all fifteen texts that are currently used in the United States as introductions to jazz or jazz history.[15] Musicians and music publishers routinely use improvisation and ability to swing as jazz characteristics. For example, in music publishers' brochures describing big band arrangements, a note is frequently included to the effect that "only the first tenor saxophone part requires jazz," meaning that the first chair tenor saxophonist is the only member of the band who must improvise during performances of a particular arrangement. Similarly, a musician's contractor might phone a player requesting he fill the "jazz trumpet" chair in a band, meaning that the player will have the responsibility of improvising solos in addition to the ordinary responsibilities of doing "section work" (playing ensemble parts).

---

14. As opposed to swinging in a general sense, a quality ascribed to any successful performance of music that has steady tempo and lively execution; see Mark C. Gridley's *Jazz Styles* (1978), pp. 14–16.

15. Leroy Ostransky, *Understanding Jazz* (1977); Frank Tirro, *Jazz: A History* (1977); Jerry Coker, *Listening to Jazz* (1978); James Lincoln Collier, *The Making of Jazz* (1978); Charles Nanry, *The Jazz Text* (1979); Joachim Berendt, *The Jazz Book* (1982); Donald Megill and Richard Demory, *Introduction to Jazz History* (1984); Paul Tanner and Maurice Gerow, *A Study of Jazz*, 6th Edition (1988); James McCalla, *Jazz: A Listener's Guide* (1982); Henry Martin, *Enjoying Jazz* (1986); Grover Sales, *Jazz: America's Classical Music* (1984); Nathan Davis, *Writings in Jazz* (1978); Otto Werner, *The Origin and Development of Jazz* (1984); Joseph Levey, *The Jazz Experience: A Guide to Appreciation* (1983); and Mark Gridley, *Jazz Styles: History and Analysis*, 3rd Edition (1988).

The interchangeability of the terms "jazz" and "improvisation" is common in the music business. A brief perusal of record and concert reviews or a little eavesdropping among musicians will also reveal that the quality and extent of swing feeling is frequently the topic of discussion among listeners describing a jazz performance. This is also a popular topic among teachers and students who are involved in teaching and learning the skills of jazz performance. It is widely assumed, therefore, that there is some general agreement on the meaning and utility of these terms.

The requirement that a performance contain improvisation allows us to differentiate jazz from other types of music that swing, such as popular music, which bears swing feeling and frequently can be heard on American radio and television broadcasts (e.g., André Kostelanetz, Ray Coniff, Percy Faith, Broadway show music of the 1950s, much music that might be jazzy or jazz-influenced though not ordinarily called jazz). This also allows us to differentiate types of music that sound quite similar. Herb Alpert's music is usually unimprovised and therefore differentiable from Chuck Mangione's, which usually contains enough improvisation to qualify for the "jazz" label. The common view that "jazz is a feeling more than anything else" implies that a musician's playing must elicit swing feeling from his listeners in order to qualify the player as a jazz musician. And the requirement that a performance must swing in a jazz way allows us to distinguish jazz from rock, Indian music, and other nonjazz idioms that use improvisation.

Problems become evident when we observe that either of these two criteria, when taken individually, applies to a larger number of styles than when both are taken together. The union of the two terms into a single definition creates difficulties. For instance, some performances that have been called jazz do swing but contain little, if any, improvisation. Some of Duke Ellington's and Stan Kenton's concert pieces fit this category.[16] Other performances have been called jazz and do contain improvisation, but don't swing. The Johnny Hodges sax solo in "Come Sunday" from Ellington's *Black, Brown & Beige* as well as some

---

16. All but the brief trombone solo in Ellington's "Work Song" from *Black, Brown & Beige*, Kenton's recording of Robert Graettinger's "Dance Before the Mirror" from *City of Glass*, Capitol W736.

performances of the Art Ensemble of Chicago[17] and Cecil Taylor[18] fit this category.[19]

Despite this difficulty of excluding so many performances that are ordinarily classified as jazz, a strict definition of jazz requires the presence of both swing feeling *and* improvisation. If we want to include as many styles that have been called jazz as possible, the best approach to framing a strict definition might lie neither in loosening the term "jazz" itself (so that it includes styles that are called "jazz" merely by association with the jazz tradition) nor in excluding either swing feeling or improvisation. It might lie instead in adopting flexible definitions for swing feeling and jazz improvisation.

In the process of framing flexible definitions for jazz improvisation, we must confront several knotty questions. For example, what constitutes improvisation in the jazz sense? How extensive must it be and how fresh?[20] Can it be no more than variations of timing and the alteration of ornaments?[21] Or must it be full-blown melodies and accompaniments?[22] Is it sufficient that a musician repeat patterns acquired either through his own creative effort or through his familiarity with the works of others?[23]

---

17. *People in Sorrow,* Nessa n-3.

18. *Silent Tongues,* Arista A1 1005.

19. On April 22, 1982, the students in a jazz appreciation class at John Carroll University said that the Taylor improvisation "doesn't swing at all." On Oct. 26, 1985, the participants at the meeting of the American Musicological Society, Allegheny Chapter, agreed that the Hodges solo did not swing. On Feb. 22, 1986, panelists and audience in Denver, at the Colorado Endowment for the Humanities "What Makes It Jazz" session, concurred that the Art Ensemble selection did not project swing feeling.

20. See Robert Brown's "How Improvised Is Jazz Improvisation" in Charles Brown (ed.), *Proceedings of N.A.J.E. Research* (1981), pp. 22–32.

21. Listen to the Johnny Hodges solo cited earlier, as well as various versions of his solo on "Things Ain't What They Used to Be"; compare, for instance, his July 30, 1945, Victor recording with his 1959 Columbia recording.

22. Compare the Paul Gonsalves sax solos on these two versions of "Cop-Out": March 13, 1957, available on a Columbia sampler called *Jazz Omnibus* (Columbia CL 1020) and Sept. 8, 1959, on Duke Ellington's *Festival Session* (Columbia CL 1400).

23. Charlie Parker occasionally reused some of the phrases first recorded by him on "Now's the Time" Nov. 26, 1945, for Savoy; Miles Davis has frequently quoted his own phrases originally recorded by him April 22, 1959, available on *Kind of Blue* (Columbia CL 1355). These are not exceptions. They constitute accepted practice. In fact, many jazz musicians can be identified by the astute listener who detects the player's favorite phrases in a new recording. Jazz musicians frequently quote each other's favorite phrases, sometimes an entire chorus being re-created. Gridley once attended a nightclub performance in which Sonny Stitt inserted note-for-note Lester Young solos into his tenor sax solos and note-for-note Charlie Parker solos into his alto sax solos. Jon Faddis has crafted a jazz trumpet style by quoting Dizzy Gillespie phrases, and Wynton Marsalis has done similarly with Miles Davis phrases.

If we are to be flexible, perhaps it behooves us to realize that no poet or novelist can be expected to write in a language entirely original to him, purged of all idioms and clichés. Likewise, it would be unfair to expect that jazz musicians create not only fresh "paragraphs" and "sentences," but even the "phrases" and "words" they use. So the frequent recurrence of standard patterns should not by itself disqualify a passage as improvisation. In a strict definition for jazz, it might be useful to allow that an improvisation can be constructed from preexisting elements, but only if these elements are reorganized and this reorganization takes place at the very moment they are performed.

How extensive must improvisation be in order to qualify a performance as jazz? We ought to ask, "What minimum amount of improvisation should be necessary in a performance before we can call that performance 'jazz'?" Some of a jazz performance certainly needs to be improvised, such that significant aspects of each performance are not preset. For a flexible application of the improvisation requirement, let us suggest that the amount of nonpreset material be just low enough to include performances in which improvisations are the outstanding feature and just high enough to exclude works that do not exhibit improvisation as a prominent feature. Note, however, that this would result in removing the jazz label from much of the big band dance music of the 1930s and 1940s, thereby taking out of the jazz category a large body of music that many usually consider to be jazz.

We also have to classify cases in which a performer arranges or simply repeats someone else's improvisations. The music of Supersax and Manhattan Transfer are examples.[24] The strict definition would exclude these cases perhaps justifiably because the premium that many jazz musicians place on spontaneity is well worth preserving, and it is dangerous to confuse this jazz kind of spontaneity with other forms of musical expression that are essentially interpretive. Therefore, in defining jazz improvisation, let us rule out improvised alterations of

---

24. On *Supersax Plays Bird* (Capitol ST 11177), Buddy Clark has arranged phrases from Charlie Parker improvisations and scored them for five saxes. Manhattan Transfer is a vocal group that specializes in re-creations. Their version of Joe Zawinul's "Birdland," for instance, takes not only the ensemble parts from the original recording by the band called Weather Report, but also the sax and piano improvisations and sets lyrics to them for vocal performance.

timing and ornaments when such alterations constitute the only changes that occur from performance to performance, changes that should be classified as "interpretation" rather than "improvisation."

If we adopt a strict definition of jazz, then what can be said about performances in which the music does not seem to be improvised? Some of Duke Ellington's concert music, as well as the nth repetition of his band's hits, fall into this category. (For instance, many recordings of his "Cottontail" differ very little from each other.) If we define jazz rigidly so that some improvisation is always required, then such performances cannot be jazz. This may seem to be a ludicrous conclusion, but it is both logical and useful. In fact, a term for such works already exists: swinging concert music. And this term not only saves the marriage of jazz and improvisation, but it also creates a category for a musical tradition that, though deriving from jazz, might better be kept separate.

We also confront several knotty questions when we try to frame a flexible definition for jazz swing feeling. Ordinarily the feeling is described as a quality of experience elicited by music, and it is frequently characterized as a buoyant, lilting feeling that pulls the listener along. Scholars and music psychologists remain unclear about precisely what causes listeners to report that a given performance swings, but a few ideas have received wide discussion. One is the presence of "swing eighths," patterns in which alternate eighth notes are slightly lengthened or shortened, yielding a ratio of about 60:40, rather than the straight 50:50. (This may remind music historians of the phenomenon of improvised *notes inégales* in the music of the baroque era.) The 60:40 pattern is significant because it is a discernible and quantifiable component in the music that has traditionally been considered "swinging."[25] A second, objectively quantifiable predictor of swing feeling is steady tempo, and a third, somewhat less easily measurable predictor is a balanced proportion of syncopated rhythmic figures.

The prediction of swing feeling via the presence of swing eighths, steady tempo, and syncopation provides some of the methodology necessary to categorize any performance as swinging, since those features

---

25. See Richard Rose's "Computer-Assisted Swing," *Jazz Educators Journal* (1985), 17, 3, 14–15.

can be verified by acoustic analysis. But the mere presence of any of these is not sufficient to allow us to reliably predict the listener's judgment of a performance's swingfulness. The presence of syncopation, for instance, is not sufficient to evoke swing feeling in the listener. In fact, there is a good possibility that the amount of syncopation in a performance corresponds in a curvilinear fashion to perceived swing feeling. In other words, if amount of perceived swing feeling were plotted against amount of syncopation, the resulting graph would take the shape of an inverted U.[26] For example, too much syncopation might be part of the reason that some of Cecil Taylor's playing does not swing.

A fourth suggested cause of jazz swing feeling is the alternation of tension and relaxation that has been described by Hodeir in 1956, Pekar in 1974, and Gridley in 1985. Gridley said that the alternation in density of activity might be an objective correlate of the subjective impression of tension/relaxation.[27] Hodeir described the ride rhythm (quarter note, dotted eighth note, sixteenth note, quarter note) as possessing the same properties. Gridley believes that not only does this occur in the typical jazz drummer's work but also in the rhythms of an improvised line. In other words, on the suggestion of Peter Manuel of Columbia University, Gridley thinks that syncopation might constitute density of activity and function as an anacrusis while on-the-beat playing might constitute diffuseness. To alternate such characteristics is to alternate the subjective impression of tension with that of relaxation.

As a fifth suggestion, there is also a relationship between the detectability of the tempo and the degree of perceived swing feeling. In other words, even in pieces that are constant in tempo, naive listeners have ranked the music as less swinging if they had, also and independently, rated the beat as "difficult to detect."[28] Not entirely consistent with this finding is a sixth possible cause for jazz swing feeling: the spontaneous, slight expansions and contractions of the duration for each measure. (This would mean that absolutely constant tempo is incompatible with swing feeling.) Related to this is a seventh element: the common type of rhythmic displacement that toys with the beat

---

26. See André Hodeir's *Jazz: Its Evolution and Essence* (1956).
27. Mark C. Gridley, *Jazz Styles: History and Analysis,* 2nd edition (1985), pp. 7–8.
28. Gridley, unpublished study, presented to Society for Ethnomusicology, April 24, 1982, Kent, Ohio.

within the improvised line—*à la* "tempo rubato." It is also possible there is an interaction such that we cannot measure or even estimate the relative contribution of each individual element.

Even the availability of a methodology for predicting the listener's response to the objective determinants of swingfulness, however, is not sufficient to settle all doubts about what jazz swing feeling is. Musicians and critics tend to agree that swing feeling constitutes a dimension of musical perception. This means that some performances swing more than others. We also need to note that swing feeling is not only a quantifiable dimension but also a multifaceted group of qualities, amenable to description in terms of distinctive varieties. For example, few listeners would argue with the statement that pianist Count Basie swings in a way that is qualitatively different from that of pianist Duke Ellington and that pianist Bill Evans swings in still a third way. (And some listeners claim that Evans fails to swing at all.) Additionally, many suggest that the swing feeling that typifies dance bands of the 1930s differs qualitatively from the swing feeling typifying jazz/rock bands of the 1970s. If this is not already confusing enough, listeners frequently disagree as to whether a given performance swings a lot or not at all—although both might agree that the performance was highly spirited. The most flexible view is best exemplified in a classic article, "Swing as an Element of Jazz,"[29] in which Harvey Pekar made clear distinctions among the earliest jazz musicians in terms of the extent of swing feeling that each projects in his playing, and he made clear distinctions between the swingfulness of Sonny Stitt and Ornette Coleman. Yet at the end of his piece, Pekar encouraged us to remain open to "nonswinging" jazz, music that comes from the jazz tradition but fails to swing. He also asked whether swing feeling would continue to be as important in jazz of the future as it was in jazz of the past. Before responding to Pekar's suggestions, let us propose that, in a strict definition of jazz (requiring both improvisation and swing feeling), the definition of swing feeling would have to include performances about which listeners disagree—which elicit swing feeling in at least some listeners.[30]

---

29. *Coda* (Aug./Sept. 1974), pp. 10–12. [Updated and republished in *Jazziz* (June 1996).]

31. Note that swing feeling here is a purely rhythmic phenomenon. A band can play out of tune yet still swing.

Although listeners may agree that certain performances are rhythmically similar and other performances are rhythmically different, they disagree about whether those same performances swing, because listeners use the term "swing" to denote their own emotional response to a given sound; some listeners are pleased by the same sound that fails to move other listeners. (Gridley has interviewed jazz musicians who felt that John Coltrane's playing on *Interstellar Space,* Impulse ASD 9277, swings, and other who felt that it does not swing at all.) It is important to note that these listeners are not hearing differently; they are responding differently to what they hear. We are dealing here with situations in which the percept is the same but the affect is different.[31] At the earliest stages of processing the sounds, all listeners agree. This is the recognition stage. At later stages in processing those same sounds, listeners disagree. This is the result of differences in what happens at a deeper level, the associative stage. After the sounds are first perceived, the perceptions interact with the listeners' own idiosyncratic ways of thinking and feeling, ultimately leading to a response ("That's really swinging!" or "These guys just don't swing!").

Harvey Pekar's suggestions, especially because they reflect so much historical perspective, lead us to the question of whether a strict definition for jazz is truly workable, especially if it requires that a performance swing. Pekar's observations force us to consider reclassifying the music of players who do not swing but whose music is improvised and stems from the jazz tradition. Perhaps it should instead be called improvised concert music. Pekar's suggestions cause us to remove so many performances that have been loosely called jazz that we question the utility of framing a strict definition. However, if the swing requirement is applied with some flexibility, defining jazz by requiring it allows us to include most of the music that has traditionally been called jazz. On the other hand, the more flexible form of the definition is still useful enough to exclude music like *Rhapsody in Blue* that does not swing, though this definition also excludes some music that most

31. See Morris Holbrook and Stephen Bertges' "Perceptual Veridicality in Esthetic Communication," *Communication Research* (1981), 8, 4, 387–423; and Holbrook and Joel Huber's "Separating Perceptual Dimensions from Affective Overtones," *Journal of Consumer Research* (1979), 5, 272–283.

listeners would call "jazz": many of Cecil Taylor's post-1960 works, because they do not swing; "Come Sunday" from Duke Ellington's *Black, Brown & Beige,* because it is neither swinging nor largely improvised, Manhattan Transfer's vocal recreations of instrumental jazz, because Manhattan Transfer is not improvising, and so on.

A "Family Resemblances" Approach

Practical application of the strict definition requires an impossible-to-attain degree of precision in specifying swing feeling and a considerable loosening in the way many of us ordinarily define improvisation; even with such loosening, it still excludes many styles that have traditionally been accorded the jazz designation. So perhaps we should try an entirely different approach. This would not seek common elements in all the styles that have ever been called jazz but instead look for ways in which some styles resemble and differ from others, and in which those others resemble and differ from still others. Instead of searching for a single fiber that continues throughout the entire thread of jazz history, we would satisfy ourselves with finding links between adjacent styles and thereby appeal to Ludwig Wittgenstein's metaphor that "the strength of the thread does not reside in the fact that some one fibre runs through its whole length, but in the overlapping of many fibres."[32]

Wittgenstein believed that, for many words, the use of the word was its meaning. He suggested that some words simply resist strict definition and we must content ourselves with observing their use instead of trying to frame definitions. It would be inconsistent with Wittgenstein's approach to force a change in the way a speaker uses the word "jazz." To the person who is using the word, jazz is whatever he thinks it is, whatever he is using it to describe.

Acceptance of the above perspective leads us to consider that perhaps some music is called jazz simply because it has similarities with some of the musical events that were previously called jazz. We know, for instance, that during the 1920s almost any lively popular music

---

32. *Philosophical Investigations* (1953), p. 32a. In other words there may be no hidden unity in the diverse forms called "jazz."

could be called jazz. The title of the Al Jolson movie about a Jewish vaudeville singer was *The Jazz Singer.* According to former Lombardo trombonist George West, when Guy Lombardo first came to America, he felt that the music he played was jazz. From all the elements that have ever been felt to help qualify a sound as jazz—syncopation, improvisation, saxophones, drums, blue notes, etc.—at least one must be present for any performance to be called jazz, but no one particular element must always be present; i.e., no single element is necessary and no single element is sufficient. By adopting such a stand, we would be able to include any style that has ever been called jazz, thereby placating everyone who would be outraged at the suggestion that certain works of Cecil Taylor, certain movements of Duke Ellington's *Black, Brown & Beige,* or some of Glenn Miller's biggest hits are not jazz. We could even include most of the lively popular instrumental music of the 1920s, much of which is routinely excluded by jazz scholars on the grounds that it is not improvised, though it is included by most laymen because it is lively and stems from what F. Scott Fitzgerald dubbed "The Jazz Age." We could include *Rhapsody In Blue* because it is bluesy and syncopated, even though it is not improvised or swinging. And we could include Manhattan Transfer's vocal re-creations of jazz instrumentals because the re-creations sometimes swing, even though they lack improvisation.

If you feel that a definition requiring jazz performances to be improvised and to be perceived as swinging excludes too much to be useful, then you probably agree with Wittgenstein's suggestion that some terms cannot be subjected to quasi-mathematical treatment. The things to be defined are just too varied—like members of a family. No single trait is necessarily common to each and every one of them. Applied to the term "jazz," Wittgenstein's suggestion would allow a large number of styles to be sheltered under a very comprehensive umbrella. It would not require that all the styles exhibit even one common defining characteristic. Two entirely dissimilar styles, such as Guy Lombardo's and Woody Herman's, might be linked by a third style, such as big band music in general—or even by a chain of styles in which each pair of adjacent links would share a common feature but in which no single feature would characterize every style. For instance, the music of the Modern Jazz Quartet does not resemble that of Guy Lombardo, but because of the MJQ's use of improvisation and swing feeling, its work does resemble that of the Woody Herman band, which, in turn, resembles the work of Guy Lombardo because both Lombardo and Herman have similar instrumentation.

This "family resemblances" way of characterizing jazz might have its appeals but, like a strict definition, it has serious problems. Whatever gains we make in clarity and comprehensiveness, we lose in simplicity and usefulness. For instance, applying Wittgenstein's idea of family resemblances to jazz means that two jazz styles need not share any predetermined set of defining characteristics. Yet in doing this, we leave several questions unanswered. For example, what are real jazz musicians doing when they play jazz? Do they have to swing? No. Or is it enough that they play in bands with musicians who do swing or improvise? Maybe. It is important that aspiring performers develop an improvisatory technique? Not necessarily. Is it sufficient that they copy the genuine improvisations of others? No. There is no single element that is sufficient.

Considering the practical inadequacies, why is the family resemblances approach useful? With sufficient historical perspective, a theorist finds the family resemblances approach plausible; it includes all the styles that have ever been called "jazz." But this historical view, in fact, lacks real perspective. An analogy should clarify this point. Dividing the history of music into periods requires stepping back and seeing the gross differences rather than the long-term continuities. For example, though Palestrina's melodic writing is chantlike, his masses do not belong in the Gregorian chant bin of the record stores—even though both the chant and his masses derive from the same tradition. Similarly with jazz, the theorist who is familiar with the entire span of jazz history can link the playing styles of Fats Waller and Cecil Taylor. Yet, though both have roots in jazz, their products are so dissimilar that they may demand separate categories. This is a realization that the historically minded observer might overlook, especially if he is partial to a family resemblances approach to characterizing jazz. Wouldn't it be more useful to separate things that are different? Isn't that part of what we do when we make a definition? In other words, the family resemblances approach is good at letting us rule in styles, but it provides very little help in showing how a given style can be ruled out of the jazz category.

Another attraction of the family resemblances approach might stem from observing a timbral similarity among many jazz-related styles. Many listeners have observed that much jazz is rough in tone and features drums and saxophones.[33] However, if we make too much of this similarity, we would be led to define jazz in terms of timbre, despite the fact that timbre has never been sufficient to define a style.[34]

What about "blues tonality" as an element that links many jazz styles? We might cite this in a family resemblances characterization of jazz. But no matter what definition of "blues tonality" is used, this feature falls far short of characterizing a majority of jazz styles. Some listeners call "bluesy" a preponderance of chromatically lowered thirds and sevenths in melody lines. Others think of a preponderance of pitch bendings akin to vocal ornamentations common in Afro-American folk music. Some call "bluesy" a combination of these properties.[35] Even during the 1920s, jazz musicians did not choose a characteristically high percentage of chromatically lowered thirds and sevenths. And the very existence of piano and vibraharp in jazz groups refutes the notion that "neutral thirds" (heptatonically equidistant tones, exemplified by the pitches "in between the cracks" that hornmen occasionally play) are essential for jazz. When tuned in the standard well-tempered system, these instruments are incapable of producing such "blue" pitches. And the contention that many pianists favor "crushed tones" (simultaneously sounding the major third and minor third, thereby approximating the "blue pitch" sound) does not hold up; "crushed tones" are not very common in the work of jazz pianists.

Although family resemblances solve some of the problems that accompany a strict definition, this approach creates at least as many problems as it solves.

---

33. But many jazz sounds are smooth in tone quality and lack drum or saxophone timbres.

34. During the late 1960s, the presence of horns in the popular group called Chicago is thought to have been part of the reason the group was classified as "jazz-rock," although the music had little else in common with jazz tradition.

35. See William Tallmadge's "Blue Notes and Blue Tonality" in *The Black Perspective in Music* (1984), 12, 2, 155–165.

Approaching Jazz as a Dimension

Aspects of both the strict approach and the family resemblances approach can be used in forming a third approach to defining jazz. This approach hinges on the idea that, of those elements that have been previously associated with jazz, the more that are present and the more clearly they can be heard, the more a particular performance qualifies as jazz. In other words, jazz is not an all-or-none event, but is a continuum, a dimension: jazzness. It accepts the history of musical elements that have been associated with the term jazz, elements that recur in the links between adjacent styles already discussed. This approach acknowledges that different weights are attached to various elements by the listener who is trying to determine whether a given performance is jazz. However, this does not necessarily imply a hierarchy of elements, although many listeners attach considerable weight to improvisation and swing feeling and less weight to instrumentation. Furthermore, it does not deny the situations in which only one or two elements are present or in which the presence is barely detectable. This approach simply says that little jazzness exists in such situations. For example, it is likely that little jazzness would be perceived in Stan Kenton's recording of "Reflections" from Robert Graettinger's *City of Glass,* while much jazzness would be evident in Charlie Parker's "Ko-Ko" (Savoy, November 26, 1945). *Rhapsody in Blue* would be perceived as jazzy, but not unless there were more steady tempo passages and improvisation would it qualify as bearing as much jazzness as Count Basie's 1937 recording of "One O'Clock Jump." Manhattan Transfer's first recording of Joe Zawinul's "Birdland" would qualify as jazz because of its syncopations and swing feeling, but more jazzness would be evident in Weather Report's original version of "Birdland" because of its use of saxophone and improvisations.

We suggest that, in the mind of the listener who is trying to categorize a performance, the jazzness approach derives from: 1) taking each element that has, in the past, been associated with jazz and accepting it as a dimension of its own; 2) weighing the relative representation of each element; and, finally, 3) taking the number of elements together to lead to a decision of whether to call a given performance jazz. For the jazzness approach, improvisation need not have a strict definition;

it can be present in greater or lesser degree. Swing feeling need not have a strict definition; it, too, can be present in greater or lesser degree. Bluesy flavor need not have a strict definition; like improvisation and swing feeling, it can be present to a greater or lesser degree. A determination can be made of the total number of elements present, each taken with respect to prominence. From this, a fix on the jazzness of the performance is made.

We are now in a position to return to the original questions. Is jazz art music? To address this question we must have definitions of jazz and art music. Depending on the definition of jazz chosen, some of these examples qualify, others do not. For instance, can we accept as "jazz" the music of the singing group Peter, Paul, and Mary that won first place in the vocal division of the "jazz" popularity polls run by *Playboy* in 1964, 1965, and 1966? Should we include the music of Al Jolson from his 1927 film *The Jazz Singer?* By a strict definition, requiring full-blown melodic improvisation and jazz swing feeling, none of the music of Peter, Paul, and Mary qualifies as jazz. Therefore it would not matter how we defined art music. We could not use those styles to support or refute the contention that jazz is art music. But, if we followed Wittgenstein's admonition to look at how the word is used, we would say anything that has ever been called jazz is jazz. So the Al Jolson and the Peter, Paul, and Mary music would be jazz, and we could match their music against art music criteria to argue whether jazz is art music.

Was jazz popular during any given era of twentieth-century music?[36] As we have seen, the question becomes problematic, especially for music of the 1930s and 1970s, when certain best-selling records contained brief improvisations. Following Wittgenstein, any music that was ever called jazz still warrants the label "jazz." Music of the very popular Ted Lewis of the 1920s, Rudy Vallee of later periods, Paul Whiteman of any period, could be called jazz, although they employed little improvisation and projected far less swing feeling than Count Basie and Duke Ellington. We could then say that jazz was popular during those periods. During the 1980s, pianist George

---

36. See "Is Jazz Popular Music" by Mark Gridley, *The Instrumentalist* (March 1987), Vol. 41, Issue 8, pp. 19–26, 85.

Winston's records appeared in the "jazz" bins of many stores. So, by the reasoning associated with Wittgenstein, we also could apply "jazz" to these quite popular recordings, although most jazz musicians agree that the music does not swing, and Winston himself refuses to label his music "jazz." Manhattan Transfer's tremendously popular vocal recreations of jazz instrumentals could qualify because, even though they are not improvised, they do sometimes swing. By this reasoning, we could say that jazz has been and continues to be popular. However, if we use a strict definition of jazz, then we find that the music never has achieved widespread popularity in that (with a few exceptions such as Louis Armstrong, Benny Goodman, and Miles Davis) many of the critically acknowledged greats in jazz rarely sold many records or packed many nightclubs and theaters.

How should we interpret discographer Brian Rust's statement about Glenn Miller's output, ". . . the majority of the Bluebird and Victor sides are of little or no jazz interest . . ."?[37] Rust is referring to the fact that improvised solos are infrequent, brief, and often constitute inconsequential portions of a Miller performance. He is not implying that the band fails to swing, only that the band's priorities are not on improvisation.[38] He is also revealing his own adherence to a strict definition of jazz.

Conclusion

The overwhelming strength of the strict definition is its simplicity. And this is the most telling weakness of the dimensional approach because this approach does not allow one to make unequivocal decisions. The family resemblances approach and the jazzness approach are more relativistic, with a flexibility that accommodates jazz as an evolving art form and thereby excludes far fewer performances than the strict definition excludes. The jazzness and the strict definition are both problematic because they require us to determine the extent to which a given element is conspicuous. For example, in both the jazzness and the strict definition, we must determine the percentage of fresh material in every performance in order to address the improvisation requirement,

37. *Jazz Records,* Vol. 2 (1970), p. 1125; Storyville Publications, Chigwell, England.
38. Personal communication to author, July 13, 1987.

though this is more severe in the jazzness approach than with the strict definition. In the strict definition, the amount of improvisation must exceed a critical minimum before we can call the performance improvised, whereas in the "jazzness" approach, the amount of improvisation affects only the degree to which the performance is likely to be called jazz.

As appealing as any one approach might seem, it will remain problematic because an adequate definition of swing feeling remains to be crafted. For example, how is a performance supposed to make you feel before you can call it "swinging"? How is this different from the way a successful performance of any other kind of music should make you feel? Can we legitimately (arbitrarily) take the rhythmic conception of one particular jazz style—bop, perhaps—and adopt it as the epitome of what constitutes jazz swing feeling? And in determining the contribution that improvisation makes to jazzness, what is the minimum extent of change and the minimum percentage of nonpreset material that qualifies a performance for the label of "improvised"? And should the listener be able to determine this, just by listening? Can any change in the practical meaning of these terms be tolerated from decade to decade, so that we can still call the music jazz, despite how much it has changed from Louis Armstrong to Albert Ayler, from Jelly Roll Morton to Keith Jarrett?

In conclusion, we feel that the definition having the greatest utility for scholars is the strict definition. Its simplicity allows us to determine what is not jazz, though it excludes much music that the public ordinarily calls jazz. That having the greatest utility for the public is the family resemblances approach because it allows the public to continue calling "jazz" anything they ever thought was jazz. The reprioritization of elements that is possible with the jazzness approach might reflect most adequately the changing nature of what is regarded as jazz from decade to decade, improvisation being most important sometimes, swing feeling other times, bluesy flavor other times. The definition by jazzness is probably the way the majority of jazz fans are responding. (Mark Gridley, Robert Maxham, and Robert Hoff, "Three Approaches to Defining Jazz," *Musical Quarterly* 73, no. 4 [1989])

I would like to add one tangential point that does not affect the main argument of the above article. As I understand Wittgenstein's philosophy, he meant that words are defined by the way they are *commonly* used, not by *any* way they are used. In other words, he would not have denied that one can use a word incorrectly! He would not have advocated, as suggested here, that Peter, Paul, and Mary must be a jazz group because a poll in *Playboy* listed them as such. He would have agreed with Nick Straus, however, that in the 1920s the word *jazz* actually meant something different than it does today, because then it was typical, rather than unusual, for it to apply to all bouncy popular music.

Gridley has provided me with an update to the preceding article for inclusion in this book.

The three approaches outlined above are extremely useful in attempting to classify newer music, such as saxophonist "Kenny G," acid jazz, and rap. Kenny G's music has been dismissed by many jazz musicians who consider it to be nonjazz instrumental pop, and Gridley has classified it as "jazzy pop" (*All Music Guide to Jazz,* [San Francisco: Miller-Freeman, 1994], p. 13) and as "background music with a beat" (*Jazz Styles: History and Analysis,* 4th edition, [Englewood Cliffs, N.J.: Prentice-Hall, 1991], p. 350). In fact, Kenny G's music would qualify as jazz by the family resemblances approach because much of it is improvised and derives from the jazz tradition. However, because it fails to swing in as pronounced a fashion as earlier styles, his music would fail to qualify by a strict definition that requires considerable syncopation and swing eighth notes.

Acid jazz, on the other hand, qualifies as jazz to the extent which it both conveys swing feeling and overdubs freshly improvised material. Its jazzness increases when its creators, the disc jockeys and rap artists, add piano chords typical of jazz, or a Harmon-muted trumpet improvisation, or excerpts sampled intact from, say, an Art Blakey or Lou Donaldson album. (For a further discussion of this point, see Gridley's *Concise Guide to Jazz,* 2nd edition, [Upper Saddle River, N.J.: Prentice-Hall, 1997], pp. 174–176.)

Rap music without jazz elements does not qualify under any of the three approaches to defining jazz. However, apparently because both rap and jazz are African American forms, a number of journalists and listeners classify rap as jazz. In that case, they are applying the family resemblances approach.

Thus, the issue of "What is jazz?" is still a hot one. The question returns in the discussions of avant-garde and fusion later in this anthology.

3

Analyzing Jazz

Jazz, many maintain, resists analysis. Well, yes and no. Because so much of jazz is improvised, it is not as easy to analyze as a piece of music that is fully or mostly notated. For that reason, scores by jazz composers Gil Evans and Fletcher Henderson—or Ludwig von Beethoven or Wolfgang Amadeus Mozart, for that matter—are easier to analyze than improvised solos by Charlie Parker and John Coltrane.

So far, so good. But it is plain anti-intellectualism to suggest that analyzing jazz is somehow wrong or that analysis can ruin jazz. Moreover, it is plain snobbery to suggest, as I've been told several times by classical musicians, "Since it's improvised, what's there to analyze?" Jazz musicians themselves have promoted this skepticism about analysis, but their own behavior contradicts the belief that jazz cannot be analyzed. Paul Berliner's massive and important study, *Thinking in Jazz* (Chicago: University of Chicago Press, 1994)—and my own experience as a performing pianist—confirms that jazz musicians will talk about music for hours and often in quite specific terms, naming particular chords, humming particular phrases to play on those chords, and so on. If that's not analysis, what is? To put it differently, how could one possibly learn to perform such a technically demanding form of improvisation as jazz without bringing some kind of analytic thinking to the task? The fact that the training for jazz has been primarily outside "the academy" and that the kind of analysis the musicians engage in is not written down or formalized helps to perpetuate the idea that no analysis occurs.

The musicians may dislike certain approaches to analysis, the ones that seem far removed from practice. If we transcribe an improvised solo from a recording and write it down on a piece of music paper, we can then analyze it just as we would a Beethoven sonata. But that approach would be misleading. On the one hand, Beethoven often took months to write a piece of music, and he could take the time to revise it during that time and to make connections musically that probably couldn't have been accomplished on the spur of the moment. (He was a great improviser, by all accounts, but that doesn't mean his improvisations were exactly like his writings.) On the other hand, a jazz solo is the product of years of training and practice and of more recent, specific practice on the particular song that is the basis of the improvisation being studied. So a jazz solo should be analyzed as a result of that process, not of a writing and revising process.

Many analytical pieces have been written on jazz in recent years—some of my own included—and this is not an attempt to survey them. Rather, this chapter offers an historical look at some of the ways that jazz has been analyzed over the years.

Teaching jazz requires one to analyze the music into its component parts and to make very specific judgments about which elements need to be taught and in which order. Instruction books for jazz began to appear soon after the first records were issued in 1917. A book for trombonists appeared in 1920. Glenn Waterman of Los Angeles began advertising his piano school, and in 1924 he came out with a book that included material copyrighted as early as 1917 (I think this may have applied to some of the more general music theory material that was not specific to playing jazz). Here are some excerpts of the text and music.

Cover of the 1924 edition of Glen Waterman's *Piano Jazz*. *Courtesy of Lewis Porter*.

Preface

Unwritten music has had no textbook, heretofore. The results produced by those who have never taken a piano lesson, are a source of wonderment, even to students of Harmony. One object of this volum[e] is to supply ANYONE a practical-working-method for accomplishing the same, and greater, results—serving as a short cut to the actual playing of the piano.

THIS IS TRUE: Popular Songs demand embellishing. Notes must be added and the time altered. The instant any deviation is made from the strict note reading, that moment you are knowingly or unknowingly following the harmonic structure taught in this System.

The Course is particularly designed to enable ANYONE to treat a melody; whether that melody is played by ear; spontaneous improvision; original composition; or obtained from the upper Treble Notes of instrumental pieces; lead sheets; the Voice Part of a Song; or from any other Melody Source. For the sake of furnishing a uniform vehicle for experimenting, the melody printed in the Voice Part of a Song is sighted and used as an example throughout the Course. However, it is the Grand principle of treating any melody by FORM (and not specifically the Voice Part) that this method aims to embrace. A Course of Invention based on a given Melody. . . .

Jazz Hints

TEN RULES. (1) Pedal down on Count 1, up on 2, down on 3, up on 4. Stamp right pedal regularly. (2) Avoid expression, crescendo, ritards, entirely. (3) Wrist action in both hands. Semi-staccato touch—positive—crisp. Equal density of stroke. (4) Employ full harmony in *both* hands—5 or 6 toned chords in Treble where possible—complete volume. (5) Don't play fast. (6) Memorize the melody. Think ahead. Visualize the air and chords several measures in advance. (7) Repeat melody notes . . . on long or short spaces. Passing Notes ad lib. (8) Buy a Metronome. Play Long-Swing-Bass . . . on counts 1, 2, 3, 4. *Must* be exact, perfect, accurate, precise. Any deviation from this insistent rhythm is *fatal.* Left hand beats the time. Right hand does the Jazzing. (9) Never sprinkle (arpeggios) a right hand chord. Strike solidly at once, or ADVANCE any tone, *i.e.* strike *before* the regular beat. Bass tenths, similarly. (10) To syncopate: Move Voice Notes left or right to the "and". Accent these off-beats. . . . The octave (filled-in) is universally used in carrying the Melody-Voice-Part. Break these octaves down (or up) thus dividing quarter-notes into two-eighths. The upper-voice-note is advanced to the "and": balance of chord struck on regular beat. The exact "way" of striking these two-eighths (also *written* as dotted eighth and sixteenth) produces good or bad Jazz. They *must be played* as a triplet with the first note tied. Analyze the following. Adopt *Example 4.*

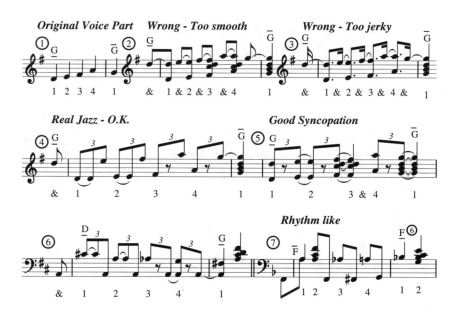

Hot Rhythms

Select a Foxtrot measure having 2 Melody Notes. Exchange the Voice Notes found in the Song, for the notes shown in Rhythm #1. Observe the Treble-octave is Double-filled, and broken. Voice Notes are numbered: v̇v̇. Letter "H" is Harmonic (Fill-in) tone, from chord. Forms #16 to 40 substitute for, and "erase" original melody, in *any* measure of same harmony.

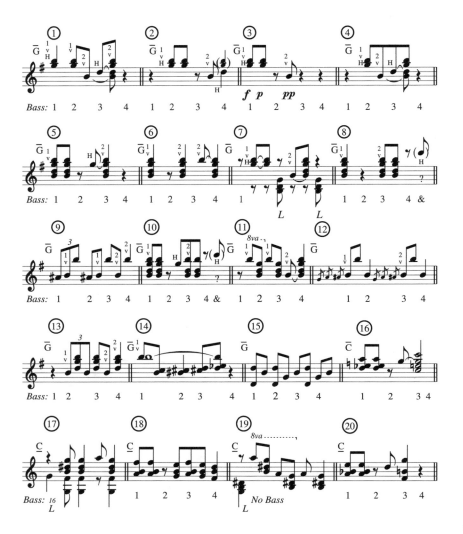

Space Fillers and Breaks

Embellishment consists in filling unoccupied spaces. . . . Forms and Figures may be applied to sustained tones only. A whole note lends itself to invention. A measure containing 8 eighth notes necessarily has the embellishment limited.

This is an axiom: "The MORE the notes are read, the LESS the Jazz." Therefore read from the LEAD. Professional pianists, without exception, play from the Voice Part, employing an artificial bass, and an improvised melody. If you want success, utterly ignore the piano score and confine yourself 100% to the Voice Part. Any other plan is a makeshift and waste of time. (Glenn Waterman, *Piano Jazz* [Los Angeles: self-published, 1917, 1924])

As clearly illustrated by the last excerpt, Waterman recognized the importance of improvisation in this music. He also understood, as shown at the end of his "Jazz Hints," that a triplet feeling was more swinging than plain eighth notes or dotted eighths and sixteenths, even though the sheet music was generally written in the last two ways. He assumed that players would know how to adapt the rhythms to make them swing. To this day most jazz is written in plain eighth notes, with the same assumption.

Nevertheless, the nature of swing, which Mark Gridley and company discussed briefly in the preceding chapter, continues to be a mystery. Just playing triplets is clearly not the whole answer. That's just a shortcut that Waterman uses to get his students on the right path.

Virgil Thomson (1896–1989), a remarkable American composer and critic, has a kind of blunt manner in the following article that may strike some readers as condescending to jazz. He makes some bold and provocative statements: the melodic matter of jazz is never "especially novel or significant," jazz is not dance music ("nobody dances to jam," he writes, and by "jam" he means jamming, improvising, jam sessions) and it doesn't swing! When one reads Thomson dispassionately, however, one realizes the value and originality of what he has to say. His comment on jazz melody is not meant to insult but to point out that those melodies would not have so much impact were it not for jazz rhythm. When he says jazz is "not dance music," he really means that it is too subtle and complex to be just dance music; it reflects an "imaginative intellect" and a freedom that is, as he says, "real and exciting." By "swing," he means a back-and-forth feeling like a Viennese waltz, and he's right that in jazz we find a different pulse. Near the beginning of his discussion and again at the end, he compares jazz to baroque music and especially to Johann Sebastian Bach. He must be onto something, because Bach is a favorite of jazz musicians and his music has probably been "jazzed" more often and with more success than that of other classical composers. (Thomson's comment that Benny Goodman's Carnegie Hall concert was "quite uninteresting," by which he may mean that nothing new happened from a strictly musical point of view, is worth taking seriously as well.)

Thomson's main point is based on an important observation about the jazz 4/4: it is composed of four even beats of equal value, relatively undifferentiated. While true at his writing, over the years his point has become even more valid as jazz musicians have emphasized a smooth flow. He says this *smoothness* creates a "quantitative rhythm"—that is, a rhythm marked off simply by the equal duration of each beat—as opposed to a "qualitative rhythm," in which the first beat, for example, might get a special accent and the fourth might be held a bit longer. Thomson notes that while the second and fourth beats appear to be accented—and this point has often been made—that cannot be true. If they were accented, the beat would soon "turn around," and one would think that 2 is 1, the beginning of a measure, but in fact one always knows where "one" is.

Supporting Thomson's view, jazz musicians have often noted that swinging in meters other than 4/4 is harder, although it is often done, of course. For all the work in other meters, most often 3/4, four beats are still the norm in jazz (as they are for most Western music). John Coltrane himself once said that, for all the pleasure he derived from playing the waltz "My Favorite Things," the 3/4 meter put him in a kind of straitjacket (liner notes by Ralph Gleason to the recording *Olé Coltrane*).

In Thomson's previous article, to which he refers, he postulated that Latin American dance music was a crucial ingredient in the formation of the swing feel. This is an important point that has often been suggested by other writers, but only Thomson spells it out explicitly, with musical examples, so that one may properly consider and evaluate his claims. (Virgil Thomson, "Swing Music," *Modern Music* 13, no. 4 [May–June 1936], reprinted in John Rockwell, ed., *A Virgil Thomson Reader* [New York: Dutton, 1981])

In the present piece, Thomson also makes the rather surprising suggestion that the reason we find ourselves tapping with our feet or hands while listening to jazz may not simply be that we are moving to the beat. He thinks we may *need* to do this in order to keep time, because the music itself suggests a variety of rhythms at once. In other words, taking Thomson's point a bit further, the music may demand the audience's participation by its very nature. Whether or not one agrees with him, Thomson is thought-provoking and well worth reading.

Swing Again

VIRGIL THOMSON

In May 1936 I stated in this magazine that "swing-music is a form of two-step in which the rhythm is expressed quantitatively by instruments of no fixed intonation, the melodic, harmonic, and purely percussive elements being liberated thereby to improvise in free polyphonic style."

That definition is pretty pompous, but I think it still holds. However, since quantitative rhythm is a term and a conception that a great many people do not understand, my definition has remained not only uncriticised and undisputed, but also unaccepted. I am therefore taking this occasion, which arose from an invitation to review Benny Goodman's concert in Carnegie Hall (a quite uninteresting concert on the whole), to talk some more about quantitative rhythm and its function in swing-music, in the hope of further clarifying a little the bothersome question of what is swing-music anyway.

The melodic matter of swing, though frequently charming, I have never found to be especially novel or significant. The elaborate *fioritura* of the New Orleans school and the tighter contrapuntal texture of the Chicago school are equally mannerisms of style. They are not of the essence. They are only significant as indicating, by their presence at such a high degree of elaboration, that there must be some pretty solid underpinning somewhere in the structure to make such elaboration possible. The constant use of the air-and-variations form is of no significance either, the variation being the loosest of all musical forms and at its best only a shape, never a structural system. Similarly as regards the contrapuntal freedom, the harmonic and instrumental variety. That is all superstructure too. It certainly astonishes no one who is acquainted with modern musical resources. The existence of such a practical superstructure makes it certain, however, that there is a method somewhere in the whole thing. The important place that improvisation has in swing-playing is conclusive. Nobody improvises publicly much without a method. Communal improvisation without it is a clear impossibility.

Now the sleuths, amateur and professional, who have looked for this basic method have mostly been taken in by the lingo. Let me remind them that *hot* does not mean passionate in expression. It means rhythmically free and it applies only, in consequence, to melody or to percussion. More important than that, that swing-music rarely has any literal swing in it. Certainly nothing like the Viennese waltz music has. At most it sort of quivers or oscillates rapidly like a French clock. At its best it has no motor effects at all. Good jam invariably sounds not unlike a Brandenburg Concerto, where every voice wiggles around as rapidly as you please, the rhythmic basis or center remaining completely static and without progression or development of any kind.

If dance-music doesn't swing, is it dance-music? Answer, no. Motor impulses in dance-music are of the essence. They are the *sine qua non*. But nobody dances to jam anyway. What kind of metrical routine then has replaced the rhythmic beat? That there is a metrical routine of some kind is obvious. Otherwise the rhythmically free (or non-metrical) "hot licks" would not be free. They would be just a vague melopoeia without tension. Their freedom is real and exciting only because it exists by contrast to a fixed measure of some kind. Also collective improvisation is not possible without a fixed metrical basis. There is only one answer, because there is only one other known form of metre besides the metre of beats. That is the metre of quantities.

Here is the root of the matter. Beat-music is accentual music. Its rhythmic measure-unit is a succession of blows of varying force. Its effect on the listener is muscular. It is the music of the march, the dance, the religious or secular orgy. Quantitative music has no accent. It is serene. Its rhythmic measure-unit is a unit of length. Its effect on the listener is likely to be hypnotic. When practised with sufficient subtlety it becomes not only the lullaby, but also the ballad, the music of prose declamation, of high religious rite, of contemplation, of the imaginative intellect.

The pianoforte, the drums, all the stick-and-hammer family, are primarily accentual instruments, although the length, or vibrating-time of the tone produced is usually controllable. The bowed instruments are primarily quantitative, though they can play a fairly presentable accent too. The wind instruments, both brass and wood, are almost completely quantitative, their bravest attacks being always more vocal than percussive, and their diminuendos having always a very audible stopping-place. The organ (reed or pipe) is one hundred per cent quantitative, no accent of any kind being possible at any time, and all tones being completely sustainable. Likewise for the modern electrical instruments, though a fairly successful imitation of string pizzicati is often added to their organ-like range of sounds. The plucked instruments are equivocal. Banjo, guitar and harp are chiefly accentual. The lute less so. The harpsichord not at all, because it has no accents. Harpsichord music, therefore, is always quantitative, in spite of the non-sustaining tone of the instrument. It resembles organ-music far more than it resembles piano- or harp-music. I am now going to explain how in swing-music a similar phenomenon takes place, whereby the foundational underpinning, its basic rhythm, although purely quantitative in character, gets expressed by non-quantitative instruments, by drums, guitars, cymbals, pianos and hand-plucked double-basses.

The basic routines of the rhythm-section in a swing-band are as follows:

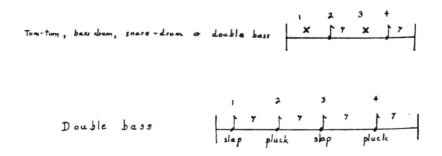

Cymbal (with hard stick)

x represents the stroke, o the damping.

Snare-drum (with sticks, brushes or dragging brush)

non cresc.   non cresc

There are some variations on the above, such as the double cymbal-stroke on counts 2 and 4 (with damping on 1 and 3) and the double brush-tap on the snare drum (also used on counts 2 and 4). Also the combinations of all these. The hot drum-solo is not a basic routine but a cadenza. It is made to sound as different as possible from the basic routines by the use of *sfz* stresses in unexpected places and the temporary introduction of new patterns, sometimes in a variant metre and sometimes in free prose. It is only cadenza, however, a little spurt of very exciting freedom in the midst of the grind.

Notice in the routine exposed above the consistent placing of what looks like a strong accent on counts 2 and 4. This cannot be what it looks like, because a musical structure of any length cannot be made on a routine of strong off-beats, since the tendency of any regular strong beat is to become itself the down-beat of the measure. Robert Schumann was fond of playing around with off-beats and frequently got his interpreters into a lot of trouble on their account. No. 1 of the *Phantasiestücke* is a celebrated example, a clear rendition of its rhythmic content (as written down by the composer) being one of the more difficult feats in piano-playing.

By what agency is the tonic measure-accent expressed then in swing-music if not by the rhythm-section of the band? Certainly not by the melody-instruments, the saxes, trumpets, clarinets, etc. These play with the greatest rhythmic freedom, varying continually both their accents and their quantities to exploit the rich fancy of the arranger and the tonal resources of the instruments. The harmony-section, that is, piano, guitar and the like, seems to string its chords on a rhythmic routine not unlike that of the rhythm-section itself. I repeat that there is no tonic measure-accent, that the measure-unit in swing-music is a measure of quantities and not of accents at all.

Let me represent the quantities in a measure of four-four time by the following pictures. I presume an instrument of unvarying pitch.

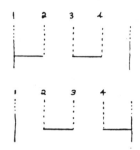

The numbers represent the four counts of the measure. They are theoretically of equal length. In musical performance, number 4 is usually a shade longer than the others. This imperceptible hold (familiar to all organists and harpsichordists) serves to define the measure's limit and to produce a tiny semblance of down-beat at the beginning of the following measure. The horizontal lines represent the duration of the unvarying sound, the blanks between them its absence. There are no stresses. You could play it all perfectly on an electric buzzer. These two patterns are for theoretical purposes identical, because, unless there is in any measure of repeating-pattern, a tonic accent on 1 and 3, there is no tonic accent at all (or any measure either, except of two counts) and nobody can ever know which came first, the sound or the silence.

Now superpose on these theoretical, quantitative designs the formulae given above for basic swing-rhythm and you will see what happens in a swing band. Remember that the instrumental strokes cannot be considered as marking tonic measure-accents, because they are all off-beat strokes. Yet they must mark something, or they wouldn't be there. They must therefore mark the quantities. The taps and plucks do coincide, as a matter of fact, with the beginning and ending of the units of the quantitative pattern. The cymbal and the snare-drum roll, having a sound of some duration, can actually express these quantities. More often than not, however, in good swing-playing, the continuing, or exactly quantitative sounds are dispensed with on account of their insistent character, the taps and plucks being left to play the perverse role of indicating and defining a kind of rhythmic pattern that they are by nature incapable of stating in all its plenitude.

Now the two quantitative measure-patterns drawn above, although identical when expressed in pure quantitative sound, are not identical when expressed by dry taps. Such taps, if placed on counts one and three, would create a tonic measure-beat. Consequently they are placed on two and four in order to make it clear that there is no tonic measure-beat. The cymbal and snare-drum occasionally add their precise statement of quantitative pattern no. 2 to reinforce the same point.

The result of all this elaborate procedure is an amplification of the expressive range. The listener, like the improvising player, is not whiffed back and forth by any muscular reactions to regular beats. So marked, in fact, is the absence of regular beats that most players are obliged to keep themselves aware of musical time by rapid foot-patting. Neither is the listener lulled to sleep by an expressed quantitative routine (which can be very monotonous indeed). The pluck-and-tap rhythm is equal and delicate. It never becomes a beat. But it reminds one at all times of the underlying measure of length which is the structural unit of the whole music, reminds one so gently but so continuously that both the invention and the comprehension of complex musical structures is greatly facilitated.

Notice the high degree of intellectual and nervous excitement present in any swing-audience. The listeners do not close their eyes and sink into emotional or subjective states. They sit up straight, their eyes flash, they applaud the licks. They occasionally jerk on the absent down-beat, but on the whole they seem to be enjoying one of those states of nervous and muscular equilibrium that render possible rapid intellection.

Quantitative rhythm in music has long been known to have special characteristics, not the least noticeable being a tendency to develop complex textures for non-emotional purposes, the organ-works of Sebastian Bach and his predecessors being pretty spectacular in that way. Beat-music, on the other hand, is always emotional and tends to hide rather than parade its complexities. The whole matter, however, has been very little discussed theoretically. Even the term quantitative rhythm is unknown to many musicians, although the musical notation we all use is as strictly a quantitative conception as though accents didn't exist. Musicians all know there is something rather special about the pipe-organ, but they mostly consider the unvarying nature of an organ tone to be a defect rather than a special characteristic of that instrument. I don't want to go into all that any further just now. But I do want to note that quantitative music is having under our very noses a renaissance and that the plucked or tapped instruments are occupying an important place in that renaissance, a place not unlike that occupied by the harpsichord in the equally quantitative music of the seventeenth and early eighteenth centuries. (Virgil Thomson, "Swing Again," *Modern Music* 15, no. 3 [March–April 1938])

I would like to add another note about swing. First and foremost, swing is an experience, or a kinesthetic sensation of "swinging," that is felt in the body, not a "decision" made in the mind. Swing may result partly from the relationship between the bass and drums, but it does not arise from that relationship alone. Rather, it is the resulting *sensation* that may evolve partly from those things. When I saw the drummer Jo Jones, famed for his work with Count Basie in the late 1930s and many bands since, at the Museum of Modern Art in Manhattan around 1966, I knew he was swinging like mad, not because I decided as much, but because my leg was bouncing wildly up and down without my even thinking about it!

With his book *Jazz: Hot and Hybrid*, Winthrop Sargeant is often thought of as one of the first critics to analyze jazz, and his text was surely the first to analyze it in detail with musical notation. The book was first published by Arrow Editions in 1938; it was revised in 1946 and 1964 and reprinted in 1975 (New York: Da Capo Press). Sargeant was a classical music critic who wrote for *Time* and the *New Yorker*, among others. He had also written about the music of India and Latin America. He approached jazz from a classical point of view; he had the benefit of his technical knowledge of music but the disadvantage of looking at jazz condescendingly. Alain Locke, an important African American essayist from whom we shall hear more, approved of the book because Sargeant treated jazz seriously:

Winthrop Sargeant's *Jazz: Hot And Hybrid* is the best and most scholarly analysis of jazz and Negro folk music to date; all the more welcome because it is objective in attitude and technical in approach. The
Negro source influences are freely admitted and correctly traced, the
important basic denominators of idioms common to the Negro's religious and secular folk music are clearly seen, the periods of development are competently sketched with the possible exception of the
post–Civil War period, where there is little documentation anyway;
and most important of all, the musical idioms of modern jazz are carefully analyzed. (Alain Locke, "Negro Music Goes to Par," *Opportunity,*
July 1939)

But Locke also noted the condescension that crept into Sargeant's
work.

Although I readily agree that "Jazz does not attempt to sound the pro-
founder depths of human emotion, but gives a meaningful account of
some of the shallows," and would equally discount much of the faddist
delusions and pretensions of the first decades of symphonic or classical
jazz, I do not share Mr. Sargeant's skepticism over the potential contributions of jazz and Negro folk music to music in the larger forms.
Jazz does not need to remain, I contend, even "at its most complex"
still "a very simple matter of incessantly repeated formulas," or even,
as is later hinted "most successful in the looser forms of ballet and
opera, where music plays a subsidiary atmospheric role." (Alain Locke,
"Negro Music Goes to Par")

Sargeant's problem was that he held a common misconception
about early jazz—that it was a kind of folk music and thereby limited. There are many problems with this idea—often still used today
in the context of "jazz evolved from a folk music to an art music"—
not the least being that the categories of folk, popular, and art music
that were used one hundred years ago have exploded in the twentieth century. Roughly, in their original senses, *folk music* referred to
the songs—religious, secular, children's—that we all learned by
ear; *popular music* meant published and performed material of

professional songwriters in the entertainment field, such as Stephen Foster and minstrel writers; and *art music* described the European "classical" tradition oriented around concerts. In an age when all kinds of music are available in stores, on radio and television, and in films; when people know "popular" songs by ear just as well as they know "folk" music; and when opera singers Luciano Pavarotti and Placido Domingo can be "pop" stars just like Judy Garland, it is very difficult to apply the same three distinctions today. Some kinds of classification will be useful, but they must be rethought and applied carefully.

Even if the folk music category were still valid, it never made sense for jazz, which has always been familiar only to a select group of musicians and fans and which has been learned from recordings, radio, and live performances. Even the first jazz musicians, contrary to common mythology, had to understand harmony and chord progressions, at least by ear; had to have a good facility with their instruments; had to have (for the most part) some experience with written music; and had to be able to compose new melodies over the chords on the spot—that is, to improvise. (Paul Berliner's *Thinking in Jazz* documents much of these prerequisites for more recent generations.) These requirements are hardly typical for "folk" musicians.

Finally, it wouldn't matter that people like to call early jazz "folk" music, except that they often use that label as a way to denigrate jazz. In the following passage Sargeant classifies jazz as folk music and then makes a common intellectual error: he feels compelled to justify his decision by making statements that oppose anyone's experience of jazz, probably including his own. He says that jazz is neither the result of any intellectual effort (I suppose he never tried to improvise over chord progressions) nor that of any training. He maintains that folk music never develops while art music does, and although he admits that jazz does change "from time to time," he shrugs that off since it is incompatible with the point he wants to make. This issue is where Sargeant's intellectual dishonesty shows, for if there's one thing all observers agree on, it's this: jazz has been continuously evolving and changing as the result of study and thought by its musicians.

Jazz, for all the enthusiasms of its intellectual fans, is not music in the sense that an opera or a symphony is music. It is a variety of folk music. And the distinction between folk music and art music is profound and nearly absolute. The former grows like a weed or a wild flower, exhibits no intellectual complexities, makes a simple, direct emotional appeal that may be felt by people who are not even remotely interested in music as an art. It may be pretty to listen to, but it is not subject to intellectual criticism, for it lacks the main element toward which such criticism would be directed: the creative ingenuity and technique of an unusual, trained musical mind.

The latter (art music) is an art as complicated as architecture. It begins where folk music leaves off, in the conscious creation of big musical edifices that bear the stamp, in style and technique, of an individual artist. Its traditions—the rules of its game—are complicated and ingenious. They are the result of centuries of civilized musical thinking by highly trained musicians for audiences that are capable of judging the finer points of such thought. Art music is no weed patch. It is a hothouse of carefully bred and cultivated masterpieces, each one the fruit of unusual talent and great technical resourcefulness. You may prefer the open fields of folk music to the classical hothouse. That is your privilege. But if so, you are simply not interested in music as an art. And it is no good getting snobbish about your preference, and pretending that your favorite musical wildflower is a masterpiece of gardening skill. It isn't . . .

Having no intellectual principles of structure, jazz is incapable of development. Aside from a few minor changes in fashion, its history shows no technical evolution whatever. Boogie woogie pianism, for example, has recently come into a tremendous vogue among the long-haired jazz addicts. But it differs in no structural particular from the blues that were sung in New Orleans at the turn of the century. This lack of evolution, which is an attribute of all folk music, is another of the outstanding differences between jazz and concert music. The history of art music shows a continuous development of structural methods. Such variations as do occur from time to time in the style of jazz are usually merely the result of trial and error, public demand, or changes in the types of instruments it is played on. The basic idiom of jazz is the same today as it was two generations ago. . . .

Jazz appeared in the first place because the poor Southern Negro couldn't get a regular musical education, and decided to make his own homemade kind of music without it. His ingenuity has proved him to be one of the world's most gifted instinctive musicians. But as his lot improves, and with it his facilities for musical education, he is bound to be attracted by the bigger scope and intricacy of civilized concert music. Give him the chance to study, and the Negro will soon turn from boogie woogie to Beethoven. (Winthrop Sargeant, "Is Jazz Music?," *American Mercury Magazine*, October 1943).

Toward the end, Sargeant adopts a kind of "noble savage" idea about African American jazz musicians by suggesting that they are purely "instinctive." A jazz magazine called *The Needle* reprinted Sargeant's piece in July 1944 and gave Duke Ellington space to respond. He wrote, in part: "Mr. Sargeant has evidently not been exposed to some of the more intelligent jazz, nor is he aware of the amazing musical background of some of our foremost composers and arrangers in the popular field."

Jazz is overwhelmingly an instrumental music, and singers probably account for less than 5 percent of its professional performers. Nonetheless, everyone loves a singer, and among that small percentage have been some of the most popular of all jazz artists. Yet, probably because of the instrumental bias and because of the difficulty in transcribing and analyzing sung pitches compared to instrumental notes, there has been little musical discussion of jazz singers.

Richard Rodney Bennett, born in England in 1936, is an ideal person to discuss jazz singers. He is a marvelous composer and pianist who has worked in symphonic, show music, and jazz settings. His article sheds some light on what jazz singers do, and it covers a broad range of stylists from several countries.

The Technique of the Jazz Singer
RICHARD RODNEY BENNETT

The human voice is perhaps the most mysterious, the most unpredictable and the most stimulating instrument of all. It is precisely because of its limitations of range, of timbre, of amplitude, even of expression, that the voice seems to me to remain so challenging and to present to the composer such an incentive. How far *can* it be taken? How much more can it do? What is there still to be done, without making it freakish?

Having been involved from childhood, both as a composer and as a pianist-accompanist with both the human voice and with jazz, I have spent much time exploring the ill-defined and largely undocumented world of jazz singing. In this article I hope to point out some of the extensions and varied uses of the voice in jazz. (Jazz has always been dependent for much of its vitality on pop music, whatever the period; I do not intend to suggest that the art of the jazz singer is altogether different from that of the pop or rock singer. However, within the restrictions of an article such as this it would seem more fruitful to examine only one area of popular singing in detail, rather than merely to give a general view of the whole vast area of popular singing.) I believe that for a composer—and even for a singer—an understanding of the vocal flexibility and of the wide range of timbre used by the most creative jazz singers of the recent past can suggest many new possibilities.

The freedom and spontaneity of the traditional blues singers stems directly from folk music: the voice was made to behave exactly as the singer wished, concerned only with a direct and personal expression of the material—personal in that the melody and even the lyrics could be altered and embellished in whatever way seemed relevant. There was no printed music to instruct the singer as to the 'correct' version of the song, nor was there any correct way of producing the voice. The only limitations were those of artistry and of vocal range. However banal the song (jazz singing has almost always been entirely concerned with the popular music of the day), the singer could use it as the basis of a personal statement, if it seemed to provide a musical and emotional stimulus.

The first true *jazz* singer (as opposed to a blues singer) who comes immediately to mind is Billie Holiday. She was never a blues singer in that she always sang the music of her own time and was not concerned with the heritage of American negro folk music and the blues, although Bessie Smith the blues singer was, with Louis Armstrong, her strongest influence. The tragic life of Billie Holiday has been often described—in any case the voice, as one listens chronologically to her recordings, provides sufficient documentation. It turned from the almost mocking lightness of many of her early performances—the voice touching deftly on the notes of the melody, sketching curves and slides between them, the more serious emotions half-disguised, a marvellous combination of cynicism and warmth—to the terrible dragging sadness of the late recordings. The vibrato became uncontrolled, the typical glides and scoops became a parody, and the emotions were too naked for comfortable listening. Nevertheless she always had the ability to turn the most thin and frivolous song into a quite unique statement, full of emotional depths which the song itself does not necessarily reveal. She was without doubt the strongest single influence on almost all of the singers who were to follow her. A purely musical examination of her art only skates across the surface, but it is perhaps the most fruitful approach.

The basic qualities of all the best jazz singing were present in Billie Holiday's voice. Certainly a great voice is not essential—indeed it can often obscure the spontaneous, mercurial quality of the performance. Her voice was always limited in range, slightly raw and edgy, and she seemed to use it with total unconcern for its limitations. Her performances were as free and (in the best sense) unrepeatable as those of any good jazz instrumentalist. It is impossible to think that her delicate shadings, glides and half-sung tones could be either calculated or reduced to a "standard" performance, to be repeated even once again. (Compare an artist of today, such as Shirley Bassey, whom I consider grossly over-rated: she even cries in the same place every time she sings certain songs.) However many times Billie Holiday recorded—let alone performed—the same song, there were always different nuances and new variations. In the same way that a good jazz player always gives a feeling of improvisation, of invention, even when merely stating a melody, so I believe that a true jazz singer is constantly improvising, even if this involves only a rethinking of the rhythmic structure of a song. Later singers, such as the technically amazing Sarah Vaughan, based their improvisations largely on embellishment: Billie Holiday's great strength was that she almost always simplified. A typical example of this technique of "pruning" is given in her 1936 recording of Kern's *A Fine Romance*. (Ex 1—in all the following transcriptions I have tried to notate something of the singer's rhythmic quality as well as a suggestion of the vocal devices employed. Notes in brackets are "ghost-notes," which are implied rather than fully sung.) The lagging rhythm and "flattened-out" melody, together with her plaintive insistence on the upper notes of each phrase are an elegant equivalent of the gentle cynicism of the lyrics.

Even Billie Holiday's most deep-rooted mannerisms were entirely personal, and stemmed from her emotional attitude to the material rather than from a self-consciously "stylish" manner. She began more and more to slide wearily towards and away from each note, almost dragging her voice up to the next, and even to start a phrase with a fall to the "right" note from a half-sounded higher note, giving a touchingly poignant quality to her singing. Her harmonic sense was excellent: all these inflections touched instinctively on other notes which were essential parts of the harmonic structure of the song, as though she were sketching out the supporting chords. This is, of course, an essential part of jazz improvisation, and all the more improvisatory jazz singers—Fitzgerald, O'Day, Vaughan and the younger generation of McRae, Laine, Connor and Jordan—have a well-developed ear for harmony. The rhythm depends typically on speech rhythms, the voice floating freely over the solid pulse of the accompaniment, sometimes slipping behind it, sometimes moving ahead, occasionally landing right on the beat, and altogether producing complex and subtle patterns which create the indefinable "swing." Her highly inflected vocal lines made the simplest phrase extraordinarily expressive (Ex 2). Her last recordings [with Ray Ellis] (CBS Realm Jazz 52540) have a tragic intensity beyond anything else in jazz.

Example 1: Billie Holiday [improvises on] "A Fine Romance"

Example 2: Billie Holiday [improvises on] "You Don't Know What Love Is"

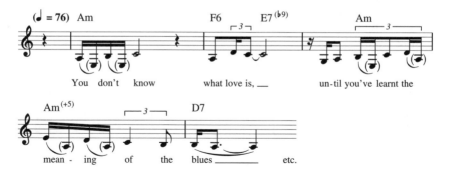

Nobody has ever disputed that Billie Holiday was a true jazz singer. Since her death in 1959 there has been an extremely tedious tendency among critics to argue about what makes a jazz singer and which artists can be said to have this apparently magical quality—one could be forgiven for thinking they were discussing the gift of second sight. Their conclusions have ranged from Edith Piaf to Nobody, and the general impression is that, if a critic likes a singer, then he or she is a jazz artist. I feel simply that a singer who is at his best with jazz accompaniment and who naturally sings freely and 'swings' is singing jazz. Many singers, for example Sinatra and Peggy Lee, have moved with ease in and out of this area of jazz, and many young pop singers, such as David Clayton Thomas and Laura Nyro, are merely sailing under a more commercial flag, but from now on I shall be discussing my *personal* choice of singers who use a particularly inventive approach to their material. I make no apologies for stressing some little-known names at the expense of others, much more widely known.

Ella Fitzgerald [1917–1996] is unquestionably the greatest of all in terms of public acclaim. Her technique and musicianship are faultless, and she generates a warmth and involvement which are remarkable. For my taste, however, her singing is a little too smooth and cozy, relying too much in recent years on well worn clichés and a tired repertoire.

Anita O'Day is a splendidly eccentric and idiosyncratic artist, who has learnt much from Billie Holiday. Although she lacks Holiday's intensity, there is a welcome and quite personal humour in her singing, together with a great flair for melodic invention. Consider her hilarious improvisation on, of all things, *Tea for Two* (Ex 3). One of the most notable features of her style is the instrumentally inclined tendency to split syllables up into melismata containing many notes, generally sung non legato (Ex 4).

Example 3: Anita O'Day [improvises on] "Tea for Two"

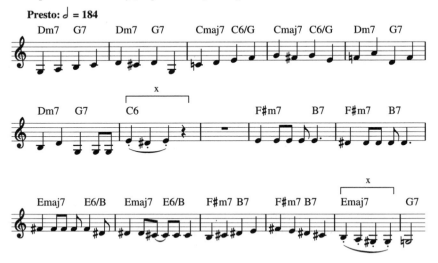

Example 4: Anita O'Day [improvises on] "I Never Realized"

The voice is wry, warm and husky. Needless to say, like all jazz singing it would not be possible without a microphone to pick up the smallest inflection of the voice—and this is in no sense a criticism. (Surely many of the most intimate features even of classical singing are frequently destroyed by the need to project even the simplest song audibly through a large concert hall, while balance problems may force a singer to disregard a composer's dynamic markings totally, in an effort to be heard above the accompaniment. The use of the microphone in more advanced music could open up a wide field of delicate nuances and shadings, at present unavailable to the classical singer.)

Like most post-war singers, Anita O'Day uses a minimum of vibrato, and when vibrato is used it is made to colour or change a note. One of the most noticeable details of her style is the way in which a sustained sound, sung without vibrato melts slowly into a gentle vibrato, just before its release.

Carmen McRae [1920–1994] is in many ways the ideal jazz singer. She started—like many others—as a jazz pianist, which gave her a thorough understanding of harmony and an almost instrumental fluency of improvisation. (Other notable singers having an instrumental training include Sarah Vaughan, Jeri Southern, Blossom Dearie, Shirley Horn and Mark Murphy.) In Carmen McRae's case this is linked with great emotional power and projection. She moves easily from a savagery reminiscent of Piaf or Lenya to passages of extreme delicacy and tenderness (Ex 6b).

My personal favourite among the more recent singers is Chris Connor. Gunther Schuller has written of her: "Chris Connor has always been one of the most original and personal of jazz singers . . . She is exclusively concerned with the essentials of music-making in a terribly personal and inner-directed manner which is easy to misunderstand or reject." Her performances can be uncomfortable in their intensity, simply because one is unprepared for such powerful and uncompromising statements to be made in the night-club atmosphere in which most of these singers have to work, or shocking in the extremes of invention and emotion to which she will take a simple popular song. The voice is deep, husky and powerful. She will so drastically revise the rhythm of a song that one has the feeling of watching a brilliant tight-rope walker, apparently in constant danger of losing his balance (or, in this case, the beat). In both cases one is aware of the absolute security which permits such risks to be taken. Her improvisations, particularly in live performance, are on occasion wilder than those of almost any other singer. Example 5 incorporates one of the more instrumental details of the style—an accented turn or trill, placed on the strong beat. This often gives a vivid touch of colour to a word or a phrase, and seems to have been characteristic of the singers (O'Day, Connor and June Christy) who at one time worked with the Kenton band (Ex 6a).

Example 5: Chris Connor [improvises on] "Chinatown"

Example 6a: Chris Connor [improvises on] "Skyscraper Blues"

Example 6b: Carmen McRae [improvises on] "Midnight Sun"

Example 6c: Sheila Jordan [improvises on] "You Are My Sunshine"

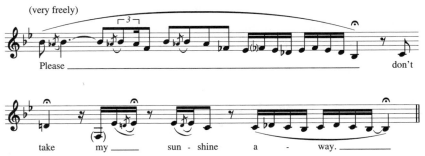

Chris Connor is one of the few singers, first prominent in the 1950s, who have made their way successfully into the stormy musical world of today. This is certainly due to her insistence on singing the most important songs of the period—whether jazz, ballads or rock—and to a strong awareness of important musical developments. Many of the best singers of the past [40] years have vanished from the musical scene because of their inability to adjust to changing tastes in popular music.

It is worth looking for the recorded work of some of the more experimental and less-known American jazz singers, such as Betty Carter or the quite remarkable Sheila Jordan—perhaps the best musician of any jazz singer whom I have known (6c).

A very strong influence on today's jazz singers is the gospel-based Soul style. Notable features are a pronounced vibrato, a very well-developed head voice and an elaborately decorated melodic line. The melodic decorations often trail like streamers *after* the main notes of the phrase, sometimes turning upwards into the head voice at the end of a note. This type of singing is invariably best suited to black singers, and is of course directly linked with today's rock music. Soul singers, such as Lorraine Ellison, Aretha Franklin or Lou Rawls, are by any standards fine jazz artists.

Throughout this article I have spoken almost exclusively of female singers, but with rare exceptions—such as Mark Murphy, Jimmy Scott and Joe Carroll—male singers seem less inclined to experiment, perhaps because of the slightly less agile and flexible nature of the male voice. [Today we have a few—McFerrin, Jarreau, Elling.]

Although European jazz singers are in general less well known to the public than their American counterparts, much interesting work has been done over here. Cleo Laine's singing is happily widely known and needs no recommendation. She has a remarkably beautiful voice with a range going from the C below middle C to the G or A on four ledger lines, and a huge variety of vocal colour. These qualities are linked to faultless intelligence and musicality and a great ability to project her material. At times she seems to rely on over-elaborate routines, with too many changes of key, tempo and rhythm: an average singer may be greatly helped by such fanciful packaging, but Cleo Laine has no need of it. She is possibly at her best when least encumbered and least concerned with technical display.

Another English singer, Norma Winstone, is involved almost exclusively with jazz and is a totally uncompromising and innately musical singer. I personally regret the fact that she is so often used as an ethereal wordless voice in avantgarde jazz works, rather than being allowed to project her own very interesting personality.

On the continent two singers stand out. Rita Reys lives and works in Holland and has sung at the Bath Festival as well as winning many awards at jazz festivals, for example in Antibes and Prague. Within a fairly conventional format she is a charming and inventive artist.

The Norwegian, Karin Krog, is perhaps the most experimental jazz singer in Europe. She has an intensely probing mind, strong convictions and a vivid jazz style; she has been recently working with ring modulator and synthesiser, the voice being electronically modified; and has taken part in experimental theatre. Her work runs the risk of seeming pretentious, but it undoubtedly represents one of the most promising and forward-looking developments in jazz.

To sum up this brief survey of a neglected art, the main characteristics of jazz singing would appear to be the following:

(a) totally personal and individual attitude to the material: this may transform the simplest and most ephemeral song into an original and powerful statement;

(b) a constant quality of improvisation: this requires an almost instrumental flexibility of voice coupled with the ability to use any vocal timbre, however unorthodox, and a constant use of decoration of various kinds;

(c) a strong and inventive rhythmic feeling, which may change the whole rhythmic structure of the basic material and will often come into conflict with the basic pulse.

One of the most fascinating things about vocal jazz is that the singer is always expressing the lyrics, even when creating quite new melodic lines. This apparent limitation can, paradoxically, be one of the most productive elements of the style. I have never been interested in attempts to use the voice wordlessly as an extra instrument. In the first place an instrument can usually do it better, but more important this approach seems to deny the *raison d'être* of singing—the element of human expression.

The dangers of jazz singing are considerable: it can degenerate into a mere parade of mannerisms—a totally artificial approach. Vocal experiments can often obscure the sense and innate qualities of the basic material, or may simply disguise bad singing, giving rise to appalling intonation and a forced and unnatural voice production. Much recent work has tended to be pretentious and self-conscious in its search for new and "meaningful" developments, but I feel very strongly that at best the jazz singer's approach to the voice is worthy of serious consideration by any unprejudiced listener who is interested in exploring a fascinating and rewarding area of music. (Richard Rodney Bennett, "The Technique of the Jazz Singer," *Music and Musicians*, February 1972)

To conclude, we return to Lawrence Gushee. In excerpts from an analytical piece about saxophonist Lester Young (I reprinted the complete piece in my previous anthology, *A Lester Young Reader* [Washington, D.C.: Smithsonian Institution Press, 1991]), Gushee outlines the approaches that have been used to analyze jazz. In the parts of the article that are not given here, he used Young's music to illustrate an eclectic approach that fully appreciates the improvisational nature of the music. He does not try to analyze jazz the way one would a written score, for as a clarinetist himself, he knows enough about improvisation to understand how decisions are made, and how it feels to work with a rhythm section.

Written and *oral* per se are rather crude, if not misleading terms, each covering a variety of specific cultural or historical circumstances, and not very useful for a taxonomy of music, an analysis of poetic or "creative process," or an explanation of musical change.

My discussion of Lester Young's "Shoe Shine Boy" seems in retrospect to recommend a versatility in analysis, not simply as an exercise in the exhaustion of possibilities, but in recognition that in music—perhaps especially with functionally differentiated or stratified ensembles (as in jazz bands)—different kinds of relationships operate over different time spans. It may be that within one and the same kind of music, performers differ greatly in the emphasis or control of one kind of relationship, and in the way their memory functions at the various levels. And finally, I discover that my subject is chiefly oral composition, although the proximity in time of the two performances examined can be considered to involve a kind of transmission. . . .

From "Lester Young's 'Shoe Shine Boy'"
LAWRENCE GUSHEE

Preliminary Note on Jazz Analysis
There is no commonly accepted coherent method of jazz analysis. The most thorough and consistent applications of analysis to jazz to date are those of Thomas Owens dealing with the playing of Charlie Parker and of Gunther Schuller dealing with the playing of Afro-Americans during the 1920s. These represent, in my opinion, two distinct approaches, which I designate "formulaic" and "motivic," respectively. Two other approaches, called here "schematic" and "semiotic," are encountered, along with eclectic mixtures. My understanding of the characteristic features of the four approaches or types are summarized in table 1. Whether these types of analysis correspond to types of creation or perception is a question with no general answer. In the present instance I believe they do. . . .

Table 1

Type of Analysis	Methods Objectives/Content	Assumptions	Boundaries
MOTIVIC Tirro[a] Schuller[b]	Demonstration of organic relations, development, climactic (tension-release) structure. Logically connected ideas.	Criteria of logic. Aesthetic merit of the work.	The work itself
FORMULAIC Owens[c]	Labeling of phrases according to the lexicon. Appropriate choice of compatible formulas, with relaxed logical requirements.	Learning and performance by rote or imitation.	The collective style
SCHEMATIC Dauer[d] Hodeir[e]	Generation of specific expression by transformation of fundamental structures (including a tune or chord progression as well as other patterns).	Separable levels of mental activity.	The process of forming
SEMIOTIC (A great deal of the popular literature of jazz)	Meaning as given by the system of signs. Decoding of mythic structure.	The apparatus of general semiotics; or sociopolitical theory.	The culture

[a] Frank Tirro, "Constructive Elements in Jazz Improvisation," *Journal of the American Musicological Society* (1974):285–305.

[b] Gunther Schuller, *Early Jazz: Its Roots and Musical Development* (New York: Oxford University Press, 1968); idem, "Sonny Rollins and the Challenge of Thematic Improvisation," *Jazz Review* 1 (November 1958):6–11, 21.

[c] Thomas Owens, "Charlie Parker: Techniques of Improvisation," 2 vols. (Ph.D. diss., University of California, Los Angeles, 1974).

[d] Alfons M. Dauer, "Improvisation: Zur Technik der spontanen Gestaltung in Jazz," *Jazzforschung/Jazz Research* 1 (1969):113–32.

[e] André Hodeir, *Jazz: Its Evolution and Essence,* trans. by David Noakes (New York: Grove Press, 1956).

The Collective Structure of Jazz Performance

The discourse of "classic jazz" is carried out in four- and eight-measure phrases, choruses, and three-minute recordings, features that it shares with the U.S. popular song of the period. In jazz these units of structure are not "deep," whether internal (in each player and fully explicable by him) or external (in the activity of the rhythm section). The listener's (or participant's) knowledge of such things is perhaps more tacit, with, in any event, strong reinforcement from dancing or knowing the words of a tune. In addition the rhythm section is part of the performance, and its behavior is articulated at various levels (pulse, harmonic rhythm, hierarchical punctuation of the larger units). Within this highly predictable binary structure, there is much opportunity for briefly playing "against" the prevailing pulse, but not to the extent of muddling the major points of arrival or departure.

The jazz rhythm section is also noisy and resonant, with percussive time-keeping counteracted by cymbal shimmer, indistinct decay of the string bass, and the timbral liaison provided by guitar. Not only does such noise and resonance make for continuity, they may also be understood as "energizing" or giving a kind of meaning to single pitches that may be played by soloists (a concept more usually encountered in discussions of African musics).

These features combine to produce a merciful and supportive environment for the jazz soloist. It is difficult to become completely lost: at the rapid tempo of a "Shoe Shine Boy," there are points of reference passing by every four seconds or so. Errors are made, however, and in places that suggest the importance of eight-measure units in terms of memory encoding. In an AABA structure a performer may forget the second A section (or play the bridge too soon, however you wish). Another related error is to play the wrong bridge, or to forget the correct one.

In this already strongly connected environment, a soloist may play "ideas" of quite incoherent character—as judged by the norms of written composition—in successive four-measure units or, sometimes, especially in the bridge, in successive two-measure units. They can be taken as surface detail floating on the rhythm section: thus Schuller's dictum that "the average improvisation is mostly a stringing together of unrelated ideas." Often such decisions as to incoherence do not take into account such features as timbral continuity or a characteristic personal timing with respect to the rhythm section. The piece is already so strongly connected in its rhythmic order that a time-span of four measures may be perceived as linked to a preceding one merely by virtue of a note-group, or even a single pitch, played in the equivalent metrical position. Pitch-centered or motivic analysis will often not take this sufficiently into account. Also, such connections, clearly as they may be *heard* in performance, lose much of their force when *viewed* in a transcription.

Dramatization of the Collective Structure

In any popular song as well as in the harmonization that a jazz performance may follow, there are major and minor points of repetition and arrival in the timing cycle. Immediate repetition is relatively weak, but one that comes after significantly contrasting material at the same durational level is strong. The approach to measure 25 of a thirty-two-measure chorus (repetition after contrast) is more portentous than to measure 9 (repetition). While such weighting factors may be given their full expression in the performance of a popular song (or, even more, in an art song) and in the behavior of a jazz rhythm section, the situation is different for the jazz soloist. This is because practically all jazz solo performance avoids literal or close to literal repetition of four- and eight-measure units. If encountered, such repetition is immediately labeled as "composition." If the strategic or weighty places of the timing cycle are to be recognized in the solo, some means other than literal repetition must be found.

There is another kind of weight in the solo enterprise. To play a solo is to step out of, emerge from the band, eventually to return. During whatever period of time that is given by prearrangement to the soloist, or that he can lay claim to, his goal is to demonstrate "chops" (technique), "soul" (expressivity), and "ideas" (originality and, to some degree, logic). While these need not be used separately to mark off one part of a solo from another, or used in the service of a rhetoric corresponding to the social and formal articulations of a solo, I believe that they may be, and *are,* in the performances of "Shoe Shine Boy" by Lester Young.

Formulas and Formulaic System

The distinction between formulas—more or less literal motive or phrase repetitions—and formulaic system—a more generalized structural outline embracing many specific formulas—would seem to be more obvious to the student of music than to the student of literature. Music claims transformation and varied repetition as a fundamental forming process. Whether we can isolate levels of organization in music so neatly as in language (see Nowacki) is to me questionable. In any event, my ensuing discussion of formulas in these performances will deal with melody, then phrase and harmonic structure as reflected in melody. But according to my table above, these last two topics can be seen as instances of schematic, not formulaic, analysis. . . .

Phrasing and "Changes"

Much solo jazz performance of the twenties and thirties can easily be regarded as melodic paraphrase. Even when this is not the case, one hears a solo quite frequently as following the phrasing of the melody. Obviously this cannot be simply a matter of binary construction, which would hardly be enough to differentiate one tune from another, but must involve preservation of other features of the tune in a solo, such as the actual duration of phrases or the number of tones in them. There is some possibility for self-deception, however, when a listener knows the tune very well himself and "hears" it along with a performance. But I have no doubt that it is part of the perception for the jazz musician as listener. . . .

Jazz performance is sometimes explained as based on harmonic progression. This is often meant in some fairly strict sense; that is, jazz uses the pitches of the "vertical" harmonies as the primary constituents of "horizontal" phrases. An extreme example would be a solo consisting only of the arpeggiation of the changes. Approaches to such an extreme do exist but are not generally admired, unless in some instances as tours de force. Generally the changes are not considered so much as a schematic feature greatly facilitating improvisation but as a measure by which one may determine a player's originality, for example, Bix Beiderbecke playing accented ninths and thirteenths, Charlie Parker playing on the tertial extensions upwards of seventh chords, and the like. It is my opinion that the changes are most important for the act of performance—as opposed to that of analysis—in their ability to orient a player in the thirty-two-measure time cycle. Be that as it may, analysts of jazz are sometimes rather incautious in their assumptions about what the changes are, especially in deriving them from sheet music or a lead sheet or fake book rather than from the rhythm section as actually recorded. In "Shoe Shine Boy," for example, it is clear from listening to the various performances that the augmented V^7 is much favored by Count Basie and his sidemen as well. Thus, a feature that might be considered a deviation from the sheet music harmony is normal with respect to the changes actually used. . . .

Perhaps my questions so far might be considered as addressed to the how and the what of these performances. Be that as it may, I take the subsequent remarks to ask or answer, in part, why.

Should we relabel as "motives" the phrases or bundles of features I have designated formulas or expressions of an underlying scheme, the thrust of analysis shifts from the oral to the composed, from the performance as one possible arrangement among many to the performance as a unique creation, from the variations of a basic form to the repetitions or transformations of a motive that make form. I don't believe such a shift to be profitable. . . .

There is no reason, though, to rule out intentional motivic work from the oral poetic of jazz, especially at slower tempos or in the longer time cycles of more recent jazz. It is simply that in this style, at such a tempo, the time cycle's demands for change of any sort take precedence. In illustration of this constraint, I could mention the rather frequent judgment one makes that a pattern is ended too soon: the listener has the leisure to reflect that a process could have been continued to good effect. But the player, like Lord's epic singer, is always thinking ahead and has perhaps already forgotten what he's playing while still doing it. . . .

If our model for Lester Young's performances is that of oral composition, the actual order of performance matters little. The comparative "straightness" of version A and the adventurousness of B may be understood either as a decision in the context of a recording session to take fewer chances or a desire to play something a bit more challenging. But if the model is that of reflective composition, working toward a more socially comprehensible sequence of ideas, then B–A appears to be the necessary order. . . .

It may be that we must carefully distinguish immediately successive performances from those separated by an interval of time sufficient to diminish muscular memory. Also, conventionalization may be more prominent in the different circumstances.

The question of recording order is not without interest, but perhaps only a scenic tour that diverts us from asking whether behind the adventurous and variable detail of the two versions there lies an overall shape—particularly one comprehensible or perceptible by the ordinary listener (a category that may include many musicians). I've already suggested above that there may be a kind of rhetorical plan, serving not only to give "meaning" to these performances but to forge two choruses together. In fact, the plan I suggest could not practically unfold within the confines of one chorus.

> 1. The first move is a move out of the band or in juxtaposition to another soloist or both. It must catch the attention, and in Lester Young's case—who at this point in his career was not satisfied with rhetorical gestures alone—must be an intelligible musical idea. It will generally fill the first four measures.

The initial idea should not be too complicated. The place for tricky stuff, that is, cute ideas or technical display, is later—but how much later? The obvious point in a two-chorus solo is at the beginning of the second chorus, although one might start after the first bridge. In any event,

> 2. Demonstration of mastery, "chops," technique identifiable with respect to the instrument, normal harmony, or rhythmic construction. In Lester Young's case this often involves polymetric or otherwise unbalanced phrasing rather than rapid playing. . . .
>
> 3. Return to the band, "wrapping it up," an expressive peak reached by using common property, a riff, or a well-known lick. . . .

I construe these processes according to the scheme of table 1 in the following way:

1. *Semiotic.* Lester Young, like many players, thought of a solo as "telling a story." This story transcends the repetitive, hierarchical

structure of the tune and its harmonization, and depends on the use of typologically different material.*

2. *Schematic.* He also affirmed the pop song structure of "Shoe Shine Boy" in differentiating measure four from measure eight cadences (*ouvert* and *clos,* if you will), in observing the conventional character of the channel or bridge, and so on. In a few cases, that structure is deliberately upset.

3. *Formulaic.* As a saxophone player Young had his bag of propensities and tricks—call them conscious style or automatisms—such as false fingerings, rips upward to the palm keys, dramatic bombs in the extreme low register, chains of thirds. Beyond that, of course, he might use favorite motives having nothing to do with the saxophone per se.

4. *Motivic.* Young knew this tune as such—witness the prominent F-sharp—and found a degree-progression filling a four-measure segment that he used in various positions and shapes in [three recorded versions]. It may well not be specific to this tune. . . .

It will perhaps seem a small accomplishment if all I have done in these pages is to reaffirm the necessity of a sense of overall structure or an image of the whole work, if that work is to be valued and remembered in detail by those who come after. (Without saying, to be sure, that this is a guarantee of survival.) More than that, I hope to have shown that oral composition, at least in the distinctly mixed oral-written tradition called jazz, in some of its expressions, proceeds along several tracks at once. I suppose that I have tried to show that in addition to the communal, highly conventional organizing schemata of jazz playing, there are others that we must invoke or imagine in order to account for the extraordinary profundity or coherence of some jazz playing, wherever and whenever we may find it. . . . (Lawrence Gushee, "Lester Young's 'Shoe Shine Boy,'" in International Musicological Society, *Report of the Twelfth Congress, Berkeley, 1977,*

---

* Richard M. Sudhalter and Philip R. Evans, *Bix, Man & Legend* (New Rochelle, N.Y.: Arlington House, 1974), 192, report the following exchange between Wingy Manone and Louis Armstrong: "Hey, Pops, how do you do play so many choruses the way you do?" . . . "Well, I tell you . . . the first chorus I plays the melody. The second chorus I plays the melody round the melody, and the third chorus I routines." Although one must doubt that this is a verbatim transcript of the conversation, it is descriptive of one of Armstrong's ways of dealing with multichorus solos.

ed. Daniel Heartz and Bonnie Wade [Kassell: Barenreiter, 1981], 151–169)

Perhaps the most important legacy of Gushee's article is his recommendation, at the outset, to pursue "a versatility in analysis." In other words, do not get stuck in one approach, but look at the music in many different ways.

4

Where Did the Music Come From?

Many white observers felt early on that African Americans had a special gift for music and dance, although the same authors usually believed African Americans were otherwise inferior. One of the most outspoken writings on this topic was anonymously published in *Dwight's Journal of Music,* a Boston publication, on November 15, 1856. (The same journal published a better-known piece on spirituals by Lucy McKim on November 8, 1862.) The author, identified only as "Evangelist," is unusually positive about black culture and decidedly critical of whites, who are described as "a silent and reserved people." Still, the author is a product of his or her time, and maintains that blacks are "inferior to the white race in reason and intellect." Although it predates jazz, this article is reprinted for its historical value regarding the era before jazz, and because it is otherwise, I believe, unavailable.

Songs of the Blacks

EVANGELIST

The only musical population of this country are the negroes of the South. Here at the North we have teachers in great numbers, who try to graft the love of music upon the tastes of our colder race. But their success is only limited. A few good singers are produced, and some fine instrumental performers, but the thing never becomes general. Music may perchance be the fashion for a winter. But it does not grow to a popular enthusiasm. It never becomes a passion or habit of the people. We are still dependent on foreigners for our music. Italian singers fill our concert rooms, and German bands parade our streets.

Throughout the country the same holds true. Singing masters itinerate from village to village, to give instruction in the tuneful art, but the most they can muster is a score or two of men and maidens to sing in church on Sunday. Brother Jonathan is awkward at the business, and sings only on set occasions. Let him be enrolled in the ranks of the choir, and placed in the front of the gallery, and he will stand up like a grenadier, and roll out lustily the strains of a psalm. But all his singing is done in public. He makes little music at home, or at most only on the Sabbath day. During the week his melodies are unheard. He does not go to his labor singing to himself along the road. No song of home or country, of love or war, escapes his lips as he works in his shop or follows the plough. Our people work in silence, like convicts in a Penitentiary. They go to their tasks, not with a free and joyous spirit that bursts into song, but with a stern, resolute, determined air, as if they had a battle to fight, or great difficulties to overcome.

Even the gentler sex, who ought to have most, of poetry and music, seem strangely indifferent to it. Young ladies who have spent years in learning to play on the piano, and sing Italian airs, drop both as soon as they are married. Enter their houses a few months later, and they tell you that they are out of practice; they have forgotten their music, their pianos are unopened, and their harps are unstrung.

Compared with our taciturn race, the African nature is full of poetry and song. The Negro is a natural musician. He will learn to play on an instrument more quickly than a white man. They have magnificent voices and sing without instruction. They may not know one note from another, yet their ears catch the strains of any floating air, and they repeat it by imitation. The native melody of their voices falls without art into the channel of song. They go singing to their daily labors. The maid sings about the house, and the laborer sings in the field.

Besides their splendid organs of voice, the African nature is full of poetry. Inferior to the white race in reason and intellect, they have more imagination, more lively feelings and a more expressive manner.

In this they resemble the southern nations of Europe. Their joy and grief are not pent up in the heart, but find instant expression in their eyes and voice. With their imagination they clothe in rude poetry the incidents of their lowly life, and set them to simple melodies. Thus they sing their humble loves in strains full of tenderness. We at the North hear these songs only as burlesqued by our Negro Minstrels, with faces blackened with charcoal. Yet even thus all feel that they have rare sweetness and melody.

Mingled with these love songs are plaintive airs which seem to have caught a tone of sadness and pathos from the hardships and frequent separation of their slave life. They are the Songs of their Captivity, and are sung with a touching effect. No song of a concert room ever thrilled us like one of these simple African airs, heard afar off in the stillness of a summer night. Sailing down the Mississippi, the voyager on the deck of the steamer may often hear these strains, wild, sad and tender, floating from the shore.

But it is in religion that the African pours out his whole voice and soul. A child in intellect, he is a child in faith. All the revelations of the Bible have to him a startling vividness, and he will sing of the judgment and the resurrection with a terror or a triumph which cannot be concealed. In religion he finds also an element of freedom which he does not find in his hard life, and in these wild bursts of melody he seems to be giving utterance to that exultant liberty of soul which no chains can bind, and no oppression subdue. As hundreds assemble at a camp meeting in the woods, and join in the chorus of such a hymn as

> *"When I can read my title clear,*
> *To mansions in the skies,"*

the unimpassioned hearer is almost lifted from his feet by the volume and majesty of the sound.

No voices of well trained choir in church or cathedral, no pealing organ, nor mighty anthem, ever moved us like these voices of a multitude going up to God under the open canopy of heaven. Blessed power of music! that can raise the poor and despised above their care and poverty. It is a beautiful gift of God to this oppressed race to lighten their sorrows in the house of their bondage.

Might not our countrymen all learn a lesson from these simple children of Africa? We are a silent and reserved people. Foreigners think us taciturn and gloomy. So we are, compared with the European nations. The Germans sing along the banks of the Rhine. The Swiss shepherd sings on the highest passes of the Alps, and the peasant of Tyrol fills his vallies with strains wild as the peaks and the torrents around him. But Americans, though surrounded with everything to make a people happy, do not show outward signs of uncommon cheerfulness and content. We are an anxious, careworn race. Our brows are sad and gloomy. Songless and joyless, the laborer goes to his task. This dumb silence is ungrateful in those who have such cause for thankfulness. Americans are the most favored people on one earth, and yet they are the least expressive of their joy. So that we almost deserve the severe comment of a foreigner, who on seeing the great outward prosperity, and yet the anxious look of the people, said that "in American there was less misery, *and less happiness,* than in any other country on earth."

Let us not be ashamed to learn the art of happiness from the poor bondman at the South. If slaves can pour out their hearts in melody, how ought freemen to sing! If that love of music which is inborn in them, could be inbred in us, it would do much to lighten the anxiety and care which brood on every face and weigh on every heart. The spirit of music would beguile the toilsome hours, and make us cheerful and happy in our labor.

Nor would this light and joyous heart make us too gay, and so lead to folly and frivolity. On the contrary, it would prove a friend to virtue and purity. The sour and morose spirit, when it recoils from its oppressive gloom, is apt to plunge into the worst excesses. The absence of a cheerful buoyancy is one of the causes which drive men into vice and sin. If every family sung together at early morn, that lingering melody would render their spirits more elastic. With his children's voices in his ear, the hard-working man would go more cheerfully to his labor, and those melodies would make his spirit sunny and joyous through the day.

If common domestic joys, home, health and fireside love, can thus fill the heart with happiness, and cause it to break forth into singing;

surely, when that heart is bounding with immortal hope, it may rise to the highest strains of exultation and of ecstacy.

"Let those refuse to sing
Who never knew our God.
But children of the heavenly King
May speak their joys abroad."

(Evangelist, "Songs of the Blacks,"
Dwight's Journal of Music, November 5, 1856, pp. 51–52)

Fifty years after the above article was published, jazz was created by a later generation of African Americans. While this fact may seem obvious to the reader, in the past white observers often avoided this simple acknowledgment by referring to jazz more generally as "American" music. Even in recent years white fans have told me that the music is just as much European as American in content. As I like to point out to them, that begs the question of who took these influences and put them together to create jazz—African Americans. The ingredients didn't combine by themselves. Master chefs were required.

In the early years white observers further complicated the issue by using the word *jazz,* as we have discussed, to refer to the popular songs of Irving Berlin as well as to the performances of black musicians and improvisers. What the white public didn't know was that black Americans saw right through these maneuverings. Some proof of their awareness comes from the pages of *Opportunity.*

Opportunity, Journal of Negro Life was begun by the National Urban League on January 1, 1923, as a forum for writing on "social and economic problems affecting Negro life" and as a showplace for creative arts. In the last issue, winter 1949, the League could write with some satisfaction that in the intervening years blacks had begun to contribute to many other publications, both for the mainstream press and for the black press. With budgets becoming limited, the League decided to concentrate its funds on services in industrial relations, vocational guidance, programs in social welfare, community studies, and programs for urban youth. (The periodical was reborn in August 1996 as the *Equal Opportunity Journal,* with hopes of publishing twice a year.)

In the July 1923 issue, editor Charles S. Johnson took to task a critic named Henry T. Finck, who had written that Negro folk music was nothing but an imitation of such writers as Stephen Foster. Johnson's anger is expressed primarily through sarcasm. He points out that even Finck acknowledged that Foster "spent his time studying plantation life and attending Negro camp meetings [religious get-togethers]. These are peculiar tactics for an original genius. It would be difficult to convince a man from Mars that he went to these meetings to inspire the Negroes." Today it should be obvious to anyone that the dialect of Foster's songs is an imitation of southern Negro speech. I doubt Foster, who was of Scotch-Irish and English extraction, said "doo-dah," as sung in his "De Camptown Races" (or "de" for that matter) when he was at home with his family. Johnson also noted that "although the Negroes are called imitators (intended as a distinctive trait and a disparagement) the songs were made popular by white men with their faces blackened. This, presumably, is not imitation." Point made!

In a short, unsigned editorial from 1928, Johnson (I assume it is he) takes the same tactic to expose the foolishness of arguments that take credit for jazz away from black Americans. He notes at the end that a white woman claimed to have invented the dance craze called "the Charleston", but she was "naive enough" to admit that she'd learned the basic steps from her black maid.

The Origin of Jazz

Scientists occasionally give expression to astonishingly naive observations. Comes now Dr. Smith Ely Jellife, noted neurologist, in an address before the New York Society for clinical psychiatry with this extraordinary explanation of jazz music: Irving Berlin's mother suffered from an irregular heart! The irregular rhythm of her heart exerted a prenatal influence upon the son, and thus jazz was born.

Proof: "I proposed the idea that Irving Berlin may have been born with a talent for irregular rhythms of jazz, the rhythms of syncopation, by the possibility of his mother's having had an irregular heart. You can imagine my astonishment when a physician arose and said: 'That is a strange fact. I was physician to Mrs. Baline, the mother of Irving Berlin, and she did have a cardiac affection, which brought about her death. . . .'"

"I remember that I inquired for the doctor's name at the time of the meeting. His name has slipped my mind now. . . ."

And so goes another of the preposterous assumptions [denying] that Negroes created jazz. There was, not so long ago, a feature article in one of the popular magazines, by a white music hall favorite with the caption: "How I Created The Charleston". It is barely possible that some forebear suffered from St. Vitus' dance. She was naive enough, however, to explain that she had learned the essential steps from her Negro maid, and by transferring them from the servants' quarters to the stage, presumably, supplied the element of creation. (Charles S. Johnson, "The Origin of Jazz" (editorial), *Opportunity, Journal of Negro Life,* April 1928)

(By the way, the song "The Charleston" was written by a marvelous black American composer and pianist—a great influence among jazz musicians—named James P. Johnson.)

Once we acknowledge that jazz is clearly an African American invention, it is equally clear that all kinds of African American music have certain distinctive characteristics that owe something to the African origins of black American culture. This bit of deduction, obvious to us today, was not so obvious to writers in the early days of jazz. They expressed a general sense, as we will see in chapter 6, that the music owed something to the "wildness" or "savagery" of black culture, but this concession is rarely meant as a compliment. Typical were the English authors Norman Sargant and Tom Sargant, who acknowledged the African influence but saw it as a danger to modern society. In *Musical Times,* they wrote:

Jazz is a reversion, a retrogression, to the primitive. The person whose whole life is immersed in it, without any uplifting influence, whose sole interest in music is swaying before a gramophone [record player] to the latest rag [ragtime music, as we will see, was often not distinguished from jazz in those days], will find that some unconscious, psychological change is taking place in his outlook on life. . . . So, when our fathers so cruelly ravished Africa of her men, women and children, they never thought that to-day we should be reaping where they had sown, and that jazz would be visited upon the children of a later generation. (Norman Sargant and Tom Sargant, "Negro-American Music or the Origin of Jazz," *Musical Times,* September 1, 1931)

The Sargants make jazz sound like a punishment to modern society for having engaged in slavery. It's a most ironic comment, because when the English began bringing slaves to the so-called "New World" they never in their wildest dreams imagined they would one day need to learn how to live with Africans as equals. Likewise, the English (and other) settlers who became the founders of the United States had the same difficulty accepting blacks as partners in the new country.

It's all too easy to see the slavers as evil people, but slavery has been a nearly universal fact of human life since ancient times and is mentioned in the beginnings of recorded history. As soon as two tribes came upon one another, the human response seems to have been a battle to the death. And when one side won, what were the victors to do with the enemy survivors? Let them go to fight again another day? Certainly not. They became the slaves of the victors. Thus slavery began, and as human populations grew, so did the magnitude of slavery. For all their enlightenment, the ancient Greeks had slaves. In Africa, as in other parts of the world, one tribe would force another into slavery, and when Europeans originally explored there, the first Africans they purchased were already slaves to other Africans. Many of the African men were destined for execution had they not been bought by the Europeans. No one seriously questioned slavery until the late 1700s (the English Quakers were in the movement's forefront), just when the English in America decided to break free from English rule. In the meantime, selling African people as slaves had become an international business dominated by the English, Spanish, Portuguese, and Dutch.*

The numbers involved in the slave trade have been mythologized. In reccent times some have suggested that 100 million (or more) Africans died while in transit from Africa to America alone. Since the population of the entire African continent did not surpass 100 million until after 1850, that figure is clearly fabricated. Scholars have estimated the number of Africans who were brought to the United States, the Caribbean, and Central and South America by the end of the U.S. Civil War at between ten and twelve million, and the number who died in transit at perhaps a million, which is still horrifying. The point is that if even one person died, that is one too many. A much larger number of Africans were enslaved in the Middle East, where the business began as early as 650 and was not totally banned until 1962. (It still goes on, albeit undercover, in Sudan and possibly elsewhere). According to the *Encyclopedia Britannica*, "approximately 18,000,000 Africans were delivered into the Islamic trans-Saharan and Indian Ocean slave trades between 650 and 1905." (Other sources give a lower number, but in any case it is clear that this is a major story not well known in the Western world.)

Of the millions of Africans brought to the New World, only about 427,000 landed in what became the United States. But for a variety of reasons, including the more temperate climate, better living and

---

* The idea that Jews were leaders of the slave trade is so obviously false it is a wonder that Louis Farrakhan and others continue to promote it. During the slave trade period, Spain and Portugal had virtually no Jews—they had expelled all Jews in the 1490s and made it illegal to practice Judaism on pain of death. England successfully banished its Jews in 1290 and only began to allow a Jewish community to be built up again by the late 1690s. Holland, which was more tolerant, did have a Jewish community, and it appears that a few Dutch Jews may have been active in buying and selling slaves from Africa. In America, where less than six thousand Jews lived until the 1800s, a few were involved in the business side of slavery. I know of none who were plantation owners, nor of any who kept more than a few "house" slaves, nor of any who kept slaves for longer than seven years, in accordance with biblical law. Although Jews were not blameless, they were involved in proportion to their population, which was less than 1/16 of 1 percent, and they had virtually no political power or leadership to exercise.

The final and most telling proof that the Jews were minor players in the slave trade is that virtually all African Americans have names originating from the British Isles, because they were named after the plantation owners—Armstrong, Parker, Davis, Smith, and Jones are British names, Gillespie is Irish, Coltrane is Scottish. No one has ever documented any African American who was named after a Jewish "master." (By the way, Whoopi Goldberg's birth name was Johnson, a British name, and Louis Farrakhan was born with the British name Louis Eugene Walcott.)

working conditions, a higher proportion of women among the slaves, the fact that white farmers had on average only ten slaves, and the fact that farmers encouraged Africans to raise children, the African American population grew while the number of Africans south of the U.S. border drastically declined. By 1865, the U.S. was home to four and a half million black people, more than were living in all the other countries of the Western hemisphere combined. They represented about one seventh of the total U.S. population. Roughly 10 percent were free citizens, distributed equally between the South and the North. The remaining 90 percent who had been slaves remained in the Southern states until the 1910s, when the great migration north began in earnest—taking with it the new music called jazz.

England's plan had been to send small numbers of its people to America (itself named after a Portuguese explorer, Amerigo Vespucci) to oversee the farming of its land with the actual work to be done by slaves. The English immigrants who ran the plantations at first thought of America as a remote, godforsaken place that nobody would really choose as a permanent residence. Of course, many English did eventually settle here permanently, and the growing African slave population was to become a major moral issue (not to mention the fate of the native peoples already living here, but that's a whole other story). The slavery issue was hotly debated during the framing of the U.S. Constitution, since slavery so blatantly contradicted some of the stated principles of the new country.

Eventually European descendants had to learn to accept their African slaves as equals. This cultural process was incredibly painful—and it's not fully resolved yet—not only because of white Americans' racism toward the Africans. Compounding the problem, the Africans had, for the most part, not been educated properly to enable them to perform as equals with the other Americans. Also there was the perceptual problem. In order to maintain slavery, the whites had convinced themselves that Africans were inferior, and to break fully and quickly through hundreds of years of this kind of indoctrination was impossible. Finally, since white Americans had known black people when they were at their lowest station, even when they met an accomplished black person, many could not break the perception that "we knew you when you were slaves."

As Leroi Jones (Imamu Amiri Baraka) points out so clearly in *Blues People* (New York: William Morrow, 1963), to be an African American is very different from being an African—different in language, in religion, in music, in types of instruments, in lifestyle, in political situation. So when we are looking for residuals of African culture in jazz, and I believe they exist, we are not looking for African melodies or instruments, but African concepts—concepts of sound quality, of structure, and of the role of musicians in cultural life. (Also refer back to Gushee on page 70.)

A writer named Rebecca Hourwich was, in 1926, one of the few white writers who actually heard and liked both African music and jazz and could write about the connections she heard. I know nothing of her, but I gather from the article and from her name that she was an American Jew who had traveled to South Africa, perhaps to visit relations there. Hourwich heard a general similarity between African music and jazz—nothing scholarly about it, but it's an observation few in her day were making. Some of her language is clearly condescending, however; for example, she talks of the black girls' "greedy little claws."

Where the Jazz Begins

REBECCA HOURWICH

Aboard a train creeping across the monotonous African veldt, I was approached by a little brown beggar girl. She shuffled her feet, wriggled her tummy, rolled her eyes, opened and closed her greedy little claws and wailed her blues, punctuating them with "Sheelin', meesus, sheelin'."

For a fleeting instant, until the first demand for a "sheelin'," I thought I was back home. Suddenly I was seized with a violent attack of homesickness.

One evening about three months after I had returned, someone brought me to the Harlem extension of Broadway. In one of the black-and-white dens of dance a singing high yaller ["high yellow,"a light-skinned black woman] came up to our table. She shuffled her feet, wriggled her tummy, rolled her eyes, opened and closed her greedy little claws, wailed her blues.

And suddenly, in the tropical stuffiness of that chamber in the black man's Broadway, a pang of homesickness swept over me and I was seized with a violent attack of nostalgia for Africa.

Sisters under their skins, indeed, are the priestesses of jazz in Africa and America.

Jazz, as we know it, is unmistakably American. But it is derived directly and indirectly from the music of Africa. If you could hear the native music makers and watch their dances, you would easily recognize the strange lyric bond that links the Dark Continent with the New World.

From early morning, throughout the day and well into the night, the African makes music. From Capetown, across the lower strip of the continent, through to Portuguese East Africa are native tribes distinctly different in racial appearance and type from the American Negro. But start the natives singing or dancing and the ensuing scene is one that might be enjoyed at the old market in Montgomery, Ala., the levees at New Orleans or in darktown anywhere.

To the American it is the one authentic touch of "back home." Inevitably comes the realization: why, this is jazz! This is the land of jazz! This is the birthplace of jazz!

There is a quality in jazz, a let-go prankishness, a wildness and a certain plaintive wistfulness of which the Negro is creator and master. From the cakewalk to the Charleston it would seem that the black man has proved his title to the body and soul of jazz.

The World's Noise Record

In Africa I heard on all sides lilt and swing and twanging that seemed to yearn for some friendly hand which would set to it "banana" and "mammy" lyrics. And I saw everywhere the perfect, the original shimmy, bunny hug, turkey trot and the entire group through which ballroom dancing has passed since it wandered away from the Blue Danube.

Music in Africa had its origin not as an independent art but as an accompanying chant to poetry and dancing according to Professor

Kirby of the Witwatersrand University of Johannesburg. From the start this chant held hint of music, for rhythm and melody are as old as man.

We know little of the earliest evolutionary stages of native music in Africa. From that continent, however, we do know that it traveled to Spain by way of the Moorish occupation.

Here it left its stamp in the barbaric abandon of the Spanish dances and in the Spanish music, where there are long stretches without tune or melody—only the rhythmic tum-te-ta sufficient to dance to.

In the heyday of Spanish maritime supremacy Afro-Spanish music spread widely, but intrenched itself most firmly in South America, especially in the Argentine. Thence its subtle influence and appeal reached up to North America, to Mexico and the coast cities of the South.

On other continents African music was sugared and dressed so that it became well-nigh unrecognizable. But here in America we had more than the indirect influence of the native music. We had the added weight of the direct effect of the importation of Gold Coast West African natives as slaves.

This slave strain has affected not only our dance music, but our whole body of religious tunes. Our Negro minstrelsy and spirituals are more developed, more intense than any tunes evolved from the natives in Africa. This possibly can be explained by the sufferings of the Negroes, their emotional conversion to Christianity and the more intimate influence of white over black in the United States.

More even than it is a land of flamboyant flowers and riotous color, Africa is a land of music. Music is everywhere, and you cannot escape it. Every native has some musical instrument, bought perhaps from slender wages, but more likely fashioned out of any material close at hand—from hundred-gallon oil containers to sun-dried calabashes.

. . . And whether it's made by black man or white man, jazz is the same music—music which has come winging down the years from its obscure origin in the jungles of the Dark Continent. (Rebecca Hourwich, "Where the Jazz Begins" (*Collier's,* January 23, 1926)

Of course, African Americans saw the connection between jazz and Africa. James A. Rogers wrote "Jazz at Home," found in Alain

Locke's edited anthology *The New Negro,* in a section entitled "Negro Youth Speaks." Locke's important anthology presents the work of young poets, playwrights, essayists, and other members of what is now known as the Harlem Renaissance. Useful bibliographies relating to literature and music appear at the end of the volume. One might think that Rogers himself was not black, because he writes of happening upon "a Negro revival meeting" and describes black youth as "urchins" and black dancers in a show as "a bobbed-hair chorus"; but he is identified as a "journalist and correspondent" on the staff of two black newspapers, *The Messenger* and *The Amsterdam News.* In any case, he showed himself plainly aware of both the direct influence of ragtime and the more indirect one of Africa on jazz:

> The direct predecessor of jazz is ragtime. That both are atavistically African there is little doubt, but to what extent it is difficult to determine. In its barbaric rhythm and exuberance there is something of the bamboula, a wild, abandoned dance of the West African and the Haytian Negro, so stirringly described by the anonymous author of *Untrodden Fields of Anthropology,* or of the *ganza* ceremony so brilliantly depicted in Maran's *Batouala.* But jazz time is faster and more complex than African music. With its cowbells, auto horns, calliopes, rattles, dinner gongs, kitchen utensils, cymbals, screams, crashes, clankings and monotonous rhythm it bears all the marks of a nerve-strung, strident, mechanized civilization. It is a thing of the jungles— modern man-made jungles.
>
> . . . [It] is of Negro origin plus the influence of the American environment. It is Negro-American. (James A. Rogers, "Jazz at Home," in *The New Negro,* edited by Alain Locke [New York: Albert and Charles Boni, 1925])

Probably the first person to attempt serious scholarship on the relation between African and African American music was the French ethnomusicologist, André Schaeffner (1895–1980). In November 1926 he and André Coeuroy published *Le Jazz,* a work of 150 pages, in a limited edition of 1625 copies. Coeuroy's name is listed first, but according to French jazz critic Lucien Malson (writing in *Revue de Musicologie* after Schaeffner's death) Coeuroy only wrote the last three chapters and was overall editor. The general characteristics and instruments of "Afro-American" jazz, as it's called in the book, are treated at length, but the only groups mentioned by name are popular white bands, in particular Paul Whiteman's. Malson places the blame for the absence of black artists on Coeuroy, since it was his task to research the bands, although as we have seen it was quite common for jazz publications of the 1920s to omit African Americans. Schaeffner writes at length about two aspects of jazz that were derived from African music: the translation of vocal styles onto instruments, and a passion for rhythm, differing from that of other cultures in its subtlety and in the constant struggle between the rhythms of the melodies and the steady pulse underneath. These observations still seem valid today.

It should be pointed out, though, that the African origins of jazz are rather distant—something like seeking the influence of Josquin Des Pres on Mozart. The African Americans who originated jazz had their own vibrant culture to draw upon. The first generation of jazz musicians, born roughly between 1880 and 1890, were not directly conversant with African languages, melodies, or instruments; however, they were immersed in their own ragtime music and later the blues, both of which developed at the end of the 1800s, as well as classical music (especially opera and the so-called light classics) and popular music in general.

Lawrence Gushee is, in my opinion, the leading researcher into the questions surrounding the early years of the twentieth century, when somehow jazz crystallized and eventually began to be perceived as distinct from other types of music. His mastery of archival and musical materials is evident in his article below.

Black Americans are often barely visible in early writings about jazz, Gushee notes, and that makes giving them due credit difficult. He adds that general descriptions of black American dances and celebrations are useful in tracing black music of the 1800s, but they do not lead to specific musical antecedents of jazz.

As Gushee points out, researchers keep running into dead ends when they try to pinpoint the origin of jazz by starting with the present and going backwards. At a certain point the informants were born too late to add anything else. So he suggests starting with what is known of black music around New Orleans in the 1800s, well before jazz originated, and working one's way forward. Gushee presents an astonishing array of data about blacks' participation in the musical culture of New Orleans that helps bring these formerly unknown persons to life. He is not afraid to venture his opinions as to which music may have prefigured jazz and which did not, and when he quotes observers of the 1800s he does so critically, without taking each report as "fact" but carefully evaluating each one.

Gushee notes that dance music and the distinct types of dances themselves are vital in the study of early jazz, and he finds that around 1895 a number of reports surfaced about "new dance styles" and accompanying new music styles. Gushee concludes with his respect for the "astonishing expressiveness" that African Americans brought to dance music, and with an appreciation of the fact that they were not allowed, in those days, to bring that same creativity into the concert hall or other venues.

In the course of the article, Gushee also discusses the origin of the word *jazz*, adding to what we have already presented.

The Nineteenth-Century Origins of Jazz

LAWRENCE GUSHEE

The question of the origins of jazz has, one might well imagine, received many answers in the seventy-five years since the music burst like a rocket over the American musical landscape. The least palatable perhaps is that offered by reactionary champions of the musical originality of the Original Dixieland Jazz Band (ODJB), for example, Horst Lange. Much of his evidence is easy to dismiss, but one point at least makes us pause and think. He writes:

> It was always a riddle for the serious friend of jazz, why the fabulous and legendary New Orleans jazz hadn't already been discovered around 1900 or 1910 in the city itself, since not only was it full of home-grown talent and musical professionals, but also received a constant stream of visitors and tourists. Shouldn't there have been someone, among all these people surely interested in music, who was struck by

this novel music, which was later designated "jazz" (Lange 1991, 28; my translation)?

In fact, there's no question that the particular instrumentation, manner of playing, and repertory of the Original Dixieland Jazz Band, decisively assisted by the superb recording technique of the Victor Talking Machine Company, were copied by hundreds of young musicians, many of whom never had visited and never would visit New Orleans.

Someone who came close to fitting Lange's music-loving visitor to New Orleans was J. Russell Robinson (1892–1963), a pianist and songwriter who had worked in that city around 1910 and was eventually to become a member of the ODJB. Many years later he recalled his reaction to these recordings: first, it was a new, interesting, and exciting sound, a bit blood-curdling; second, the musicians were recognizable as nonreaders; third, jazz was nothing but ragtime, played by ear (Robinson 1955, 13). Thus the sound, while strikingly novel and surely deserving of the acclaim of Lange, was recognized by an experienced professional as being but one species of the genus, ragtime played by ear by "fakers," to use the usual term of the day.[1]

Even at the time, however, New Orleans colleagues and competitors of the ODJB fully acknowledged the debt all of them owed to African Americans. For example, Walter Kingsley reported the views of clarinetist Alcide "Yellow" Nunez:

> In 1916 Brown's Band from Dixieland came to Chicago direct from New Orleans, and with it came Tutor Spriccio. They knew all the old negro melodies with the variations taught by Spriccio. . . . This bunch from New Orleans played by ear entirely (Kingsley 1918, 867).

Then after a discussion of the "Livery Stable Blues" and the break routines for which Nunez claimed credit: "All this, however, was derived from the New Orleans blacks and John Spriccio" (Kingsley 1918, 867).

---

1. Or *routiniers,* to use the somewhat less derogatory and more descriptive French term. The fact that orchestral ragtime was undoubtedly played by ear in many parts of the country accounts for many musicians' rejection of New Orleans's claim to originating jazz.

These statements are offered not only to refute Lange's revisionism, but as one more illustration—Is one needed?—of the pervasive bias that constantly obscures investigation of the contributions of African Americans. Spriccio has a name, but not the "old negroes" or the "New Orleans blacks."

As is often the case, things look different from the other side of the color line. It is interesting to go back to what seems to have been the first published attempt by an African-American native of New Orleans to plumb the mystery of the origin of jazz. The year was 1933, the author E. Belfield Spriggins, social editor of the *Lousiana Weekly*. He wrote, under the title "Excavating Local Jazz":

> For quite some years now there has been an unusual amount of discussion concerning the popular form of music commonly called "jazz." . . . Many years ago jazz tunes in their original forms were heard in the Crescent City. Probably one of the earliest heard was one played by King Bolden's Band. . . . The rendition of this number became an overnight sensation and the reputation of Bolden's band became a household word with the patrons of the Odd Fellows Hall, Lincoln and Johnson Parks, and several other popular dance halls around the city (Spriggins 1933, 6).

The tune in question was "Funky Butt"—the unexpurgated text of which Spriggins was unwilling to print. More widely known as "Buddy Bolden's Blues," as copyrighted by Jelly Roll Morton, this was a descendant or a cousin of the second strain of the 1904 rag "St. Louis Tickle," which, though designated a rag, is clearly a different species from Scott Joplin's compositions.

Be that as it may, Spriggins makes no unqualified claim for the priority of Buddy Bolden, hedging his remarks with a caution that was to be lost in succeeding years, as in the designation of Bolden as "First Man of Jazz" (Marquis 1978). Still, there seems to be no question that his band made an unforgettable impression, not always to the good, on many of those who heard it around 1905.

Other expert witnesses would come up with different candidates for the position of giant of early jazz. Guitarist Johnny St. Cyr (1890–1966) remembered toward the end of his life that

Every band had their specialties that they played hot, one out of every five or six selections. . . . But the Golden Rule band played everything hot, . . . they were the original hot band that I knew. . . . [Bolden was] not hot, just ordinary, but he had a little hot lick he used. To me he was not as hot as the Golden Rule Band (St. Cyr 1966, 6).

Cross-examination of the witnesses being out of the question, there is ample room for the free play of preconceptions and foregone conclusions in preferring one bit of evidence over another. But there seems to be no reason to doubt that at least by 1905 some bands, whether Bolden's, the Golden Rule, or some other, were playing a music that we might consider an ancestor of jazz. To be sure, St. Cyr was not of an age to testify to bands, events, and sounds much earlier than that.

Stymied by the mortality of our informants, we might well consider another strategy: instead of carrying things backwards as far as we can, perhaps we might begin early in the nineteenth century and advance toward 1900, thus cornering the elusive quarry.

This was the intention of Henry Kmen, a historian whose pioneering work on music and musical life in New Orleans up to 1841 has contributed much to the field. But until I reread his book in preparation for this discussion, the degree to which he thought of his own work as a prelude to the history of jazz had escaped me.

Although he could find comparatively little evidence for music making by African Americans, in his final chapter Kmen was able to cite an impressive list of activities which provided him justification for a startling and provocative concluding paragraph.

Is it not here, . . . in the whole overpowering atmosphere of music in New Orleans that the Negro began to shape the music that would eventually be Jazz? Certainly all these strands were a part of his life, and if to the weaving of them he brought something of his own, it was as an American rather than as an African. Or so it seems to this writer (Kmen 1966, 245; note capital "J").

From this point of view, every musical activity of the African American in antebellum as well as postbellum New Orleans could be considered part of the prehistory of jazz. This seems to fit David Fischer's description of the "fallacy of indiscriminate pluralism":

> It appears in causal explanations where the number of causal components is not defined, or their relative weight is not determined or both. . . . [It is] an occupational hazard of academic historians, who are taught to tell comprehensive truths (Fischer 1970, 175–176).

There is also a categorical problem, namely that a variety of social activities involving music are seen as ancestors of a distinctive kind of music, something Kmen seems to recognize: "The method used is that of the social historian. Which is to say, the book is not concerned with the structure and development of the music itself—that is left for the musicologist" (Kmen 1966, viii).

No small challenge, particularly given the inadequacy of notated music in indicating the distinctive features of music of the oral tradition. To be sure, thanks to Dena Epstein (1977) one can consult hundreds of verbal descriptions of antebellum African-American musical practices in the United States generally, most of them from the Southern states. But these are often too vague for us to imaginatively reconstruct the sounds the writer heard; none of the thirty-odd references to New Orleans or Louisiana appear to describe specific practices that might be related to the hot or ratty[2] ragtime played around 1900.

Likewise for the few instances of local practice reflected in musical notation: the "Creole songs" that Louis Moreau Gottschalk used for some of his piano pieces presumably are a sampling of music he heard in the New Orleans of the 1830s. Charming and historically important, but no more nor less an ancestor of jazz than some of the raggy banjo pieces transcribed or collected by Dan Emmett (Nathan 1962, 340–348).

On the other hand, the rhythms notated in the seven songs in Creole dialect which conclude Allen, Ware, and Garrison's pioneering ([1867] 1951) collection of slave songs sound to me more pertinent. They seem distinctively West Indian in their various ways of singing five notes in the time of four. In strong contrast to the rest of the collection, the

---

2. The slang term "ratty" is commonly used to describe "hot" music or the older ragtime style or a kind of "strutting walk" (see Russell 1978, 7+; Rose 1974, 177; Merriam-Webster 1986, 1871).

songs are also all secular, and a case can be made for the "urban" character of three or four of them, despite their having been collected on Good Hope Plantation in St. Charles Parish—or rather because of having been collected there, a half-day's journey or less from the metropolis. Also of great interest is the fact that the first four of the songs, those which, in fact, could be said to have West Indian rhythms, were danced to "a simple dance, a sort of minuet, called the *Coonjai;* the name and the dance are probably both of African origin" (Allen, Ware, and Garrison [1867] 1951, 113).

We know, of course, that at the outset and for decades to follow jazz was functionally music for dancing. Nothing was more clear to Henry Kmen than this, and surely it was the reason why he began his work with chapters on dancing. But he conveys virtually no details concerning the participation of African-American musicians in what, after all, would have been the bread and butter of the professional musician.

Kmen terminated his history at 1841, a fact all the more regrettable because of the great shift in social dance style—and its accompanying music—which took place in the 1840s and 1850s all over urban Europe and America, North and South. The change was not only a shift from the quadrille, cotillion, and contradance to the closed couple dances of waltz, polka, and the other new dances to follow in their wake (mazurka, redowa, etc.), but also of social meaning, well described by Jean-Michel Guilcher:

> It's true that dancing remained a pleasure. But the nature of the pleasure has changed. Under the Consulate and the Empire, any personal expression, whatever amplitude it might take, was within the social forms inherited from the past. After 1840, the closed couple dance took over. Although other periods had already given much room to the expression of the couple, none had allowed it to take on the character it was now to assume. The series of courantes and minuets had expressed at the same time both solidarity and hierarchy. . . . The waltz and the polka made no pretense at expressing anything whatever. Closed in on itself, the couple danced for itself alone, . . . the ball no longer manifested unanimous agreement; it juxtaposed solitudes (Guilcher 1969, 173–174; my translation).

This new configuration of dances was to last until the century's end. Already challenged by the two-step circa 1895, it was definitively replaced by a cluster of new dances around 1910. Of this, more below.

There is clearly much work to be done in continuing the story of music in New Orleans after 1841. My own research into music for dancing begins some twenty years later, with a few tentative forays into the massive city archives held by the New Orleans Public Library. As an example of what can be learned, one might cite a ledger of permits issued in 1864 by the acting military mayor, which included some 150 licenses for balls, private parties, and soirées between January 1 and March 12. Included are the names of the licensees, the locations of the events, whether wines were permitted, the ending time, whether the event was masked or not, and whether it was "colored." A good many of the balls are so designated, but more important, perhaps, a number of entrepreneurs are African American, still designated "free persons of color" as the Thirteenth Amendment was not to take effect for nearly two more years. These entrepreneurs were A. J. Brooks, Paul Porée, Eugene Joseph, and John Hall; those often sponsoring "colored" balls were Emile Segura, Madame Charles (patroness of the quadroon balls), Benjamin Graham, Aaron Allen, Benjamin Colburn, J. J. Bouseau, Josephine Brown, and John Reed. It appears that similar documents have not been saved, except for several after 1900.

We do not need these data to show that New Orleans was a dancing city—a long-established fact—but the fact that African Americans were so much involved in the *business* end is most interesting. Did such entrepreneurship entail substantial employment for African-American musicians? Did it continue following Reconstruction in a city increasingly repressive of its African-American population?

Another kind of documentation to consider is offered by the five extant post–Civil War censuses, 1870 to 1910. One assumes that the majority of African Americans calling themselves musicians were earning most of their money playing dance music.[3]

---

3. There is, to be sure, a difficulty involved in using census data as evidence for the practice of music. Some of those who are enumerated as musicians may have frequently practiced another trade, depending on the season of the year and the state of the economy.

Of the 222 musicians, teachers of music, and practitioners of the music trades enumerated in the 1870 census, 44 percent were of German, Austrian, or Swiss birth, 15 percent French, 10 percent Italian; in all, including some smaller groups, a staggering 80 percent were of foreign birth and only 20 percent were born in the United States. Of this small fraction three were black, seven mulatto, and one is listed as white, but is known to be African American. The African-American musicians then, although making a poor showing overall—that is, about 5 percent—make up about a quarter of this native-born contingent.

The passage of one decade from 1870 to 1880 made a great difference. There is a substantial overall increase in the number of musicians, but also a drastic shift in favor of the native-born. The total of all foreign-born musicians is at this point a mere 45 percent, now overtaken by the 55 percent born on North American soil. (It is interesting that only 4 percent of the 55 percent were *not* from the South.) Much of this change is accounted for by the fact that somewhere between fifty and sixty individual musicians or music teachers were African American, a number that remains more or less constant for the next twenty years, although the overall total of musicians increases by 25 percent.[4]

The 1910 census marked a dramatic change from those of 1890 and 1900. While the overall total of male musicians and music teachers increased by a striking 33 percent, the number of African Americans doubled, thus forming 30 percent of the total. Perhaps the ragtime craze was good for the African-American musician.

The story of musical opportunity told by the census—or rather, the story it allows us to tell—is amply confirmed by the complaint of a New Orleans correspondent to the trade magazine *Metronome* at the end of 1888: "We have here some twenty to twenty-five bands averaging

---

4. The overall total of musicians and music teachers increased by leaps and bounds between 1880 and 1910: this was largely due to the increase in the number of female music teachers, very few of whom were known as professional musicians. For the complete list of African-American musicians in the 1880 census as well as a provisional comparative table of decennial census numbers, see Gushee (1991, 61–62). The publication of this essay was unauthorized; additional research conducted between the original submission and eventual publication could have corrected or augmented much of the biographical data presented, as well as the census statistics presented.

twelve men apiece. The colored race monopolize the procession music to a great extent as they are not regular workers at any trade, as are most of the white players, no musical merit in any of these." It would be easy to assume that the writer meant this derogatory remark to apply to the "colored" bands, but it is possible that he means it to apply to the twenty to twenty-five bands, as he goes on to say: "We have only one really fine military band, that is the one at West End" (*Metronome* December 1888, 14).

It is, to be sure, only too common for African Americans to be treated as a stereotyped group by the nineteenth-century press. While we are beginning to remedy this by painstaking sifting of city directories, census returns, license registers, and other primary source materials, such names are, as it were, "faceless" and otherwise unremarkable.

Someone who is far from faceless is Basile Barés (1845–1902), bandleader to New Orleans society of the 1870s and perhaps later. Disappointingly, his nearly thirty dance compositions lack—to my ears—any of those novel and vigorous rhythms beginning to show up in music published in Cuba or Brazil. No pre-rag, no proto-habanera; just excellently crafted dance music or *morceaux de salon.*

There is no necessity, of course, that such exotic traits appear only or principally in works by African Americans. It was not the free persons of color who embodied "characteristic" rhythms in their antebellum works for the piano, but Louis Moreau Gottschalk. One also fails to find "characteristic" traits in the early works of the African-American Lawrence Dubuclet (1866–1909) who, in a manner of speaking, takes the torch from Barés, still writing waltzes, polkas, and mazurkas in the 1880s, then adapting to changing fashion and writing cakewalks, marches, and two-steps in 1890s,[5] and finally moving to Chicago after 1900 to pursue a more cosmopolitan career than was feasible in his native city.

What are we looking for, after all, in written music? Think for a moment of the several ways in which the new idiom of blues made tentative appearances in popular song and piano music for at least fifteen years before the minor blues explosion of 1912. Blues traits,

---

5. I compare his probable first composition, the self-published waltz "Bettina" of 1886 (dedicated "to my professor signor Giovani Luciani"), followed by his op. 2 of the same year, "Les yeux doux" (also self-published), with his op. 7, the "World's Fair March" of 1893, and the march and two-step "The Belle of the Carnival" (1897).

however, stick out like the proverbial sore thumb in certain idiosyncratic harmonic progressions, phrase structures, and melodic turns. For that matter, the syncopations that characterize cakewalks and rags are equally obvious. Here too, there is a long period of preparation in which what we might call "proto-ragtime" syncopation pops up, often together with pentatonic melody, both of them no doubt going back to the minstrel shows of 1840–and of course before that in oral tradition. But jazz lacks such easily transcribable and readily recognized distinctive features. We surely need to keep looking; it would be a great help if we had an authoritative bibliography of New Orleans music imprints before 1900.[6]

Surely, to ask Lange's question again with a change of venue, if there had been some kind of striking African-American music in New Orleans in these postbellum years, some visitor would have attempted a description in a diary, a letter home, a travel book, or some other means that would make up for the lack of traces in published music. One immediately thinks of the extraordinary Greek-born Lafcadio Hearn (1850–1904), who during his stint as a reporter in Cincinnati in the late 1870s wrote exceptionally detailed descriptions of roustabout songs and dancing in Ryan's dance-house, a riverfront dive (Hearn 1924, 161–164).

Hearn moved to New Orleans in 1877, where he remained for some ten years. One could hardly ask for a better observer: Hearn, a European, was enthralled by folklore and sympathetic to people of color; not only that, his dear friend was the critic and musicologist Henry Krehbiel, who published the first book on African-American folksong in 1913. In response to his friend, who was even then fascinated with the folk music of black Americans, Hearn wrote a number of letters reporting what he heard in New Orleans.

---

6. We ought not limit ourselves to published music, per se. G. F. Patton's exhaustive *A Practical Guide to the Arrangement of Band Music* (1875) can surely be seen as reflecting the best New Orleans practice, as the author acknowledges the professional assistance of New Orleanians Robert Meyer, John Eckert, and Charles Bothe. Also, Patton cites as an example of an interpolated passage in another key, the "Washington Artillery Polka," "a well known *Polka Quickstep* played by all the New Orleans bands" (Patton 1875, 29). Patton further devotes some forty pages to the various genres of dance music, if we needed any convincing that brass bands counted playing for dances among their manifold functions; and the comprehensive discussion of the functions of the second cornet part might almost have been written with Louis Armstrong in mind. There are no references, however, to African Americans.

One observation in particular has been widely cited. Hearn wrote in a letter of 1881: "Did you ever hear negroes play the piano by ear? There are several curiosities here, Creole negroes. Sometimes we pay them a bottle of wine to come here and play for us. They use the piano exactly like a banjo. It is good banjo-playing, but no piano-playing" (quoted in Bisland 1906, 232).[7]

And then there is what must be the most evasive will o' the wisp to investigators of the prehistory of jazz. Walter Kingsley (1876–1929), a press agent for the Palace Theatre in New York City, was quick to discuss the jazz phenomenon which had taken the metropolis by storm, contributing an article to the *New York Sun,* August 5, 1917, headlined "Whence Comes Jass? Facts from the Great Authority on the Subject." His fateful words were:

> In his studies of the creole patois and idiom in New Orleans Lafcadio Hearn reported that the word "jaz," meaning to speed things up, to make excitement, was common among the blacks of the South and had been adopted by the Creoles as a term to be applied to music of a rudimentary syncopated type.

You can imagine how many hours have been spent by how many people, plowing through the voluminous published writings of Hearn in an attempt to nail down this earth-shattering remark—with nothing to show for it, alas. Although it seems that the remark might be found in Hearn's (1885) dictionary of creole proverbs, *"Gombo Zhèbes,"* it is not there.[8] It is possible, however, that Hearn conveyed such information to Krehbiel in a letter, or even in conversation, the few times that he was in New York. And it is possible that Kingsley knew Krehbiel.[9]

But one of the lessons we have finally learned from jazz history is that New Orleans musicians did not know that their music was called

---

7. Surely these "curiosities," whom Hearn had taken the trouble to ask to leave their normal place of business for the purpose of demonstrating their art, had names.

8. Hearn states in his introduction that he was "wholly indebted" to Professor William Henry, principal of the Jefferson Academy of New Orleans, for the Louisiana proverbs included, as well as a number of explanatory notes and examples of the local patois.

9. It is unfortunate that Krehbiel's books and papers, in principle preserved after his death in 1923, seem to have been dispersed. Some are at the New York Public Library; but no such statement by Hearn has yet been found in those documents that are available. In addition, despite the many books and essays that have been devoted to Hearn and his voluminous correspondence, some letters are still unpublished and others have reached print in censored form.

"jazz" until they went north. Certainly many of them said so; here and there, however, in the interviews collected by Russell and Allen, now held in the William Ransom Hogan Jazz Archive at Tulane University, the contrary is stated. For example, Eddie Dawson—a professional musician from about 1905 on—asserts that the term was first used in bands around the time he began and was only applied to music (Dawson 1959).[10] Similarly, Tom Albert, a violinist born in 1877, maintained that "in the real old days they called it jazz and ragtime. . . . There wasn't any real difference between ragtime bands and the jazz bands. . . . Jazz was [the term] used mostly though" (Albert 1959, reel 2 digest, p. 6).

To return to Hearn after this substantial digression, one might hope that someone with such broad and unfettered tastes as his, and with such a musically knowledgeable and curious friend as Krehbiel, would tell us something about how African-American musicians played dance music in New Orleans in the 1880s. In the first place, Hearn seems not to have been much of a partygoer. Second, and far more consequential, he was not, I think, fond of Creole music that he perceived as strongly Europeanized. For example, in a letter written to Krehbiel just before he left Martinique after a first brief trip in 1887, Hearn states:

> My inquiries about the marimba and other instruments have produced no result except the discovery that our negroes play the guitar, the flute, the flageolet, the cornet-à-piston. Some play very well; all the orchestras and bands are coloured. But the civilized instrument has killed the native manufacture of aboriginalities. The only hope would be in the small islands, or where slavery still exists, as in Cuba (quoted in Bisland 1906, 411).

Still, we can not rule out the possibility that African or West Indian rhythms were largely absent from the New Orleans dance music of the 1880s. One remark, from an 1887 letter to Krehbiel, seems to support this: "My friend Matas has returned. He tells me delightful things about Spanish music, and plays for me. He also tells me much

---

10. Manuel Manetta, also present at the interview and a professional who began at about the same time as Dawson, averred that older bands from uptown were called "ragtime" bands and were later called "Dixieland" bands.

concerning Cuban and Mexican music. He says these have been very strongly affected by African influence—full of contretemps" (quoted in Bisland 1906, 380). What an opportunity for Hearn to add, "just like I've heard here in New Orleans"! Or for that matter, such a comment might have come from Rudolph Matas (1860–1957), himself a New Orleans native. No such confirmation occurs, however, despite the fad for Mexican music, which was at the time in full swing after having been triggered by the appearance of various groups of Mexican musicians at the Cotton Exposition of 1884–1885 (Stewart 1991). Alas, when Hearn wrote his essays—well over 100,000 words—about his eighteen-month stay in Martinique, he made but one solitary reference to New Orleans, that having to do with architecture (Hearn 1890, 36).

Nevertheless, there is an inherent plausibility to the notion that New Orleans was receptive to all kinds of "Latin" music, perhaps because of geographical proximity as much as traditional ethnic preferences. The New Orleans composer W. T. Francis, visiting New York City in 1889 and commenting on the differing musical tastes in the United States, had this to say:

> It does not seem to be a matter of states or divisions of the land, but rather of particular localities. New York, Boston, Chicago, New Orleans, Brooklyn, Philadelphia and Baltimore are the best music centers of the east; San Francisco and Denver in the west. . . . Among the cities named, there is a great difference in their preferences regarding the style of music they will patronize. The two most widely differing cities in this regard are Boston and New Orleans. In the former, everything runs to classical music. . . . In New Orleans, the most popular music is that which is marked by melody. As a result, every new song and dance which appears in Paris, Madrid, Florence, Vienna, or Berlin appears in [New Orleans] anywhere from six months to two years before it is heard in [Boston]. Another interesting result is that you can listen in New Orleans to the melodic music of the Spanish nations. . . . It would seem as if the love of melody decreases as you come north from the gulf of Mexico and reaches its smallest development when it encounters the northern tier of the states of the union ("New Orleans Taste in Music" 1890).

Francis here suggests two favorite themes in discussions of the nineteenth century origins of jazz. I will call one the "French Opera hypothesis" and the other the "Spanish tinge hypothesis," both of them accounting for a love of lyrical expressiveness in music, but the second specifically accounting for the presence in New Orleans of Caribbean or Mexican rhythms.

This is not all Francis had to say in the New York interview. He goes on to state a seductive theory that can account for much of what has taken place in the development of American vernacular music since 1890, not just New Orleans music or jazz:

> The rewards of music are far larger in the north than in the south. In the latter, they are regarded as a necessity and paid for, as most necessities are, in small amounts of money. In the north they are classed with luxuries, and are paid for in accordance. Business principles alone will, therefore, soon compel the production of southern music in the north, if merely for the sake of testing its commercial value. When once heard, I am certain that the northern public will want it a second time ("New Orleans Taste in Music" 1890).

To be sure, this is no theory of origin. But at least it is conceivable that there never would have been such a thing as jazz without the economic force that brought it to the ears of the wider American public.

We may eventually find another musician, not necessarily or perhaps not even preferably an American, who describes specific musical practices which we can reasonably see as like or leading to jazz. In 1917 the Music Teachers' National Association held its thirty-ninth annual meeting in New Orleans. Among the speakers was Walter Goldstein, a music teacher at Newcomb College who was born in New York in 1882 and graduated from Tulane in 1903. His contribution was entitled "The Natural Harmonic and Rhythmic Sense of the Negro." It had been Goldstein's intention to illustrate some of his points with "the singing of a quartet of Negroes. . . . [B]ut the unreliability of our dark brother in the matter of keeping an appointment has made this impossible." Accordingly, he had recourse to Victor record 16448 by the Fisk University Quartet (Goldstein 1918, 38–39). The author's opening words are poignant:

It is only a desire to "do my bit," rather than any special fitness for the task, that has led me to accept the appointment to make an investigation into the harmonic and rhythmic talent of the Negro as I find him here in his natural environment. . . . It is not very easy, as I have learned in the last two months, to get very near to the primitive Negro, in a large city like this, but the attempt has been something of a lark, and I have run the gamut all the way from being the unexpected orator at a Sunday service of the most aristocratic Negro congregation in the city, to being ordered off the public docks as a German spy with incendiary motives (Goldstein 1918, 29).

He did get around a bit—for example, to the biweekly sacrament service of the Gretna Colored Baptist Church as well as to St. James AME Church—and had a few interesting things to say, particularly in describing ragtime—but not a whisper about jazz. The situation of being surrounded by a vibrant new music and not hearing it is in hindsight almost inconceivable to us; on reflection, though, it is just one more testimony to the power of received categories to mold our perceptions, unless, of course, the usual run of dance music was not anything special, and the unusual—that is, hot ragtime and blues with a local accent—rather rare. Perhaps this is another instance of what we could call the "Lange problem."

Bringing ragtime into the picture may seem to offer clarification to the beginnings of jazz, inasmuch as we know when ragtime began. But actually we know nothing of the sort; all we know is when ragtime sheet music in its various forms began being published in Chicago and New York and, consequently, everywhere in the country, not to speak of Western Europe. But just as the origins of jazz become fuzzy once we begin looking for jazz *before* jazz, so it is with ragtime. A couple of explanations offered by knowledgeable African-American musicians close to the events may illustrate the complexities of the question.

First, Will Foster, writing in the *Indianapolis Freeman* in 1911 under the pseudonym of Juli Jones Jr., contributed a fascinating article on the "great colored song writers":

The success of the Mobile buck found its way to the river cities on the Ohio and Mississippi rivers, when steamboats held sway in this country. . . . Sometime along in the early eighties a triple combination of song, walk and dance by the name of "Coon Jine, Baby, Coon Jine," sprang up among the roustabouts on the many boats and spread like wildfire. The song and dance found its way into the levee resorts, where all prosperous houses had old hand-me-down square pianos with a half dozen broken keys; yet these instruments were considered jewels in those days, as it only required a few keys to play the "Coon Jine." This is where the original ragtime started from— the quick action of the right-hand fingers playing the "Coon Jine" (Jones 1911).

While this kind of single-origin theory is obviously inadequate to explain a multifaceted phenomenon like ragtime in general, it nonetheless singles out a particular dance song with a complex history that may, in fact involve New Orleans (see, e.g., Krehbiel [1913] 1962, 116, 121, 138). One imagines that Hearn's "Creole Negroes" who played the piano like the banjo had "Coon Jine" in their repertory.

Another witness to his time, the eminent composer Will Marion Cook (1869–1944), contributed a brief overview, "Negro Music," to the *New York Age* seven years later. He singled out the period 1875–1888 as one of stagnation because the Negro had been taught too well by whites that he was inferior. "About 1888 [1898 is what was printed] marked the starting and quick growth of the so-called 'ragtime'. As far back as 1875 Negroes in questionable resorts along the Mississippi had commenced to evolve this musical figure, but at the World's Fair in Chicago, 'ragtime' got a running start and swept the Americans, next Europe, and today the craze has not diminished" (Cook 1918).[11]

Actually, Cook had expounded his views on the matter some twenty years earlier, with a rather different slant. His article was intended as a refutation of the proposition that Negro music, as exemplified by such "ephemeral clap-trap compositions as 'The New Bully,' 'A Hot Time in the Old Town,' 'All Coons Look Alike to Me,' was degenerate, when compared with the soul-stirring slave melodies." He says:

---

11. Much of the content of the *New York Age* article had already been printed in Cary B. Lewis's column in the *Chicago Defender* of May 1, 1915. The latter source gives 1888 instead of 1898, clearly erroneous in view of the other dates mentioned.

One special characteristic of these songs is the much advertised "rag" accompaniment, the origin and character of which will be discussed later on in this article. . . . This kind of movement, which was unknown until about fifteen years ago, grew out of the visits of Negro sailors to Asiatic ports, and particularly to those of Turkey, when the odd rhythms of the *danse du ventre* soon forced itself upon them; and in trying to reproduce this they have worked out the "rag."

During the World's Columbian Exposition at Chicago, the "Midway Plaisance" was well filled with places of amusement where the peculiar music of the "muscle dance" was continually heard, and it is worthy of note that after that time the popularity of the "rag" grew with astonishing rapidity and became general among Negro pianists (Cook 1898).[12]

One wonders whether this bit of history was cooked up by the author or taken from another source. To us it seems fanciful; perhaps it was the obtrusiveness of the drum rhythms traditionally accompanying belly dancing that caught Cook's ear.[13]

Neither Foster nor Cook mentions New Orleans, except by implication, the city being the southern terminus of what might be called levee low-life culture.[14] We must look further for early evidence specifically linking New Orleans to ragtime or proto-ragtime. Although they are not extensively trained musicians like Francis and Goldstein, nor articulate in the manner of Hearn, one might well think that the "old-timers" interviewed principally by Bill Russell and Dick Allen for the Hogan Jazz Archives would tell us a lot about the hot or ratty

12. The article was evidently reprinted from *The Prospect,* an Afro-American monthly of sixty-four pages, published in New York City, the first and perhaps last issue of which appeared in April 1898. No copy is extant; more's the pity, as the original article appears to have had musical examples that are missing in the Springfield newspaper.

13. That Cook was not the only musician to be struck by such a connection is shown in the piano medley "Pasquila" by W. J. Voges. (It is easily available in Baron 1980). While somewhat tame by the standards for rhythmic complexity established by Joplin and others from 1898 onward, it nonetheless is noteworthy for the insistence and variety of its cakewalk rhythms and for the inscriptions over the several sections: "Hot Stuff," "Good Thing, Push It Along." The strain entitled "Koochie-Koochie Dance" is indeed a version of the ubiquitous melody and makes prominent use of ♪♩♪ syncopation (in 2/4 meter).

14. Interesting in this regard is the 1906 song "Don't Go Way Nobody," often mentioned as part of the repertory of Buddy Bolden's band. The crudely drawn cover depicts a levee scene in the background, in accordance with Percy Cahill's lyrics: "I've worked out on the levee front,/Right in the broiling sun;/I've worked on every steamboat too,/That ever dare to run./Worked at the docks, from morn 'till night,/And burnt out lots of men;/When the whistle blew to knock off,/The boss would yell out then: Don't go way nobody, don't nobody leave."

ragtime of their youth. Certainly the interviewers asked a lot of the right questions: What kind of band did you play in when you began? What were some of the tunes you played early on? When did you first hear the blues? and so on. The biggest limitation in using this testimony as evidence for the beginning of jazz is that, by the time the project was funded and under way, very few musicians born around 1880 or before, those whose professional careers had begun before the turn of the century, were available to bear witness to the early days.

Be that as it may, certain particulars are heard over and over again: the oldest interviewees quite frequently first played in or were impressed by three- or four-piece string bands—such as violin, guitar, and string bass, or mandolin, guitar, and bass—with or without one wind instrument. Accordingly, their first instrument was often mandolin or guitar. Drums started to be used in larger dance orchestras only around 1900. Pianos entered the picture as orchestra instruments even later. The oldest interviewees were accustomed to playing polkas, mazurkas, schottisches, lancers, and varieties (these last two set dances were subspecies of the quadrille). The first blues came in around 1905, with, for example, "Make Me a Pallet on the Floor." Finally, there was a notable generation gap between the older musicians, who would not tolerate playing by ear or deviating from the notes as written, and the young turks of 1900. To the older, conservative generation belonged such musicians as cornetist George Moret, who was remembered with praise by Louis Armstrong, and the two fraternal clarinetists, Luis Tio and Lorenzo Tio Sr.[15]

There remains little doubt that important changes in instrumentation and repertory took place around 1900, give or take some number of years. This conclusion is amply supported by changes in clarinet performing style between, say, Alphonse Picou, born in 1879, and "Big Eye" Louis Delille Nelson, born sometime between 1880 and 1885. Or between that of George Baquet, born in 1881, and his younger brother Achille, born in 1885. Remarkably, all four men left recordings that surely speak louder than any verbal statements. For research purposes, the interviewers found Picou difficult to reach and an "unproductive"

15. The greatest lack in the collection is of interviews from older white musicians, as well as from musicians who have little or no identification with jazz. On some points, indeed, the latter might be helpful witnesses, being less inclined to take ragtime, blues, and jazz for granted.

source; Big Eye was long on anecdotes, but short on information; George Baquet, potentially an exceptionally rich source of data and musical insight, had died in 1949; and his brother, approached in Los Angeles in the late 1930s, rebuffed his would-be interviewer.[16]

Given the weak representation of survivors from the turn of the century in the Tulane archive, it becomes very important to locate and interpret any earlier interviews if we are to have any hope of gaining insight into music before 1900. Particularly important are those by Russell conducted outside of the Tulane project and still untapped in any systematic way, as well as those conducted by the Belgian poet Robert Goffin. Perhaps there are others we may find if we search concertedly.

In some ways the most intriguing and frustrating of all of these earlier testimonies is a brief interview with trombonist George Filhe that was conducted for *They All Played Ragtime* (Janis and Blesh 1971). The relevant extracts are as follows:

> It was a style just natural to them, and whenever I can remember, it was jazz. . . . .
> Percy Wenrich came to N.O. (between 1908 and 1909). We played it straight and the 2nd time we'd improvise. He came running up the steps: "That was my intentions and my ideas but I could not get them out!" . . . .
> In 1892—played [solo cornet] with Cousto & Desdunes, Cousto solo cornet, O'Neill cornet, Desdunes, violin & baritone. Played jazz, would always swing the music, that was their novelty. Solo B cornet came in then and replaced the old rotary valve E-flat cornet. They played quadrilles, schottisches, straight. Onward Brass Band. Younger musicians about 1892 began to "swing." Older men used lots of Mexican music (Filhe 1949).[17]

---

16. One should no doubt add Alcide Nunez (1884–1934) to this list, although his early death meant that he was never interviewed (unless one wants to count the Kingsley [1918] article that seems clearly based on an interview). Remarkably, for the clarinet, biography, recordings, and musical compositions (all four individuals mentioned have some to their credit) form a continuity against which change in musical style clearly stands out.

17. O'Neill is perhaps the father of the rather obscure violinist O'Neill Levasseur, mentioned from time to time in the Tulane interviews but also in the 1910 census as a white "musician—dancing hall" at 1558 Bienville Street.

Filhe was born in 1872, a youngster compared to Sylvester Coustaut, born in 1863, but a near contemporary of Dan Desdunes, born about 1870. What did he mean by "swing" and "older musicians," and how literally should we take the date 1892? In any event, what is really interesting here is the identification of a drastic shift, from Mexican music to a new kind that, by contrast, swung. To be sure, this is both good news and bad news for those who think that some kind of "Spanish tinge" was essential in producing the New Orleans manner of playing ragtime. It is also extremely interesting to learn of Percy Wenrich's reaction. Wenrich, an excellent and very successful ragtime composer from Missouri, can be taken as another witness from the outside, testifying to the existence of a distinctive New Orleans way of playing ragtime before 1910.

Another early interview that speaks of an abrupt change comes from the highly respected and often cited cornetist, Manuel Perez, to whom Robert Goffin spoke (in French) probably in 1944, or possibly on the occasion of an earlier visit in 1941. This interview, published in French in 1946, has been unduly neglected, first because it has never been translated and second because of the creative embroidery to which Goffin was prone. Caution is clearly required.

In any event Perez was born in 1881 on Urquhart Street in the Seventh Ward. Just as he was beginning to learn trumpet, at age twelve, there was a

> syncopated evolution. Vocal groups composed of young creoles, or even
> of whites, such as those of the spasmband, retained the rhythmic aspect
> of all the badly digested music. . . . At this time, his teacher, a certain
> Constant ["Coustaut"] who lived on St. Philip Street had nothing but
> contempt and mockery for the "fakers" who went around from street
> to street. Two musicians were popular among the creoles and had a
> great influence on the young generation: Lorenzo Tio and Doublet.
> Perez remembers that after 1895, even though they usually played
> polkas and schottisches, they [i.e., Tio and Doublet] let themselves be
> tempted by the infatuation of the audiences and went along with the
> new music. They constituted the link . . . between popular music and
> ragtime (Goffin 1946, 69–70).

There's a lot more in this interview, but I have singled out this passage because of Perez's emphatic focus on the brief period 1893–1895 and on two specific musicians of the older school, Lorenzo Tio and Doublet.

Both Lorenzo Tio Sr. and Charles Doublet were born in 1867 and were in fact cousins through the Hazeur family (Kinzer 1993). They appear to have begun operating under the name of Big Four String Band in 1887, although they soon were being advertised as "Tio & Doublet's Orchestra or String Band." Their last known advertisement comes from February 23, 1895, among the precious fragments of the *Crusader* so meticulously reassembled and dated by Lester Sullivan and held in Special Collections, Xavier University. On that Saturday night just before Mardi Gras, they played for a grand masquerade ball at Francs-Amis Hall on North Robertson Street.

It was gratifying to learn of the survival of some documents of the Société des Jeunes Amis, a benevolent society similar to the Francs-Amis, particularly in that the membership consisted significantly of persons descended from the old caste of free people of color. In the report of the finance committee for 1890, there is a payment of $30.00, dated September 8, 1890, to Fabregas for music, then a similar payment three months later of $28.00. It seems likely that "Fabregas" is the Frequito Fabregas, enumerated in the 1880 census as a nineteen-year-old white musician born in Louisiana of Spanish parents.

It is at least worth suggesting that the Jeunes Amis were thus demonstrating their taste in music, of a sort which, according to Filhe (1949), was soon to be replaced. There is no way to know, of course, whether Fabregas and his musicians—the orchestra must have been relatively large to judge from the payment—played Latin music. It is also worth noting that among their membership of over two hundred, the society included a number of eminent musicians, most notably William Nickerson and Daniel Desdunes (Société des Jeunes Amis Collection, Box 25–6).

Of course, what we would like to have, for the Jeunes Amis or for any organization giving a dance, are programs or dance cards listing the types of dances or perhaps even the specific pieces. In fact, any New Orleans–centered collection of such ephemera would be welcome, whatever the source. My steps in this direction have just begun, but some of the results are worth reporting. A typical, if rather grand, sequence of dances is that from the program of the Pickwick Club's ball, February 25, 1889: ouverture, waltz, polka, mazurka, lancers, waltz, polka, schottische, varieties, and so on for thirty dances, concluding with, predictably, "Home Sweet Home." This is not that different from the Installation and Hop given at Turner's Hall on December 8, 1894, by the Ramblers Club, which offered grand march, waltz, polka, mazurka, varieties, waltz, polka, schottische, lancers, and so forth.

At this point it should be recalled that the most important social dance innovation of the 1890s was the two-step. In the limited number of New Orleans dance programs I have seen there is a near series (1896, 1897, 1899) from the Carnival balls of the Twelfth Night Revelers. In 1896 we find a not unusual succession of waltz, lanciers, waltz, polka, waltz, and in seventh position a deux temps, at this time another name for the two-step. In the remainder of the program of thirty dances, there are two more deux temps, along with two other innovations, the glide and the York. The 1897 ball begins with a royal march and a lancers, whereupon an unbroken alternation of waltz and two-step takes over. Gone are the polkas, mazurkas, varieties, galops, and raquets of yesteryear. This alternating pattern is quite standard for the first years of the twentieth century until probably around 1912, at which point the newly fashioned one-step would begin to overtake the two-step.[18]

What I have not been able to find yet are any programs from African-American organizations. Finally, whatever we learn about these more formal events with printed dance cards may well be quite misleading with respect to rougher venues with unstructured or differently structured programs. It is nonetheless interesting to see that the date mentioned by Manuel Perez as the year in which Tio and Doublet allowed themselves to be enticed away from the polka and schottische is bracketed by the 1894 and 1896 programs above.

The two-step, although it was often associated at the outset with 6/8 time, as in Sousa's march "The Washington Post," had become by the

---

18. One relatively late program, that of the "New Orleanser Quartett Club" at Odd Fellows' Hall on March 9, 1909, gives two-step, polka, and mazurka nearly equal representation. It warns us to be on the lookout for variations depending on ethnicity and social level.

end of the decade the dance to which ragtime was played. To judge from the few programs I have seen, the adoption of the two-step in the Crescent City was a couple of years late, but perhaps that is to be expected. So far as rougher, rattier dancing is concerned, there is not a great deal of evidence. That kind of dancing surely existed, and it was fairly common for the old-timers of the Tulane interviews to talk about a drastic change in the character of the music and the dancing after midnight, when the more sedate folk went home to bed. But there do exist at least a couple of intriguing references, both of which give much food for thought and hints for further investigation.

The first of these is a type of news story frequently encountered all over the country during the reform years before World War I. It comes from the somewhat scruffy *New Orleans Item* of January 15, 1908, headlined "The Moral Wave Strikes New Orleans Dancing Schools":

> No More Turkey Trot, a Dance Which Was Developed Into Its Highest State of Efficiency at Milneburg and Bucktown.
>
> Signs Up "No Turkey Trotting Allowed"; "No Applause is Necessary"; "No Dancing With Hat in Hand"; "No Ungentlemanly Conduct Will Be Tolerated." At Washington Artillery Hall last evening, hundreds of couples arrived to do the turkey trot.
>
> Brookhoven's band played "Walk Right In and Walk Right Out Again."[19]

This is really rather startling, since every source claims that the turkey trot was a product of San Francisco's Barbary Coast dance halls and that it made the trip East only at the beginning of 1911.

Indeed it was at that time that *Variety*'s New Orleans correspondent—then and for a number of years to come, O. M. Samuels—sent in an item that, if at all accurate, turns the spotlight again on 1895 or 1896, albeit not in conjunction with the two-step.[20] Samuels wrote:

---

19. Jack Stewart was kind enough to send me this article, which had been collected by Russell Levy in his line-by-line reading of the *Item* some years ago; I had in fact seen, copied, and forgotten it about ten years ago, at a time when the last thing on my mind was the turkey trot.

20. My thanks to Bruce Vermazen who, knowing of my passionate interest in the turkey trot, called the article to my attention. Oscar Monte Samuels was born in 1885 and died in 1945 after a long career as building contractor and house-wrecker. His obituary (New Orleans *Times Picayune,* March 12, 1945, 2) states that he was recognized as an authority on the theater.

> Now that a siege of erotic dances has started in New York, it may be as well to place New Orleans on record as the home of "the Grizzly Bear," "Turkey Trot," "Texas Tommy," and "Todolo" dances. San Francisco has been receiving the questionable honor.
>
> Fifteen years ago, at Customhouse and Franklin streets, in the heart of New Orleans' "Tenderloin," these dances were first given, at an old negro dance hall. The accompanying music was played by a colored band, which has never been duplicated. The band often repeated the same selection, but never played it the same way twice.
>
> Dances popular in the lower strata of New Orleans society just now are the "Te–na–na," and "Bucktown Slow Drag." They, too, may find their way to the stage—authorities permitting (Samuels 1911).

The corner of Customhouse and Franklin is certainly a noteworthy address in the New Orleans dance hall directory. Between 1900 and 1915 three of its four corners were occupied, respectively, by Shoto's Honky tonk, the 101 Ranch, and the Pig Ankle tonk; this is according to the highly knowledgeable (if sometimes erroneous) map drawn for the Esquire Jazz Book (Miller 1945).

It is interesting that the downtown river corner of the intersection is occupied on the map by a joint called both the "101 Ranch" and "28." The former is the more recent of the two appellations; I assume that "28" was the old street number—analogous to the Big 25, also on Franklin Street but a bit closer to Canal Street. It is asserted that "28" was a haunt of Buddy Bolden's band (Rose and Souchon 1967, 220), and there are a couple of typically picturesque paragraphs in Bill Russell's essay in *Jazzmen* (Ramsey and Smith 1939, 34).

Samuels's stylistic observation is more than interesting, since so much of the earliest jazz on phonograph records is so little improvised. It gains credibility to the extent that it is quite unmotivated by the main point of a brief item, that is, that New Orleans had priority over San Francisco so far as the modern "erotic" dances are concerned.

These two references to the turkey trot clarify the lyrics to Ernest Hogan's famous song of 1895, "La Pas Ma La," which mentions, in addition to the title dance, the Bumbisha, the Saint Louis Pass, the

Chicago Salute, and finally, "to the world's fair and do the Turkey Trot."[21]

Samuels broke another lance for the honor of New Orleans five years later, when jazz was on its way to becoming a national mania. In so doing, he gave support to the notion that the music called "jazz" could not be exchanged for all New Orleans ragtime, but was a new phase of it. His dispatch appeared under the "Cabaret" rubric in the November 3, 1916, issue of *Variety:*

> Chicago's claim to originating "Jazz Bands" and "Balling the Jack" are as groundless, according to VARIETY's New Orleans correspondent, as "Frisco"'s assumption to be the locale for the first "Todolo" and "Turkey Trot" dances. Little negro tots were "Ballin' the Jack" in New Orleans over ten years ago, and negro roustabouts were "Turkey Trotting" and doing the "Todolo" in New Orleans as far back as 1890, he says. "Jazz Bands" have been popular there for over two years, and Chicago cabaret owners brought entertainers from that city to introduce the idea. New Orleans' "Brown Skin" dance is also to be instituted in the Windy City shortly, is the claim (Samuels 1916).

And so we are back where we started, both to the Original Dixieland Jazz Band and to the roustabouts who made the New Orleans levee one of the wonders of nineteenth-century America. Except that there is the perplexing remark, "over two years," which would take us back so far as jazz is concerned to early 1914, a date that may correspond to stylish New Orleans's somewhat tardy embrace of a turkey trot (and similar dances) that had managed to rise above their humble origins in Bucktown or in the unnamed dance hall at Customhouse and Franklin.

---

21. Hogan's piece was preceded in print by Irving Jones's "Possumala Dance or My Honey" (1894), which has quite different lyrics and melody. It does, in fact, bear a startling likeness to some of Ben Harney's songs, which were soon to become extremely popular. There is one point of perhaps far-fetched resemblance. Whereas Irving Jones's song repeats the rhythm ♪|♫♫|♫ ♪ in the voice part no fewer than eleven times in succession, Hogan's piece has in virtually every measure of the accompaniment, verse and chorus alike, the rhythm ♫♫. There are other pieces in the orbit of Hogan's and Jones's work, e.g., New Orleans composer Sidney Perrin's "The Jennie Cooler Dance" (1898); Paul Rubens's "Rag Time Pasmala (Characteristique Two Step)" (1898); Theo H. Northrup's "Louisiana Rag Two-Step (Pas Ma La)," with the additional title-page inscription "Description of Louisiana Niggers Dancing (The Pas Ma La Rag)" (1897). No doubt there are others.

I have suggested that the *omnium-gatherum* approach of the esteemed Henry Kmen and others in his footsteps is too indiscriminate. I have suggested that, while it is obvious that what the country came to know as jazz in 1917 came out of ragtime dance music as it was played in New Orleans in the first years of the century, it was the abandonment of the nexus of social dances first imported from Paris in the 1840s—the polka, mazurka, schottische, quadrille, and their relatives—in the course of the 1890s (although older dancers undoubtedly still kept on asking for them even twenty years later) that was the sine qua non for later developments. What replaced them was a simple walking and sliding dance—the two-step—ideally suited for ragtime, but also some new sexy dances, not yet quite fit for public consumption, of which the turkey trot and its sundry relatives and variations were eventually to emerge between 1911 and 1914 to define a new era of social dance, for which jazz was the accompaniment of choice.

Such a view leaves out any consideration of the astonishing expressiveness with which New Orleans African-American musicians (and the European-American musicians they inspired) imbued their run-of-the-mill dance music. In this, indeed, the local predilection for melody, as defined by W. T. Francis above, could well have played a role. But surely in the city of *Plessy v Ferguson* there was a need somehow to speak out, in whatever way one could—even in an arena, such as social dance music, that is by definition ephemeral and frivolous but by historical circumstance endowed with imagination and eloquence.

References

Albert, Tom. 1959. Interview with William Russell and Ralph Collins, September 25. William Ransom Hogan Jazz Archive, Tulane University, New Orleans, Louisiana.

Allen, William Francis, Charles Pickard Ware, and Lucy McKim Garrison. [1867] 1951. *Slave songs of the United States.* New York: Peter Smith.

Baron, John H. 1980. *Piano music from New Orleans 1851–1898.* New York: Da Capo.

Bisland, Elizabeth. 1906. *The life and letters of Lafcadio Hearn.* Vol. 1. London: Archibald Constable.

Cook, Will Marion. 1898. Music of the Negro. *Illinois Record* (May 14):1, 4.

———. 1918. Negro music. *New York Age* (September 9):6.

Dawson, Eddie. 1959. Interview by William Russell and Ralph Collins, August 11. William Ransom Hogan Jazz Archive, Tulane University, New Orleans, Louisiana.

Epstein, Dena J. 1977. *Sinful tunes and spirituals: Black folk music to the Civil War.* Urbana: University of Illinois Press.

Filhe, George. 1949. Typescript of an interview by Harriet Janis and Rudi Blesh. Held in the author's personal collection.

Fischer, David Hackett. 1970. *Historians' fallacies: Toward a logic of historical thought.* New York: Harper & Row.

Garner, Fradley, and Alan Merriam. 1960. The word jazz. *The Jazz Review* 3, no. 3:39–40; no. 4:40–42; no. 5:40; no. 6:40–41; no. 7:36–37.

Goffin, Robert. 1946. *La Nouvelle-Orléans, capitale du jazz.* New York: Editions de la Maison Française.

Goldstein, Walter. 1918. The natural harmonic and rhythmic sense of the Negro. In *Studies in musical education: History and aesthetics.* Papers and proceedings of the Music Teachers National Association (MTNA) at its 39th Annual Meeting, New Orleans, December 27–29, 1917. Hartford, Conn.: MTNA.

Guilcher, Jean-Michel. 1969. *La Contredanse et les renouvellements de la danse française.* Paris: Mouton.

Gushee, Lawrence. 1991. Black professional musicians in New Orleans c. 1880. *Inter-American Music Review* 11:53–63.

Hearn, Lafcadio. 1885. *"Gombo Zhèbes." Little dictionary of Creole proverbs.* New York: Will Coleman.

———. 1890. *Two years in the French West Indies.* New York: Harper.

———. 1924. *Miscellanies: Articles and stories now first collected by Albert Mordell.* Vol. 1. London: William Heinemann.

Janis, Harriet, and Rudi Blesh. 1971. *They all played ragtime.* New York: Oak.

Jones, Juli, Jr. 1911. Great colored song writers and their songs. *Indianapolis Freeman* (December 23):6.

Kingsley, Walter. 1917. Whence comes jass? Facts from the great authority on the subject. *New York Sun* (August 5): sect. 3, 3.

———. 1918. Vaudville volley. *Dramatic Mirror* (December 14).

Kinzer, Samuel. 1993. The Tio family: Four generations of New Orleans musicians, 1814–1933. Ph.D. diss., Louisiana State University.

Kmen, Henry A. 1966. *Music in New Orleans: The formative years, 1791–1841.* Baton Rouge: Louisiana State University Press.

Krehbiel, Henry Edward. [1913] 1962. *Afro-American folksongs: A study in racial and national music.* New York: Frederick Ungar.

Lange, Horst. 1991. *Als der Jazz begann, 1916–1923.* Berlin: Colloquium Verlag.

Marquis, Donald M. 1978. *In search of Buddy Bolden, first man of jazz.* Baton Rouge: Louisiana State University Press.

Merriam-Webster. 1986. *Webster's third international dictionary.* Springfield, Mass.: Merriam-Webster.

Miller, Paul Eduard. 1945. *Esquire's 1945 jazz book.* New York: A. S. Barnes.

"The moral wave strikes New Orleans dancing schools." 1908. *New Orleans Item* (January 15).

Nathan, Hans. 1962. *Dan Emmett and the rise of early Negro minstrelsy.* Norman: University of Oklahoma Press.

New Orleans taste in music. 1890. *New Orleans Daily Picayune* (January 2):3.

Patton, G. F. 1875. *A practical guide to the arrangement of band music.* Leipzig: John F. Stratton.

Ramsey, Frederic, Jr., with Charles Edward Smith. 1939. *Jazzmen.* New York: Harcourt, Brace.

Robinson, J. Russell. 1955. The story of J. Russell Robinson. *The Second Line* 6, no. 9/10:13–15, 30.

Rose, Al. 1974. *Storyville, New Orleans, being an authentic, illustrated account of the notorious red-light district.* University: University of Alabama Press.

Rose, Al, and Edmond Souchon. 1967. *New Orleans jazz: A family album.* Baton Rouge: Louisiana State University Press.

Russell, William. 1978. Albert Nicholas talks about Jelly Roll: Part II of an interview. *The Second Line* 30 (Spring):3–10.

[Samuels, Oscar Monte]. 1911: New Orleans makes a claim. *Variety* (July 1).

———. 1916. Cabaret. *Variety* (November 3).

Spriggins, E. Belfield. 1933. Excavating local jazz. *Louisiana Weekly* (April 22).

St. Cyr, Johnny. 1966. Jazz as I remember it. *Jazz Journal* (September):6–9.

Stewart, Jack. 1991. The Mexican band legend. *Jazz Archivist* 6:2.

Printed Music

Barney and Seymore. 1904. *St. Louis tickle.* Chicago: Victor Kremer Co.

Dubuclet, Lawrence. 1886a. *Bettina,* op. 2. New Orleans: Author.

———. 1886b. *Les yeux doux.* New Orleans: Author.

————. 1893. *World's Fair march,* op. 7. n.p.

————. 1897. *The belle of the carnival.* New Orleans: Louis Grunewald.

Cahill, Percy. 1906. *Don't go way nobody.* Music by P.A.G.T. New Orleans: Ashton Music Co.

Hogan, Ernest. 1895. *La pas ma la.* Kansas City: J. R. Bell.

Jones, Irving. 1894. *Possumala dance or My honey.* New York: Willis Woodward.

Northrup, Theo H. 1897. *Louisiana rag two-step (Pas ma la).* Chicago: Thompson Music.

Perrin, Sidney. 1898: *The Jennie Cooler dance.* New York: Stern.

Rubens, Paul. 1898. *Rag time pasmala (Characteristique two step).* London: Geo. L. Spaulding.

Voges, W. J. 1895. *Medley: Pasquila.* New Orleans: W. J. Voges.

Archival Documents

Carnival Collection. New Orleans Public Library, Louisiana Room.

New Orleans Public Library, Louisiana Room. New Orleans City Archives. AA670 / 1864. Mayor's Office. Permits issued by acting military mayor.

Société des Jeunes Amis Collection. University of New Orleans, Earl K. Long Library, Special Collections Department. Box 25–1–25–10. (Lawrence Gushee, "The Nineteenth-Century Origins of Jazz," reprinted from *Black Music Research Journal* 14, no. 1 [spring 1994])

(Gushee, Lawrence. "Lester Young's 'Shoe Shine Boy.'" In International Musicological Society, *Report of the Twelfth Congress, Berkeley, 1977.* Kassell: Barenreiter, 1981)

5

Responses to Early Jazz, 1919 to 1934

As Lawrence Gushee noted, because black and white cultures have been so separate in the United States, black people are sometimes invisible to white writers. As a case in point, consider the frequent claim in the white press that blacks don't write about jazz. True, a survey of jazz magazines and books on jazz reveals almost no black writers until the 1960s. This discovery, however, is based on the assumption that blacks who write about jazz would be featured in those publications. Instead, one needs to look at publications specifically for black readers. There is no better proof of the black community's support of and involvement in jazz than the black press. Local black newspapers around the country invariably include at least one page of national and local jazz news, listings of local jazz events, and so on—and remember, these are general, nonmusic publications. Black-oriented magazines not devoted to music still commonly carry much discussion of jazz. Thus, African Americans were writing about jazz, but since most never moved into the white press, according to those observers, they simply did not exist.

Let's return to the black press with an example from *Opportunity*. In an editorial, Charles S. Johnson again eloquently defends jazz. He begins by reprinting some of the insulting descriptions of jazz, complete with the word *nigger*, that were current in the 1920s. He points out that this decade was already becoming "the Jazz Age," despite the fact that the music was associated with African Americans, and he adds that jazz was spreading worldwide by way of the Victrola. (The Victor Company made this popular and affordable machine, which cost around ten dollars. The name "Victrola" became synonymous with "record player" just as "Kleenex" means "tissue" today.) Johnson also quotes Gilbert Seldes, whom we will read shortly. Above all, Johnson points out the irony that whites were, in effect, celebrating African American culture even though they still treated African Americans as third-class citizens.

There is a new international word—Jazz. Within the past seven years, it has flung itself impudently and triumphantly into the speech of seven nations. There is nothing vague about its meaning, even though no one seems able to define it. The Etymological Dictionary of Modern English defines it as "a number of niggers surrounded by noise—a kind of ragtime dance introduced from the United States . . . a word taken from Negro jargon." Horatio Parker, an American composer of note, decrying the decline of our taste in music, in the *Yale Review* calls it "naked African rhythm, and no more." Henry Van Dyck, the urbane, referred to it before the National Educational Association as "a species of music invented by demons for the torture of imbeciles." Clive Bell, interpreter of the modernists, back in 1921, in a ridiculously premature announcement of its death, explained that it was not merely music but a *movement* which "bounced into the world somewhere about the year 1911 . . . headed by a band and troupe of niggers, dancing."

When the subtle effects of this "movement" first began to be felt, there was a horrified revolt of the intellectuals against it. No primitive rhythms for these aesthetes! It was their duty to Art to resist the magic and lure of the African's syncopations and cacophony. "Some happy day," remarked one of these, "we shall beat our swords into plowshares and our jazz bands into unconsciousness."

If there was sandbagging of any sort, it failed to diminish the energy of this new rage. The word is now used in Europe almost exclusively to describe the kind of music and dancing imported from America. In America, its home, it describes not merely music and dancing but a national mood, or, better still, a jumble of moods. It has come to mean things typically American. Our contemporary critics speak of the "Jazz Age," the gogetters want to "jazz up" business, modern expressionism in art is jazz art. We have jazz bands, jazz murderers, jazz magazines! It is even used as a technical expression in aeronautics. If the propellor stops suddenly one must do a nose dive and "jazz" the throttle.

And here is the significant part of it: Jazz, which took its name from music—Negro music—has spread itself revealingly over the American temperament and become the expression medium for it, a sign and symbol of the American pace, of its moving spirit. This curious complexity of moods John Howard Lawson tried to portray in his play, "Processional," which Heywood Broun asserts comes closer to capturing the spirit of American life than any other contemporary play. Lawson calls it a jazz symphony. "The rhythm of the American procession as it streams about us," he says, explaining his attempt to devise something native to the American theatre, "is a stacatto burlesque carried out by a formal arrangement of jazz music."

Why has this music taken hold and what does this new movement mean? In spite of the startled protests of the classicists it is growing in popularity and meaning. It is not being foisted upon the public. As a writer in the London *New Statesman* points out, the composers and the music dealers are not the criminals. They are giving to the people what they want and can appreciate. He asks: Is jazz subsidized? Are the folk song societies contributed to by the masses? Is the passion for the good old folk songs concealed while a pretense for "Snooky-Ookums" is flaunted in order to get accepted in society? Do the popular songs cost more?

If we may believe Carl Van Vechten, "it is only through the trenchant pens of our new composers" (who are utilizing the distinctive features of ragtime and jazz) "that the complicated vigor of American life has been expressed in tone. It is the only music created in America today which is worth the paper on which it is written. It is the only American music which is enjoyed by the nation (even lovers of Mozart and Debussy prefer ragtime to the inert and saponaceous classicism of our more serious minded composers); it is the only American music which is heard abroad (and it is heard everywhere, in the trenches, by way of the victrola, in the Cafe de Paris at Monte Carlo in Cairo, in India, and in Australia)."

The secret of this vogue is that they are the kind of tunes that a large number of persons can easily enjoy, remember, play, and sing and even compose. Attention has been called to the fact that artists as gifted as Rodin and Troubetsky think that Art like true goodness flames, and is unmistakable; that it must leap sheer from the depth of feeling and be at its best understandable even to children. The great crowd is thus in good company in its appreciation of these magic tunes.

The new front toward the music and the appreciation of its relation to the new forces manifesting themselves in American life have come recently and together. It is no longer the bounden duty of the intellectuals to view these tendencies with alarm as the "enthusiastic disorganization of music"—the symptom of a national disintegration. "If, before we have produced something better," says Gilbert Seldes, "we give up jazz, we shall be sacrificing nearly all there is of gaiety and liveliness and rhythmic power in our lives. Jazz, for us, isn't a last feverish excitement, a spasm of energy before death. It is the cultural development of our resources, the expected and wonderful arrival of America at a point of creative intensity. Leopold Stokowski, leader of the Philadelphia Orchestra, thinks it is the natural expression of the times—its jerky rhythm a perfect expression of the life of today, the portrayal of the rush from one thing to another, a part of the quick transportation of modern life.

The amusing and yet profoundly significant paradox of the whole situation is the fact that it is the Negroes, who not only can best express the spirit of American life, but who have created the very forms of expression. For apart from the swirl and dash of the civilization of this country, there is, in the words and music of Negro songs, as Gilbert Seldes reminds us, an expression of something which underlies a great deal of America—our independence, our frankness, and gaiety. The distinguishing feature of the Negro part is that it is more intense. The most effective instruments and improvisations are Negro, the themes are Negro, the temperament is Negro. And yet it is American life.

Can it be that after all the creative energy of the Negro, who has been called the imitator, is sufficient in its strength to give to the Anglo-Saxon temperament a medium of expression, or complement its culture with the resistless spirit of rhythm and exultant life? May there not be in the ready appreciation of these Negro creations a recognition of common passions, instincts,—human qualities? May not, indeed, this appreciation of song and sentiment be a concealed admiration for the simple art, the spontaneity and frank intensity of Negro life, which tradition teaches us to despise? Let some analyst of the public mind explain the extraordinary vogue of George Gershwin's "Rhapsody in Blue," Al Jolson's "Mammy" songs, the "Weary Blues," the blunt, frank sentimental songs about "Aggravatin' Papa," or "Insufficient Sweetie" which make no pretences at delicately ornamented expression. Here is something to hold the interest of sociologists and psychologists as well as of artists!

At present these jumbled strains are difficult to rationalize, but there is a deep meaning in the pattern. It is the same problem which faced John Howard Lawson when he essayed to depict the American temper—with its inconsistencies and hectic march, its superficialities bored through at unexpected points with deep shafts of conflicting sentiment,—its comedy and pathos blending into feverish rhythm.

What an immense, even if unconscious irony the Negroes have devised! They, who of all Americans are most limited in self-expression, least considered and most denied, have forged the key to the interpretation of the American spirit. (Charles S. Johnson, "Jazz," [editorial], *Opportunity,* May 1925)

Now let's return to James A. Rogers's piece, "Jazz at Home," in which he provides some rather colorful descriptions of jazz.

Jazz is a marvel of paradox: too fundamentally human, at least as modern humanity goes, to be typically racial, too international to be characteristically national, too much abroad in the world to have a special home. And yet jazz in spite of it all is one part American and three parts American Negro, and was originally the nobody's child of the levee and the city slum. Transplanted exotic—a rather hardy one, we admit—of the mundane world capitals, sport of the sophisticated, it is really at home in its humble native soil wherever the modern unsophisticated Negro feels happy and sings and dances to his mood. It follows that jazz is more at home in Harlem than in Paris, though from the look and sound of certain quarters of Paris one would hardly think so. It is just the epidemic contagiousness of jazz that makes it, like the measles, sweep the block. But somebody had to have it first: that was the Negro. . . .

Yet in spite of its present vices and vulgarizations, its sex informalities, its morally anarchic spirit, jazz has a popular mission to perform. Joy, after all, has a physical basis. Those who laugh and dance and sing are better off even in their vices than those who do not. Moreover, jazz with its mocking disregard for formality is a leveller and makes for democracy. The jazz spirit, being primitive, demands more frankness and sincerity. Just as it already has done in art and music, so eventually in human relations and social manners, it will no doubt have the effect of putting more reality in life by taking some of the needless artificiality out. . . . Naturalness finds the artificial in conduct ridiculous. "Cervantes smiled Spain's chivalry away," said Byron. And so this new spirit of joy and spontaneity may itself play the rôle of reformer. Where at present it vulgarizes, with more wholesome growth in the future, it may on the contrary truly democratize. At all events, jazz is rejuvenation, a recharging of the batteries of civilization with primitive new vigor. It has come to stay, and they are wise, who instead of protesting against it, try to lift and divert it into nobler channels. (James A. Rogers, "Jazz at Home," in *The New Negro*, edited by Alain Locke [New York: Albert and Charles Boni, 1925])

When the white press needed a black person to explain jazz, it turned to James Reese Europe (1881–1919). He was one of the best-known black musicians to white audiences, for he had directed large black bands and orchestras in ragtime and popular music at Carnegie Hall as early as 1912. He also toured the United States while accompanying the ballroom dance recitals of Vernon and Irene Castle, and overseas under the auspices of the U.S. military in World War I. Europe was apparently very comfortable expressing himself publicly. His description of jazz tends to fanciful exaggerations and racial stereotypes, but he also boldly expresses pride in his people, saying, "Our musicians do their best work when using Negro material."

The negro loves anything that is peculiar in music, and this 'jazzing' appeals to him strongly. It is accomplished in several ways. With the brass instruments we put in mutes and make a whirling motion with the tongue, at the same time blowing full pressure. With wind instruments we pinch the mouthpiece and blow hard. This produces the peculiar sound which you all know. To us it is not discordant, as we play the music as it is written, only that we accent strongly in this manner the notes which originally would be without accent. It is natural for us to do this; it is, indeed, a racial musical characteristic. I have to call a daily rehearsal of my band to prevent the musicians from adding to their music more than I wish them to. Whenever possible they all embroider their parts in order to produce new, peculiar sounds. Some of these effects are excellent and some are not, and I have to be continually on the lookout to cut out the results of my musicians' originality. . . .

I have come back from France more firmly convinced than ever that negroes should write negro music. We have our own racial feeling and if we try to copy whites we will make bad copies. I noticed that the Morocco negro bands played music which had an affinity to ours. One piece, 'In Zanzibar,' I took for my band, and tho white audiences seem to find it too discordant, I found it most sympathetic. We won France by playing music which was ours and not a pale imitation of others, and if we are to develop in America we must develop along our own lines. Our musicians do their best work when using negro material. Will Marion Cook, William Tires [Tyers], even Harry Burleigh and Coleridge-Taylor are truly themselves in the music which expresses their race. Mr. Tires, for instance, writes charming waltzes, but the best of these have in them negro influences. The music of our race springs from the soul, and this is true to-day with no other race, except possibly the Russians and it is because of this that I and all my musicians have come to love Russian music. Indeed, as far as I am concerned, it is the only music I care for outside of Negro. (James Reese Europe, "A Negro Explains 'Jazz,'" originally published in *Literary Digest*, 1919)

In the general (nonblack) press, writers' responses to jazz ran the gamut from the insulting to the surprisingly understanding. They are sometimes racist or, especially in England, anti-Semitic.

In London in 1919, Francesco Berger happened to encounter a small local jazz group that he did not name in print. Although Berger clearly has a classical music bias, he found himself entranced. His review ends with an ironic comment on the commercial pressures of the music business.

A Jazz Band Concert

FRANCESCO BERGER

Not many weeks ago I had my first experience of a Jazz band, while taking afternoon-tea in a well-known West End tea-room. I had not gone there in quest of the band, so that when its strident noise burst upon my unprepared ears, it fell on virgin soil, and was a complete surprise to me.

In describing its effect (not much modified by subsequent hearings) I need scarcely affirm that I am not an agent, paid to "boom" this class of entertainment. It is already far too popular to need advertising at my hands. Neither have I any desire to exclaim against it, on the ground of its being coarse, or unmusical, or inartistic. I shall confine myself to putting into words what I thought and felt at the time, and what I think and feel since.

It was one of the strongest and strangest experiences I have undergone in an extended life, during which I have listened to much that was good, to more that was bad, to most that was indifferent. It produced an impression that was not quite pleasant, but not entirely unpleasant, a sort of comical mixture of both. Not being a frequenter of American drinking-bars, and never having tasted a real American drink, I can only guess what a copious draught of one of their cunningly concocted iced drinks would taste like on a swelteringly hot day. But I imagine that it would produce on the palate sensations akin to those produced on the ear by a Jazz band. Pleasurable though staggering, making it difficult to recover one's breath, defying analysis, repellent at the outset, but magnetically fascinating.

This Jazz band played remarkably well, with exaggerated colouring, it must be owned, but with tremendous spirit and "go," accompanied by a perfectly incongruous row, produced from a number of noise-emitting articles which cannot be called musical instruments. Its

members comprised a very clever Pianist, a clever Violinist, two excellent banjoists, a concertina-player, a cornet-player, and a "utility man"
who performed on a side drum, a big drum, cymbals, triangle, a tin-
kling hand-bell, a deep-toned large one, a dinner gong, a rattle, a rail-
way whistle, a motor hooter, and a few more deafening things.

They play a tune which may or may not be transatlantic, but is
always of a popular type, and they play it two or three times over, varying it occasionally by ingenious *fioriture* on Piano or Violin. And a
remarkable feature of their performance is the abrupt transition from
noisiest *fortissimo* to softest *pianissimo,* or *vice versa,* with very little, if
any, intermediate *crescendo* or *diminuendo.* During the soft parts the
"utility man" is silent, and you begin to hope he has gone home; but,
with the first recurrence of a *tutti* he is back again, and, like a giant
refreshed by rest, resumes his labours with redoubled energy. He
appears to have little respect for rhythm, but strikes, hits, blows,
bumps, rings, and bangs whenever "he darned chooses." Yet, whatever
his vagaries may have been during a Piece, however much he may
appear to have "set up business on his own," he is never behind-hand
nor before at the finish. And I noticed that the tea-drinking audience
applauded all the more when the *Finale* was the maddest of all mad
orgies of ROW. They would not feel they had been sufficiently "jazzed"
if a Piece ended without a hurricane and a thunderbolt.

The unanimity of accord which, in spite of ear-splitting noise, this
band is able to maintain, is one of the marvels of it all. Not one of the
players loses his head, not one of them is careless of his part, each is as
conscientious a performer as though playing a Concerto in Queen's
Hall. And when, after the final crash of a Piece, you look round for the
débris, and are preparing to count the dead and wounded on the
ground, you find the players mentally, if not physically, as cool as
cucumbers, tuning their instruments for their next encounter, or
exchanging with one another critical remarks on Puccini or Debussy. I
fancy, by their smiles, that they occasionally indulge in delicate stories
from club-land.

I am not certain whether this particular band is better than, or inferior to, others now before the public, but I can scarcely imagine one
that could excel it in precision of *ensemble,* in extravagant colouring, or

in noisy exuberance. When, on other occasions, I have had cherished ideals shattered by novel experiences, it was the music or the performer that thrilled and overpowered. But this Jazz business is quite foreign to anything else, quite unique. The Piano and Violin music is full of prominent accents and plaintive syncopations, the banjos give to it a penetrating buzzing accompaniment, and the eruptions from the "utility man" are so unexpected, that the *ensemble* becomes a medley of recognizable and unrecognizable rhythm, a blend of uncongenial elements, bewildering, exasperating, and yet appealing. Your sensations are being "brushed by machinery." Your familiar codes and laws are defied and upset. Your *terra ferma* is withdrawn. You are adrift on an unexplored ocean. The anchor of your traditions, by which you held so reliantly, has failed you. Whether you will ever reach sunlit meadows and shady groves, whether you will ever again safely tread the highroads which your forefathers trod before you, is a question which only Time, the inscrutable, can solve.

Having occasion to speak of a Jazz band to an American friend, I thought I was flattering his nationality when I described it as "an admirable performance of profaned Art." He promptly replied: "I do not claim for it that it is what has hitherto passed for *high Art*. But you must admit that it has *one* quality in which much old-world music is sadly wanting, and that is 'character.' It is thoroughly representative of Americanism; as free from conventionality and from 'schools' as my country is free from ancient history and slavery. Better stuff would probably be tamer. It is out of material such as this, brimful of spontaneous national manner, that your refined methods and artificial mannerisms have been evolved. If you take from it what is so obviously its own, including its crudity, you rob it of its distinctive quality; it becomes ordinary, often-told, undesirable." And he was not far wrong.

The Pianist in this particular Jazz band is so accomplished an artist that I remarked to him: "But you are far too good a musician to be doing *this* sort of thing. How is it you are *here*?"

"I suppose," he replied, "you mean that I ought to be doing 'the legitimate.' Well, I tried that when I first married. I played in public, I accompanied singers, and I gave a lesson when I found a pupil who would come and take it. And I earned thirty shillings a week. Then I took to *this*. When my afternoon's work is finished at six o'clock, I have a similar engagement somewhere else from nine to eleven. And I earn twenty pounds a week. I have a wife and two children to support. Do you blame me? When I shall have saved enough to afford myself the luxury, I shall go back to 'the legitimate' and to—starvation."

I could not answer him, for there is no answer.

O tempora, O mores. (Francesco Berger, "A Jazz Band Concert," *Monthly Musical Record*, August 1, 1919)

O tempora, o mores is a Latin statement attributed to the Roman statesman Cicero. It literally means, "Oh, the times, oh the mores (customs)," and figuratively Berger is using it to say, "What have our times come to?"

An American named Marion Bauer wrote about jazz in 1924 for a publication in France. Bauer's writing is filled with stereotypes about the "primitive" and "savage" nature of black America, but her intent is to defend jazz. She concludes as follows:

"Jazz" is the true child of the age; but one shouldn't forget that it is also the child of the dregs of the civilized world and that it comes from the lower classes of society. The dances that have penetrated everywhere, in our salons, in our ballrooms, were created in a quarter of San Francisco, the Barbary Coast, where one finds the outcasts of ports, the scum of all the nations and all the races; it would take the alchemy of magicians to turn material from such vile origins into a true master-piece! And possibly one might contradict me with the suites of the 17th and 18th centuries, and the mazurkas or polonaises or waltzes of Chopin which are expressions of the most high art. But "jazz" is the future, and the future remains the supreme tribunal! (Marion Bauer, "L'Influence du 'Jazz-Band,'" *La Revue Musicale,* April 1924 [this extract translated by Lewis Porter])

By her ending, Bauer seems to suggest that jazz will win out in the judgment of history, and in fact it has. Bauer doesn't seem to be aware of the New Orleans music scene—and many people weren't yet, since bands were then just starting to record there—but she is correct in thinking that San Francisco was important. Remember that the word *jazz* was first printed there. *Jazz On the Barbary*

Coast, a book by Tom Stoddard (Chigwell, U.K.: Storyville Publications, 1982), documents just how active jazz musicians were in San Francisco.

The French were familiar mostly with the white dance bands, but their reaction was generally positive. In one of André Coeuroy's chapters in the book *Le Jazz*, which as we mentioned he wrote in 1926 with André Schaeffner, he reports on a 1922 survey of French composers, among them Paul Dukas and Paul Pierné, which concluded that jazz was important and that "if so many treat jazz with contempt and levity, it's because they don't understand it." Coeuroy then presents comments he collected in 1925, which tend to be cautiously in favor of the new music. Composer Albert Roussel proclaims that jazz is very interesting, that he has "more than once" found it charming and original and that some of its musicians have "prodigious virtuosity"; though he adds that if he listens to it for a long time it starts to get monotonous and irritating. Art historian Maurice Brillant held that jazz is certainly music, and "sometimes an admirable music." All agree that jazz was having a great impact on classical composers. Coeuroy concludes the book with a defiant cry:

> In vain one closes one's ears to jazz. It is life. It is art. It is the intoxication of sounds and noises. It is the animal joy in supple movements. It is the melancholy of suffering. It is ourselves in the present (p. 145, my translation).

Meanwhile, an even more positive impression of the new music was given in Carl Engel's "Jazz: A Musical Discussion" (*Atlantic Monthly*, August 1922). Engel (born in Paris in 1884, died in New York City in 1944) had a distinguished career in music, having served as president of Schirmer, Inc. (the music publishing firm that is now separate from Schirmer Books), and of the American Musicological Society. In 1922, when he was chief of the Music Division of the Library of Congress, he read a paper at a music conference in Nashville that was later printed in the *Atlantic Monthly*. Because Engel held an influential position, his decision to come out firmly on the side of jazz is especially impressive. He wrote, "Let us admit that the *best* of jazz tunes is something infinitely more original—perhaps even musically better—than the so-called 'popular music' that America produced in the 'good old days' . . . Like any other type of music, jazz can be good or bad. I am not defending bad jazz any more than I would defend a bad ballad or the bad playing of [something by] Beethoven." (At this point he digresses to condemn Paul Whiteman and others who "jazz" the classics.)

Engel continued, ". . . [T]here exists such a thing as *good* jazz music, and *good* jazz is a great deal better, and far more harmless, than is a bad ballad or the bad playing of Beethoven." He pointed out that while many people condemned jazz because of the "lewd" dancing it inspired, in every previous generation the then-current dance, including the saraband and the waltz, had been equally condemned, whereas the music in each case had withstood the test of time. He was prudish enough to agree that the jazz dancing was "deplorable," but he suggested that the music of jazz would remain of interest "long after the dance known as jazz will happily have vanished." He wrote that good jazz—in which he included, like most of his peers, the popular songs of Jerome Kern and Irving Berlin—had blue notes and other dexterous "harmonic tricks that not only stood, but demanded and deserved, rehearing . . . [T]here sprang up a diversity of the freshest, most unexpected modulations which fell upon the ear like drops of evening rain upon a parched and sun-baked soil." Jazz also exposed the lay audience to counterpoint. Engel clearly recognized that the sheet music only represented the bare sketch of a jazz piece: "When a jazz tune is written on paper, for a piano solo, it loses nine tenths of its flavor." At its best, "jazz finds its last and supreme glory in the skill for improvisation exhibited by its performers . . . Chaos in order—orchestral technic of master craftsmen—music that is recklessly fantastic, joyously grotesque. Such is good jazz." While words like *grotesque* and *reckless* may not seem flattering, he clearly meant them as praise.

A somewhat reserved but basically positive response to jazz was offered by Edwin Stringham in "'Jazz'—An Educational Problem" (*Musical Quarterly*, April 1926). Stringham is reasonable enough to acknowledge that "there is both good and bad jazz." He felt that jazz was basically a positive development, partly in itself and mostly in that it could lead listeners to classical music. He also felt that the more jazz composers utilized classical techniques, the better the music they would make.

One of the most widely read and cited defenses of jazz was written by critic Gilbert Seldes, whose book *The Seven Lively Arts* presented individual chapters on the new movements in the arts as of 1924. (Other chapters covered film, theater, painting, and comic strips.) In his chapter on jazz, Seldes maintained, like Carl Engel, "Jazz is good—at least good jazz is good . . . " However, he also then believed that the black musicians were basically "instinctive" musicians who needed "intellectuals" like Paul Whiteman to bring the music to its highest level. In 1958, Seldes hosted the first televised educational series on jazz, with Billy Taylor as the show's musical director.

Toujours Jazz

The word jazz is already so complicated that it ought not to be subjected to any new definitions, and the thing itself so familiar that it is useless to read new meanings into it. Jazz is a type of music grown out of ragtime and still ragtime in essence; it is also a method of production and as such an orchestral development; and finally it is the symbol, or the byword, for a great many elements in the spirit of the time—as far as America is concerned it is actually our characteristic expression. This is recognized by Europeans; with a shudder by the English and with real joy by the French, who cannot, however, play it.

The fact that jazz is our current mode of expression, has reference to our time and the way we think and talk, is interesting; but if jazz music weren't itself good the subject would be more suitable for a sociologist than for an admirer of the gay arts. Fortunately, the music and the way it is played are both of great interest, both have qualities which cannot be despised; and the cry that jazz is the enthusiastic disorganization of music is as extravagant as the prophecy that if we do not stop "jazzing" we will go down, as a nation, into ruin. I am quite ready to uphold the contrary. If—before we have produced something better— we give up jazz we shall be sacrificing nearly all there is of gaiety and liveliness and rhythmic power in our lives. Jazz, for us, isn't a last feverish excitement, a spasm of energy before death. It is the normal development of our resources, the expected, and wonderful, arrival of America at a point of creative intensity.

Jazz is good—at least good jazz is good—and I propose to summarize some of the known reasons for holding it so. The summary will take me far from the thing one hears and dances to, from the thing itself. The analysis of jazz, musically or emotionally, is not likely to be done in the spirit of jazz itself. There isn't room on the printed page for a glissando on the trombone, for the sweet sentimental wail of the saxophone, or the sudden irruptions of the battery. Nor is there need for these—intellectually below the belt—attacks. The reason jazz is worth writing about is that it is worth listening to. I have heard it said by those who have suffered much that it is about the only native music worth listening to in America. . . .

More must be said of the negro side of jazz than I can say here. Its technical interest hasn't yet been discussed by anyone sufficiently expert and sufficiently enthusiastic at the same time. In words and music the negro side expresses something which underlies a great deal of America—our independence, our carelessness, our frankness, and gaiety. In each of these the negro is more intense than we are, and we surpass him when we combine a more varied and more intelligent life with his instinctive qualities. *Aggravatin' Papa* (don't you try to two-time me) isn't exactly the American response to a suspected infidelity, yet it is humanly sound, and is only a little more simple and savage than we are. The superb *I'm Just Wild about Harry* is, actually, closer to the American feeling of 1922 than "I Always dream of Bill"; as expression it is more honest than, say, *Beautiful Garden of Roses;* and *He May be Your Man* is simply a letting down of our reticences, a frankness beyond us.

I shift between the two teams, Sissle and Blake, Creamer and Layton, uncertain which has most to give. Sissle and Blake wrote *Shuffle Along;* the others accomplished the intricate, puzzling rhythm of *Sweet Angelina,* one or two other songs in *Strut Miss Lizzie,* and *Come Along, I'm through with Worrying.* Of this song a special word can be said. It is based on *Swing Low, Sweet Chariot,* and imposes on that melody a negro theme (the shiftlessness and assurance of "bound to live until I die") and a musical structure similar to that applied to the same original by Anton Dvořák in the *New World Symphony.* I am only a moderate admirer of this work; I am not trying to put *Come Along* into the same category, for its value is wholly independent of its comparative merits; nor am I claiming that jazz is equal to or greater or less than symphonic music. But I do feel that the treatment of a negro melody, by negroes, to make a popular and beautiful song for Americans ought not to be always neglected, always despised. I say also that our serious composers have missed so much in not seeing what the ragtime composers have done, that (like Lady Bracknell) they ought to be exposed to comment on the platform.

If they cannot hear the almost unearthly cry of the *Beale Street Blues* I can only be sorry for them; the whole of Handy's work is melodically of the greatest interest and is to me so versatile, so changing, in quality, that I am incapable of suggesting its elements. Observed in the works of others, the blues retain some of this elusive nature—they are equivocal between simplicity, sadness, irony, and something approaching frenzy. The original negro spiritual has had more respect, but the elements have been sparsely used, and one fancies that even in looking at these our serious composers have felt the presence of a regrettable vulgarity in syncopation and in melodic line. *Jesus Heal' de Sick* is negro from the Bahamas; its syncopation, its cry, "Bow low!" are repeated in any number of others; the spirituals themselves were often made out of the common songs in which common feeling rose to intense and poetic expression—as in *Round About de Mountain,* a funeral song with the Resurrection in a magnificent phrase, "An she'll rise in His arms." The only place we have these things left, whether you call the present version debased or sophisticated, gain or loss, is in ragtime, in jazz. I do *not* think that the negro (in African plastic or in American rag) is our salvation. But he has kept alive things without which our lives would be perceptibly meaner, paler, and nearer to atrophy and decay.

I say the negro is not our salvation because with all my feeling for what he instinctively offers, for his desirable indifference to our set of conventions about emotional decency, I am on the side of civilization. To anyone who inherits several thousand centuries of civilization, none of the things the negro offers can matter unless they are apprehended by the mind as well as by the body and the spirit. The beat of the tom-tom affects the feet and the pulse, I am sure; in *Emperor Jones* the throbbing of the drum affected our minds and our sensibilities at once. There will always exist wayward, instinctive, and primitive geniuses who will affect us directly, without the interposition of the intellect; but if the process of civilization continues (will it? I am not so sure, nor entirely convinced that it should) the greatest art is likely to be that in which an uncorrupted sensibility is *worked* by a creative intelligence. So far in their music the negroes have given their response to the world with an exceptional naïveté, a directness of expression which has interested *our* minds as well as touched our emotions; they have shown comparatively little evidence of the functioning of *their* intelligence. *Runnin' Wild,* whether it be transposed or transcribed, is singularly instinctive, and instinctively one recognizes it and makes it the musical motif of a gay night. But one falls back on *Pack Up Your Sins* [by Irving Berlin] and *Soon* [by Cole Porter] as more interesting pieces of music even if one can whistle only the first two bars. (I pass the question of falling farther back, to the music of high seriousness, which is another matter; it is quite possible, however, that the *Sacre du Printemps* of Strawinsky, to choose an example not unaffected by the jazz age, will outlive the marble monument of the Music Box.)

Nowhere is the failure of the negro to exploit his gifts more obvious than in the use he has made of the jazz orchestra; for although nearly every negro jazz band is better than nearly every white band, no negro band has yet come up to the level of the best white ones, and the leader of the best of all, by a little joke, is called Whiteman. The negro's instinctive feeling for colourful instruments in the band is marked; he was probably the one to see what could be done with the equivocal voice of the saxophone—a reed in brass, partaking of the qualities of two choirs in the orchestra at once. He saw that it could imitate the voice, and in the person of Miss Florence Mills saw that the voice could equally imitate the saxophone. The shakes, thrills, vibratos, smears, and slides are natural to him, although they produce tones outside the scale, because he has never been tutored into a feeling for perfect tones, as white men have; and he uses these with a great joy in the surprise they give, in the way they adorn or destroy a melody; he is given also to letting instruments follow their own bent, because he has a faultless sense of rhythm and he always comes out right in the end. But this is only the beginning of the jazz band—for its perfection we go afield. . . .

The title of this essay is provoked by that of the best and bitterest attack launched against the ragtime age—Clive Bell's *Plus de Jazz*. (In *Since Cézanne*.) "No more jazz," said Mr. Bell in 1921, and, "Jazz is dying." Recalling that Mr. Bell is at some pains to dissociate from the movement the greatest of living painters, Picasso; that he concedes to it a great composer, Strawinsky, and T. S. Eliot, whom he calls "about the best of our living poets," James Joyce whom he wofully underestimates, Virginia Woolf, Cendrars, Picabia, Cocteau, and the musicians of *les six*—remembering the degree of discrimination and justice which these concessions require, I quote some of the more bitter things about jazz because it would be shirking not to indicate where the answer may lie:

> Appropriately it (the jazz movement) took its name from music—the art that is always behind the times. . . . Impudence is its essence— impudence in quite natural and legitimate revolt against nobility and beauty: impudence which finds its technical equivalent in syncopation: impudence which rags. . . . After impudence comes the determination to surprise: you shall not be gradually moved to the depths, you shall be given such a start as makes you jigger all over. . . .
>
> . . . Its fears and dislikes—for instance, its horror of the noble and the beautiful are childish; and so is its way of expressing them. Not by irony and sarcasm, but by jeers and grimaces, does Jazz mark its antipathies. Irony and wit are for the grown-ups. Jazz dislikes them as much as it dislikes nobility and beauty. They are the products of the cultivated intellect and jazz cannot away with intellect or culture. . . . Nobility, beauty, and intellectual subtlety are alike ruled out. . . .
>
> . . . And, of course, it was delightful for those who sat drinking their cocktails and listening to nigger bands, to be told that, besides being the jolliest people on earth, they were the most sensitive and critically gifted. They . . . were the possessors of natural, uncorrupted taste. . . . Their instinct might be trusted: so, no more classical concerts and music lessons. . . .
>
> The encouragement given to fatuous ignorance to swell with admiration of its own incompetence is perhaps what has turned most violently so many intelligent and sensitive people against Jazz. They see that it encourages thousands of the stupid and vulgar to fancy that they can

understand art, and hundreds of the conceited to imagine that they can create it. . . .

It is understood that Mr. Bell is discussing the whole of the jazz movement, not ragtime music alone. I do not wish to go into the other arts, except to say that if he is jazz, then Mr. Joyce's sense of form, his tremendous intellectual grasp of his aesthetic problem, and his solution of that problem, are far more proof than is required of the case for jazz. Similarly for Mr. Eliot. It is not exactly horror of the noble that underlies Mr. Joyce's travesty of English prose style, nor is it to Mr. Eliot that the reproach about irony and wit is to be made. In music it is of course not impudence, but emphasis (distortion or transposition of emphasis) which finds its technical equivalent in syncopation, for syncopation is a method of rendering an emotion, not an emotion in itself. (Listen to Strawinsky.) Surprise, yes; but in the jazz of [Ted] Lewis and not in that of Whiteman, which does not jeer or grimace, which has wit and structure—*i.e.,* employs the intellect. Nobility—no. But under what compulsion are we always to be noble? The cocktail drinkers may have been told a lot of nonsense about their position as arbiters of the arts; precisely the same nonsense is taught in our schools and preached by belated aesthetes to people whose claims are not a whit better—since it doesn't matter what their admirers think of themselves—it is what jazz and Rostand and Michelangelo are in themselves that matters. I have used the word art throughout this book in connexion with jazz and jazzy things; if anyone imagines that the word is belittled thereby and can no longer be adequate to the dignity of Leonardo or Shakespeare, I am sorry. I do not think I have given encouragement to "fatuous ignorance" by praising simple and unpretentious things at the expense of the fake and the *faux bon.* I have suggested that people do what they please about the gay arts, about jazz; that they do it with discrimination and without worrying whether it is noble or not, or good form or intellectually right. I am fairly certain that if they are ever actually to see Picasso it will be because they have acquired the habit of seeing—something, anything—without *arrière-pensée,* because they will know what the pleasure is that a work of art can give, even if it be jazz art. Here is Mr. Bell's conclusion, with most of which I agree:

Even to understand art a man must make a great intellectual effort. One thing is not as good as another; so artists and amateurs must learn to choose. No easy matter, that: discrimination of this sort being something altogether different from telling a Manhattan from a Martini. To select as an artist or discriminate as a critic are needed feeling and intellect and—most distressing of all—study. However, unless I mistake, the effort will be made. The age of easy acceptance of the first thing that comes is closing. Thought rather than spirits is required, quality rather than colour, knowledge rather than irreticence, intellect rather than singularity, wit rather than romps, precision rather than surprise, dignity rather than impudence, and lucidity above all things: *plus de jazz*.

It is not so written, but it sounds like "Above all things, no more jazz!" A critic who would have hated jazz as bitterly as Mr. Bell does, wrote once, alluding to a painter of the second rank:

But, beside those great men, there is a certain number of artists who have a distinct faculty of their own, by which they convey to us a peculiar quality of pleasure which we cannot get elsewhere; and these, too, have their place in general culture, and must be interpreted to it by those who have felt their charm strongly, and are often the objects of a special diligence and a consideration wholly affectionate, just because there is not about them the stress of a great name and authority.

—and beside the great arts there is a certain number of lesser arts which have also a pleasure to give; and if we savour it strongly and honestly we shall lose none of our delight in the others. But if we fear and hate *them,* how shall we go into the Presence? (Gilbert Seldes, "Toujours Jazz," *The Seven Lively Arts* [New York: Harper & Brothers, 1924])

As the reader must have noted, Seldes appreciates jazz a bit begrudgingly. Many writers were even less charitable than he, even though they freely admitted that jazz was popular. It wasn't the first (or last) time that the experts have been against something that the layperson liked. Typical was "The Decline of Jazz," an editorial in *The Musician,* a magazine for music teachers. It assured its readers that jazz was only a passing fad driven by commercial interests, but that its legacy would be the good effect of having opened people's ears to new music.

The Decline of Jazz
Its Day—If It Ever Really Had a Day—Is Passing and Teachers Will Have Less and Less of It to Contend With

JAZZ was the voice of the Money-Changer in music. Jazz has ceased to be profitable, and hence we shall soon hear of it no more.

Only a few weeks ago the head of one of the most popular of the Mid-Western dance organizations sent out a prettily printed pink announcement to his patrons to the effect that as the "best people" were setting their faces against "jazz" the orchestras of this company would thereafter no longer discourse jazz. In a word, jazz was discovered by this keen sighted businessman to be on the verge of becoming "unfashionable" and he hastened to take his position in the van of fashion's devotees and to set the new style.

Of interest, as having the same significance, is a recent letter of considerable length sent out by one of the leading talking machine companies to its dealers, about twelve thousand, throughout the United States. This letter was a strong and well-reasoned appeal to these music merchants, probably the most influential group in the country, to cease centering their attention each month upon the "new releases" which are largely jazz numbers in dance or vocal form, and to give their time to selling the more standard numbers to be found distributed throughout the pages of the regular catalog.

This is important because probably the greatest impetus that "jazz" has received came from the strenuous sales efforts exerted by the phonograph dealers, who have found in the latest jazz numbers their greatest source of profit. This reacted, in a peculiar way, to develop the "jazz" producers, since in latter years most of the popular music publishers have been kept alive by the royalties they have received from the records made of their numbers. These royalties have gone into large advertising campaigns which have either boosted these numbers themselves later or have brought forward other new numbers of no better musical lineage. As a matter of fact clever publicity work of a highly varied character—well financed—is responsible for the seeming success of so much musical trash.

There is such a thing, of course, as a self-respecting popular song—a thing of words and rhythm and melody that really makes itself popular. But most of the stuff we have had under the name jazz has boasted of a vogue that was the artificial of the artificial—it suggests painted street harridans thrust into the lime-light.

To those who may have felt that standard music was on the wane, and jazz on the gain, it can be stated emphatically that their impression is wrong. Quite the opposite is the case. From the executive offices of the biggest of our standard music publishers comes the good news that such music publishing as is there represented is distinctly prosperous.

On the other hand it is quite evident that the so-called "jazz" publishers are having very hard sledding. The past year has not produced a single number that could really be called a "hit"—such as "Smiles," "Over There," "Keep the Home Fires Burning"—this notwithstanding the fact that popular composers today certainly have learned a thing or two about dressing up their slight melodic ideas, and will grab a resolution, or a rhythm from Debussy or Strawinsky with the utmost nonchalance. They have indeed acquired the art of giving their productions harmonic spice and rhythmic interest. And yet—failure. Simply because the public is fed up—is "on to" them.

As a matter of fact the records of the better class publishing houses demonstrate, beyond cavil, that the general taste of the American public has tremendously improved in the past decade. And so has the product of our home composers. The American public buys songs and piano solos of the very best character, and buys them in steadily increasing quantity. This is a statement proved by the figures in the order books of the big publishers. And our composers today—while we may have none of surpassing gifts—produce compositions characterized by beauty, grace, originality, and fine spiritual content—quite often showing real genius.

In the inexplicableness of this strange period of musical development of our nation, which has harbored and nurtured jazz, there is just one profitable feature. The cleverer of the jazz composers have searched far and wide for inspiration for their extravagant harmonic and rhythmic effects, and they have, in their borrowings from the masters, introduced the public to many things that were good, and that unless dished up in popular form would never have been understood or appreciated by the average listener. Latterly whole masterpieces have been "jazzed" entire, and have been received by the populace with acclaim.

We can say, undoubtedly, that jazz leaves us, as a country, with ears and intelligence wider open to the message of the newer writers. The public knows better how to listen and to appreciate. The messages of "les jeunes" have a slightly better chance of being understood by a populace that has been delighted by a Whiteman-jazz version of Rimsky-Korsakoff's "Chanson Indoue."

We are not deceived—the interment of jazz will not be immediate, but it is inevitable. In the mean time the music teacher can do his or her share in hastening the dissolution by pointing out the absurdity of jazz—and especially by showing that unquestionably it is no longer fashionable. To any up-to-date young gentleman or lady, that latter point should settle the matter at once. ("The Decline of Jazz" [editorial], *The Musician*, May 1922)

Numerous articles in newspapers of the 1920s covered the various ill effects attributed to jazz, sometimes with a touch of humor. One article, "Straton Says Jazz Is 'Agency of Devil,'" reports a meeting of the Music Forum of the American League of Professional Women, where Dr. John Roach Straton, pastor of the Calvary Baptist Church, and operatic contralto Marguerite d'Alvarez each spoke on "What Shall We Do about Jazz?"

"If I were asked to answer in a single sentence, 'what shall we do about jazz,' I would reply that we ought to consign it to a hotter place than this earth," said Dr. Straton. "I have no patience with this modern jazz tendency, whether it be in music, science, social life or religion. It is part of the lawless spirit which is being manifested in many departments of life, endangering our civilization in its general revolt against authority and established order. Jazz music is just as much a revolt against the standards of modesty and decency as is the jazz tendency in dress.

"Jazz, with its discord, its appeal to the sensuous, should be stamped out. The jazz hound is an outlaw and a musical bandit. Like the gunman, he is running amuck and should be relentlessly put down. . . ."

In reply Mme. d'Alvarez said: "Jazz is my reason for living in New York City. I prefer to live in New York because here I can best find the inspiration of good jazz music. New York is jazz incarnate. Its architecture, its businesses, its life—all sparkle to a syncopated measure.

"When I die I have only one request to make. I want music at my funeral, but no dirge or mournful laments. Play only one thing and let that number be George Gershwin's Jazz Symphony. To me it is truly great music, and certainly it is the music that best expresses us moderns." ("Straton Says Jazz Is 'Agency of Devil,'" *New York Times,* May 7, 1926)

Significantly, the article notes that the pastor received a scattering of applause, while the singer's defense of jazz was enthusiastically received. Again, the public sided in favor of the new music. A good sampling from the *New York Times* appears in chapter 2 of sociologist Neil Leonard's book, *Jazz and the White Americans* (Chicago: University of Chicago Press, 1962).

In England, Henry F. Gilbert wrote a piece entitled "Concerning Jazz" in which he gives jazz a quite mixed review. First, he notes that jazz obviously cannot be responsible for ruining people's morals, as some detractors claim, and goes on to declare that jazz is truly American, "and as such it is of great interest to all of us in America who take a serious interest in music." But then he gets critical.

This music certainly has plenty of "pep," and it certainly has plenty of "vulgarity." "Pep" and "vulgarity" are its most salient characteristics. It by no means expresses any of the higher qualities of America. "Pep," in its more noble manifestations, is that-impatient will-to-accomplish which will not be denied. No, most of the ideal aspects of Americanism are far away from jazz. Much more is jazz (as it is at present) a perfect expression of some of the worst and commonest elements in the American. For it must not be forgotten that while one half of our definition is "pep," the other half is *"vulgarity."*

But now is jazz a new kind of music? Has it anything to contribute to the art? I find that almost all pieces of so-called jazz music, when stripped of their instrumentation (i.e. the instruments upon which they are played; saxophones, muted trombones, etc.) have almost nothing new to offer in the way of strictly musical interest. And this is so, even when we consider jazz from a strictly "popular" standpoint. The amount of purely musical value, and the amount of differentiation of this music from other "popular" music, can be noted by playing a piece of jazz music on the piano. It is true that for several years the rhythmic element in popular music has been growing more insistent and nervous, and it may have reached its culmination in jazz. I rather think it has. So, as far as simple rhythmic forcefulness and iteration is concerned, jazz can claim the proud distinction of being the "worst yet." Technically speaking, however, it must be granted that the popular music of today is far richer in contrapuntal devices, in harmony, and in figuration than popular music formerly, in which the interest vested *alone* in the melody.

Another point by which jazz may be distinguished from the popular music of the olden time—say ten years ago—is the large number of cat-calls, clarinet-couacs, smears, glides, trombone-glissandos, and agonizing saxophonic contortions which occur in it. But these things are largely rendered possible by the instruments upon which jazz music is played. Take away these instruments and you take away the jazz quality almost entirely. (Henry F. Gilbert, "Concerning Jazz," *New Music Review*, December 1922)

Gilbert, however, concludes that jazz does impart an important message.

Now the lesson to our would-be serious composers is plain. The jazz composers have broken loose from tradition and have thereby been enabled to produce something which, although it is on a comparatively low plane, and is largely given over to caricature and burlesque, is at least distinctive in the domain of popular music. But our would-be serious composers have, with scarcely an exception, followed and imitated the tradition of musical beauty as it exists in Europe. They have played the conservative part, and conservatism alone precludes growth. For this, the introduction of the radical element is necessary. This element of radicalism has been introduced with all sorts of cleverness and energy, although in a boisterously vulgar style, by the composers of jazz; but it is my belief that we shall never have a distinctively American school of serious music until the would-be serious composers do, on their plane, what the jazz composers have done on theirs, i.e., cut loose to a certain extent from the dominative incubus of European musical tradition. (Gilbert, "Concerning Jazz")

One of the more insulting, mean-spirited, and sarcastic articles from England was Cecil Austin's "Jazz." Here are some excerpts:

As for the so-called tonal effects, there is no doubt that most of them were devised in the first place, not so much for their novelty as in order to disguise the diabolical tone produced by third-rate instrumentalists. It would probably be a harrowing experience to hear Mr. Paul Whiteman attempt a few bars of the Elgar "Violin Concerto" without his mute. . . .

The worse the musician and the smaller his mind the better jazz exponent he can be relied upon to make. If he has no finer feelings, no inner musical perception, and if he has never heard good music at all, the greater will be his relish in burlesque performances of masterpieces; he values not so much the novelty of the burlesque as the feeling that respectable musicians are likely to shudder in horror at his apparent effrontery. The less the jazz musician knows of rhythm, melody, harmony, and all those subjects so necessary to a correct understanding of the art of music, the more he will be convinced that of all forms in music, jazz is by far the greatest, because its prime asset is to offend all rules of decency. It is questionable whether any of the jazz composers would have broken the "rules" and "canons" of music had they known anything about them. Indeed, the leading jazz composers pride themselves on their ignorance of music.

No one jazz piece ever retains its popularity for more than eight or nine months. Every year brings the same shoal of "hits" and "latest successes," and as one tune fades from sheer anæmia, another rapidly takes its place. That, of course, is the fate of all bad music, just as it is the fate of good music to live for all time; it only ceases to be the music of an age or period when it comes to be the music of centuries. . . .

The hall mark of real music is its idealism and its purity, its truth and its fidelity. The hall mark of all great art is its honest sincerity. But jazz is neither ideal nor pure, neither is it sincere. It is faithful to nothing, an "art" without parents and without relations. No character or sentiment has ever been depicted by it. No jazz wonder-piece has ever contained even in its whole length the least inkling of that far sweeping philosophy that Beethoven often condensed in a few bars.

Truth to tell, there is no affection for jazz in this country [England]. Beneath the outward and inevitable materialism of the times, there is a real craving in millions of hearts for finer ideals in life and true conceptions of what is best in art. It is unfortunate that so many people have an utterly shallow and false sense of values and are unable to distinguish between good art and bad. At the same time, it is doubtful whether the percentage of these people is any higher than it has always been. Jazz thrives because the world is larger, and because there is more room for the humbugs who like to be in the limelight and play to the gallery. They exist because we live in a more leisured age, and in spite of industrial upheavals and unemployment, people spend far more money on entertainment than they did a decade ago. Perhaps in time many will learn to differentiate between the true art and the false, and what will happen to the stuffed scarecrow, jazz, probably long before that happy day dawns, hardly requires comment. (Cecil Austin, "Jazz," *Music and Letters,* July 1925)

Another classicist who had an extremely negative reaction to jazz was Julius Korngold, whose essay "Jazz" appeared in a Detroit Symphony program booklet in 1928. Korngold, a leading Austrian critic and father of composer Erich Wolfgang Korngold, was quite harsh in his appraisal, calling jazz a "serious menace" to good music. He recognized the "Negro" element in jazz but felt that jazz was a corruption of good Negro music, by which he meant vocal folk songs. He also disliked modern classical composition and felt that jazz was partly to blame here for opening people's ears to dissonance. Finally, he felt, as did Straton, that with the taste for new music came an overall degeneration of morals.

We can no longer be content to smile at a serious menace to culture, a menace that is also threatening the development of music. In the past there was a sharp distinction between artistic music and the music that accompanied common amusements. They were two distinct worlds. But today the two have met and the lower type threatens, nay drives out, the higher. It is infecting the best classes of people as it is infecting music itself. These modern "tendencies" have now begun to take as their foundation, material from jazz and negro dances. . . .

Let us analyze jazz itself. Does it represent in any way the product of a nation or of a race? We may echo the thought here that even with that qualification its value would not be established. We have primitive music with and without charm and significance according to the degree of musical talent in the respective races. We find much evidence of talent among the negro races. Anton Dvořák introduced negro melodies into his symphonies and chamber music and the songs, as we learned them through Hayes, the negro tenor, reveal in melancholy content that they express themselves in music with sincerity as would an occidental people. The music which the jazz band would represent as negro music is far removed indeed from the original. . . . It is interesting to note here that colored jazz players who are "artists" of rhythmical precision, are, when not playing dances, very uncertain in their rhythm. It is not really musical rhythm in which they excel or need to excel. . . .

It is decidedly doubtful if these American negro dances, with or without a jazz band, have become popular because of the fascination of their musical rhythm. The dance "urge," which developed so mightily after the war, would not wait for the opportunity presented by a "ball." New dances, which had to be practised, became the fad. Frequent changes in the steps demanded almost daily practice to acquire perfection. The suggestion of jazz music led to scantily-disguised sexual gestures—the exaggerated erotic expression of a low state of culture. . . .

In the large cities it is jazz that has prepared the way for the toleration of the ugly, false atonal linear "noise-music." The ear has become accustomed to these tonal grimaces and yowlings and it no longer notes the difference between true chords and phrases or harmony and discord. In any case it has become more tolerant and consequently less sensitive. There is an analogy between this and the state of our sense of shame in moral matters. The more obscenity occurs in words and deeds, the more we tolerate. It is not only the fashionable degeneration of customs which increases our growing callousness, but a coarsening of the senses which kills our sense of indignation. This decreased sensitiveness in the musical ear caused by false tones and sonorities gradually eliminates our musical resentment of such things. Daily jazz has furnished the anesthetic which enables atonal music to operate.

We find in this connection, however, one budding hope. Jazz without doubt is fading, as all unintellectual and superficial music must—it is rotting. (Julius Korngold, "Jazz," *Detroit Symphony Program Booklet*, 1928)

There was apparently an American film in 1927 about the ill effects of jazz, entitled *Jazz Mad*. As far as I can tell, the film no longer exists, but it inspired Svend Gade to write a novel based on the movie. The story concerns a German composer, known as Doctor Hausmann, who comes to America to make his name with his new symphony, only to find that Americans are not interested in his brand of music.

A jerk. A jerk. A jerkee rhythm. A moan. A wail. A jerkee rhythm. A bing! A clash! A wail! A mo-o-oan. A jerk. A whine. A jerk. A jerkee rhythm. Pounding, pounding. Beating. Groaning. Music for the feet. A feverish pulsation. A savage undulation. Music for the feet. Nothing for the heart. Nothing for the head. A jerk. A jerk—

And its name was jazz. . . .

[I]t was this weird yet characteristic voice of America that the Hausmanns first heard. . . .

And everywhere around them whanged, and moaned and blared, the jazz of nervous America. Jazz on the records in the boarding house parlor. Jazz over the radio in the boarding house dining room. Jazz breathed by the little colored boy on the street through his harmonica as the other little colored boy charlestoned to it. Jazz winked the signs on Broadway, proclaiming stage bands. Jazz stared [from] the painted signs, announcing delirious dancing with dinner.

But this was no concern of the Hausmanns, no, not any more say, than the gumchewing in which so many people seemed interested.

So, lightheartedly and confident of his reception Doctor Hausmann set out to bestow his great symphony on this captivating America. . . .

But day followed day, all pretty much like the first.

"Is it jazz?" someone would ask with a sudden flash of interest, when the name of the symphony was mentioned. But the interest winked right out when a negative answer was made. And came the stereotyped reception: "Suppose you write us a letter about it." Or, "Well, you might leave it here and we'll look over it." Or, "No, we don't examine the works of unknown composers." Or, in the vast majority of organizations devoted to music less austere than the few symphony orchestras, "We haven't any use for that kind of stuff. Why don't you write jazz, man? Jazz is the music to-day. Wouldn't give you a nickel for anything else." Hausmann wrote letters. They were never answered. . . .

. . . Hausmann hunted for work as a leader—theatre orchestra, band, anything. But always they demanded jazz, jazz, jazz. With his genius for transcribing into sound all the emotion of which a man is capable, he could not truckle to the cheap desire for mere motion.

Jazz, which he had thought was no concern of theirs, became the bitter topic of their meal-time conversations. It haunted his dreams at night. "This fine country is jazz-mad!" he exclaimed in despair. (Svend Gade, *Jazz Mad* [New York: Jacobsen-Hodgkinson Corporation, 1927])

In the end, Hausmann gets his piece performed, and it is well received. He wins out against the jazz "madness."

Constant Lambert (1905–1951) was a prolific English conductor, composer, and writer on music. His music was sometimes influenced by jazz, but like many classical composers of his ilk, including Aaron Copland and Igor Stravinsky, he was not a fan of jazz. These composers typically felt, like Stringham and others, that jazz was an interesting trifle that could be put to better use in "serious" music.

As the following excerpts show, Lambert appreciated the "negro" contribution to jazz, but he felt it came largely from the black musician's ability to incorporate touches of classical music in his art. In his discussion, he uses the broader definition of "jazz," which includes the songs of "Tin Pan Alley"—the district of Manhattan where many of the sheet music publishers were based. Lambert notices that many composers of those popular songs were Jewish, and talks at some length of the "masochistic" Jewish element in the music. His anti-Semitic obsession with Jews is shared by some of his English contemporaries, as we will see.

The Spirit of Jazz

By jazz, of course, I mean the whole movement roughly designated as such, and not merely that section of it known as Afro-American, or more familiarly as 'Harlem'. The negro once enjoyed a monopoly of jazz, just as England once enjoyed a monopoly of the industrial revolution, but for the negroes to imagine that all jazz is their native province is as if an Englishman were to imagine that all locomotives were built by his compatriots. Even the Harlem section of jazz is by no means so African as might be supposed.

There is a double yet opposed conspiracy to persuade one that modern dance music represents a purely negroid tradition. On the one hand, we have the crusty old colonels, the choleric judges and beer-sodden columnists who imagine they represent the European tradition, murmuring 'swamp stuff', 'jungle rhythms', 'negro decadence' whenever they hear the innocent and anodyne strains of the average English jazz band, hugely enjoying their position of Cassandra prophesying the downfall of the white woman. On the other hand, we have the well-meaning but rather sentimental propagandists of the negro race, only too eager to point out that the negroes are the only begetters of a movement that has admittedly swept all over the world and that provides an exotic influence far exceeding the localized exoticism of Cocteau and his followers. The only flaw in both these arguments is that most jazz is written and performed by cosmopolitan Jews. Were this fact sufficiently realized, it would hardly abate the fury of the colonels and the columnists, for from their point of view the Jew is just as much an enemy of the British and Holy Roman Empire as the negro; but it might slightly curb the hysterical enthusiasm of the poor-white negro propagandists whose sentimental effusions must be so embarrassing to the intelligent negro himself. . . .

The emotional appeal of jazz depends not only on its rhythms, which, though childishly simple compared with those of African folk music, may legitimately be accounted African in origin, but also on its harmonic colour, which cannot conceivably be traced back to Africa for the simple reason that harmony as we understand it does not exist in primitive African music. Hornbostel in his admirable handbook on African music records only one example of pure harmonic writing in the whole history of his discoveries, and that consisted of two chords at the end of a satirical song about the local missionary, the intention of which was obviously to parody the lugubrious effect of his harmonium.

The harmonic element in Afro-American music is an acquired element mainly due to the religious music of the Anglo-Saxon, an influence that naturally had a more powerful effect on the *déraciné* negroes of America, bereft of their language and their cultural traditions, than on the self-satisfied if not contented negroes of Africa. . . .

The superiority of American jazz lies in the fact that the negroes there are in touch not so much with specifically barbaric elements as with sophisticated elements. Negro talent being on the whole more executive than creative, and modern negro music being essentially an applied art, jazz is naturally largely dependent for its progress on the progress of the sophisticated material used as a basis for its rhythmic virtuosity. The sudden post-war efflorescence of jazz was due largely to the adoption as raw material of the harmonic richness and orchestral subtlety of the Debussy-Delius period of highbrow music. Orchestral colour, of course, is not a thing that can really be appreciated in itself; it is largely dependent for its colour on the underlying harmonies. The harmonic background drawn from the impressionist school opened up a new world of sound to the jazz composer, and although the more grotesque orchestral timbres, the brute complaints of the saxophone, the vicious spurts from the muted brass, may seem to belie the rich sentimentality of their background, they are only thorns protecting a fleshy cactus—a *sauce piquante* poured over a nice juicy steak. . . .

The most irritating quality about the Vo-dodeo-vo, poo-poop-a-doop school of jazz song is its hysterical emphasis on the fact that the singer is a jazz baby going crazy about jazz rhythms. If jazz were really so gay one feels that there would not be so much need to mention the fact in every bar of the piece. Folk songs do not inform us that it's great to be singing in six-eight time, or that you won't get your dairy maid until you have mastered the Dorian mode. In the nineteenth century there are occasional references to '*Valses endiablées*', but for the most part the music is left to tell its own tale. It is almost impossible to find a quick fox trot, however, that does not inform us that it is in a particular variant of common time, and that it is very gay in consequence. Martin Tupper, who claimed to be the first since King David to set words to a dance tune, has a heavy onus to bear if he is the father of the numerous technical songs such as 'I'm going to Charleston, back to Charleston', 'Crazy Feet, I've got those Crazy Feet', and 'I tell you Rhythm is the Thing, Rhythm is the Thing, Rhythm is the Thing of to-day'. What should we think of a concert aria which kept harping on the fact that the singer's mouth was open and that her vocal cords were in prime condition?

The third type of song—that which describes a dream world in some remote American state which the singer apparently is permanently prevented from visiting—is now happily on the wane, but in its hey-day it provided an amusing reversal of the more mawkish 'There is a Happy Land' type of hymn tune. The prosperous Anglo-Saxon having held out unctuous consolation to the poor negro, it is now, apparently, the turn of the prosperous negro to hold out unctuous consolation to the poor white. That is, if we assume that the tunes are actually written by negroes. In point of fact, jazz has long ago lost the simple gaiety and sadness of the charming savages to whom it owes its birth, and is now for the most part a reflection of the jagged nerves, sex repressions, inferiority complexes and general dreariness of the modern scene. The nostalgia of the negro who wants to go home has given place to the infinitely more weary nostalgia of the cosmopolitan Jew who has no home to go to. The negro associations of jazz, the weary traveller, the comforting old mammy, the red-hot baby, have become a formula of expression only, as empty and convenient as the harlequin and columbine of the nineteenth century. The pierrot with the burnt-cork face symbolizes not the England of yesterday but the Jewry of to-day.

The importance of the Jewish element in jazz cannot be too strongly emphasized, and the fact that at least ninety per cent of jazz tunes are written by Jews undoubtedly goes far to account for the curiously sagging quality—so typical of Jewish art—the almost masochistic melancholy of the average foxtrot. This masochistic element is becoming more and more a part of general consciousness, but it has its stronghold in the Jewish temperament. . . .

There is an obvious link between the exiled and persecuted Jews and the exiled and persecuted negroes, which the Jews, with their admirable capacity for drinking the beer of those who have knocked down the skittles, have not been slow to turn to their advantage. But although the Jews have stolen the negroes' thunder, although Al Jolson's nauseating blubbering masquerades as savage lamenting, although Tin Pan Alley has become a commercialized Wailing Wall, the only jazz music of technical importance is that small section of it that is genuine negroid. The 'hot' negro records still have a genuine and not merely galvanic energy, while the blues have a certain austerity that places them far above the sweet nothings of George Gershwin. (Constant Lambert, "The Spirit of Jazz," *Music Ho!* [New York: Faber & Faber, 1934])

Compare Lambert's writing about Jews with the following passage from Norman and Tom Sargant, whose references to Africa we have quoted earlier:

It is interesting to note that among the white peoples the Jews have been the quickest to pick up the rhythm, and they have brought modern jazz to its highest level. The music of the Bible, of the sackbut, psaltery, timbrel, and similar instruments, was almost purely rhythmical, and it is possible that Jews are more susceptible to rhythm than most Europeans. (Norman Sargant and Tom Sargant, "Negro-American Music or The Origin of Jazz," *Musical Times*, September 1, 1931)

Returning to Lambert, we note that he is not impressed with the improvisational aspect of jazz. Like many classical composers, he feels that written music has more potential and lasting interest. The one jazz artist he does single out for unadulterated praise is Duke Ellington.

The difficulty of estimating the contribution of the negro to jazz is largely due to the fact that a jazz record, unlike a valse by Johann

Strauss, is rarely the work of one man; more often than not it is the work of three composers and three arrangers plus a number of frills that are put on by the players at the spur of the moment. Of this synod only one member may be coloured and usually the negro element is confined to the actual arabesques of the execution. These arabesques may be of the most fascinating order; but the fact remains that they are improvisations over an accepted basis and not true composition at all. (It is the greatest mistake to class Louis Armstrong and Duke Ellington together as similar exponents of negro music—the one is a trumpet player, the other a genuine composer.)

Improvisation is all very well in its way, so long as its expressive and formal limitations are realized. At first sight it might seem that improvisation would lead to a greater freedom in music, but in actual practice it proves a considerable restriction—at least in music based on the European harmonic system. It is possible that a purely melodic improvisation based on a more varied range of modes than our own, such as we get in Indian music, might provide a melodic line of greater expressive and formal interest than our square-cut classical tunes; but when it comes to a number of players improvising dance music together they can only avoid complete chaos by sticking to a simple and mutually recognized ground as a basis for their cadenzas. It is the monotony and paucity of musical interest in this perpetually recurring harmonic ground that eventually makes us lose interest in the cadenzas themselves.

An artist like Louis Armstrong, who is one of the most remarkable virtuosi of the present day, enthralls us at a first hearing, but after a few records one realizes that all his improvisations are based on the same restricted circle of ideas, and in the end there is no music which more quickly provokes a state of exasperation and ennui. The best records of Duke Ellington, on the other hand, can be listened to again and again because they are not just decorations of a familiar shape but a new arrangement of shapes. Ellington, in fact, is a real composer, the first jazz composer of distinction, and the first negro composer of distinction. His works—apart from a few minor details—are not left to the caprice or ear of the instrumentalist; they are scored and written out, and though, in the course of time, variants may creep in—Ellington's works in this respect are as difficult to codify as those of Liszt—the first American records of his music may be taken definitively, like a full score, and are the only jazz records worth studying for their form as well as their texture. Ellington himself, being an executant of the second rank, has probably not been tempted to interrupt the continuity of his texture with bravura passages for the piano, and although his instrumentalists are of the finest quality their solos are rarely demonstrations of virtuosity for its own sake.

The real interest of Ellington's records lies not so much in their colour, brilliant though it may be, as in the amazingly skilful proportions in which the colour is used. I do not only mean skilful as compared with other jazz composers, but as compared with so-called highbrow composers. I know of nothing in Ravel so dexterous in treatment as the varied solos in the middle of the ebullient *Hot and Bothered* and nothing in Stravinsky more dynamic than the final section. The combination of themes at this moment is one of the most ingenious pieces of writing in modern music. It is not a question, either, of setting two rhythmic patterns working against each other in the mathematical Aaron Copland manner—it is genuine melodic and rhythmic counterpoint which, to use an old-fashioned phrase, 'fits' perfectly.

The exquisitely tired and four-in-the-morning *Mood Indigo* is an equally remarkable piece of writing of a lyrical and harmonic order, yet it is palpably from the same hand. How well we know those composers whose slow movements seem to be written by someone else— who change in the course of the same section from slow Vaughan Williams to quick Stravinsky and from quick Hindemith to slow César Franck. The ability to maintain the same style in totally different moods is one of the hall-marks of the genuine composer, whether major or minor.

Ellington's best works are written in what may be called ten-inch record form, and he is perhaps the only composer to raise this insignificant disc to the dignity of a definite genre. Into this three and a half minutes he compresses the utmost, but beyond its limits he is inclined to fumble. The double-sided ten-inch *Creole Rhapsody* is an exception, but the twelve-inch expansion of the same piece is nothing more than a potpourri without any of the nervous tension of the original version. Ellington has shown no sign of expanding his formal conceptions, and perhaps it is as well, for his works might then lose their peculiar concentrated savour. He is definitely a *petit-maître,* but that, after all, is considerably more than many people thought either jazz or the coloured race would ever produce. He has crystallized the popular music of our time and set up a standard by which we may judge not only other jazz composers but also those highbrow composers, whether American or European, who indulge in what is roughly known as 'symphonic jazz'. (Constant Lambert, "The Spirit of Jazz")

Again and again in the 1920s, Ellington won over the jazz skeptics. Even those who had no particular passion for jazz otherwise praised his music consistently.

Edward Niles (known by his middle name Abbe) was not one of the skeptics. A Wall Street lawyer and a self-described Yankee, he developed an interest in jazz and the blues, and in 1925 he sought out the blues composer W. C. Handy to interview him about his field. The two became friends, and Niles wrote long introductory essays to *Blues: An Anthology* (originally New York: Albert and Charles Boni, 1926), which collected many of Handy's songs, and to Handy's autobiography, *Father of the Blues* (New York: Macmillan, 1941). In an overview of 1929 jazz recordings, Niles too heaped the highest accolades on Ellington's work.

> *Duke Ellington's Orchestra* (also known as *The Washingtonians*), especially when playing its leader's own dance-tunes, is dogmatically pronounced to be supreme in this field. I should say that anyone who could not enjoy the savage and mournful Ellington records of "Take It Easy" (*Okeh* 41013), "Black Beauty" (*Br.* 4009, *Vo.* 15704), "Black and Tan Fantasy" (*Ok.* 40955), or "East St. Louis Toodle-Oo" (*Br. 3480*) could not enjoy jazz; save for the fact that from an orthodox atmosphere to Ellington is a formidable jump. There is more and better melody in one of the dances of this astounding Negro than in ten of the pallid tunes of the average operetta, but this fact would be obscured for a beginner by the hair-raising arabesques of the Ellington trumpet and clarinet—even, in the extraordinary record of "The Mooche" and the break-neck "Hot and Bothered" (Ok. 8623), by sounds from a human throat which most listeners would swear issued from some tortured

instrument. Yet on many hearings, there is not a note that should be changed—and what power, what attack! (Abbe Niles, "Ballads, Songs, and Snatches," *The Bookman*, January 1929)

It is difficult to sum up the attitudes found among writers on jazz in the 1920s. Certainly the most uniformly positive are the reactions of African Americans, but jazz also had many supporters among white writers in the U.S. and abroad. Those white writers who totally condemn jazz appear to be in the minority. As James Lincoln Collier has pointed out in *The Reception of Jazz in America: A New View* (Brooklyn, N.Y.: Institute for Studies in American Music, 1988), jazz historians favor a dramatic tale that tells how the music was rejected outright by the mainstream white public and then fought its way to acceptance, but when one actually takes the time to plow through all that was written, that simple tale proves to be far from true. Collier rightly points out that jazz—in the broad sense of the term at that time—apparently had a large following among the general public, especially among young audiences. Otherwise there wouldn't have been so much controversy. Partly as a result of this following, Collier notes, "the American press generally supported jazz, if only because it has never been in the business of attacking fashions that appeal to its readers" (p. 9).

On the other hand, Collier goes too far in trying to demonstrate that the Europeans were far behind Americans in their appreciation of jazz. Whites on both continents tended to be more familiar with white artists than black ones. There was some serious criticism of black artists published in America, but to be fair, Americans had much more access to the music than did Europeans on radio, on records, and in performance. The point is that Europeans were taking what they heard seriously, and in many cases they championed it enthusiastically.

6

African Americans and the Swing Era

Scholars in the 1990s often remark that the white bands of the swing era generally earned more than the black ones, except for such top names as Cab Calloway and Duke Ellington, but black commentators were always well aware of this discrepancy. In 1938, the then-current editor of *Opportunity*, Elmer Anderson Carter, wrote about this problem. Carter refers to Benny Goodman as the "so-called King of Swing" at a time when few among the white press doubted this. He throws out a question: Was it simple prejudice that denied the best jobs to the black bands, and was it true that white audiences were reluctant to patronize such bands, as was claimed? Or, as he suggests, was there a deliberate attempt among booking agents and fellow musicians to keep blacks out of the best jobs for fear that they would win out by the sheer quality of their musical performances?

Swing

A few Sundays ago [May 29] upwards of twenty thousand people, according to press reports, attended a "swing" carnival at Randalls Island, New York City. The carnival was arranged by an enterprising radio announcer: it began early in the morning and lasted until late Sunday afternoon. Most of the popular swing bands of the country participated in the carnival, which was, if we are to believe the published reports, a joyous occasion for the jitter-bugs—as the addicts of this latest evolution of jazz music are called. It remained, however, for Duke Ellington and his orchestra to send the crowd into such rapture that for a few minutes it appeared that a riot was imminent as thousands of swing-crazed young men and women broke over the barriers and attempted to storm the bandstand.

The great Negro swing bands are popular and the so-called King of Swing, Benny Goodman, has reached his eminence in a large measure through the talents of two young Negroes who have become what might be called permanent "guest artists." But the Negro bands are seldom given an opportunity to play in the better hotels and are rarely heard in sponsored programs on the radio.

In an article by Jack Gould in the New York *Times* of Sunday, July 17, an explanation of this peculiar phenomena is vouchsafed:

> Both to his and music's loss, the Negro has been asked to behave like a freak when entertaining a white audience; to put on stupid little hats and imitate a shagging inmate of Bellevue's psychopathic ward. This clowning has undoubtedly meant quick success but it has obscured some of the finest musicianship to be found.
>
> With a few isolated exceptions, the Negro cannot obtain bookings in the Grade A hotels or the cabarets not expressly of Harlem flavor. For the official records Benny Goodman's two superb soloists Lionel Hampton on the vibraphone and Teddy Wilson at the piano are listed as 'guest artists' and not as members of Mr. G.'s organization, with which they always play. The Negro musician readily acknowledges that the hotel man, for business reasons alone, cannot deny the existence of racial prejudice, but he does wonder how long he must be kicked around.

There is reason to believe that the exclusion of Negro bands from the more lucrative engagements is the result of deliberate planning. Constant propaganda in one form or another against Negro bands has been utilized to depreciate their drawing power and to exaggerate the racial antipathy which the patrons of nightclubs, restaurants and hotels are said to hold against the presence of Negro orchestras.

Mr. Gould absolves New York Local Musicians' Union 802 from any prejudice and officially this is probably true, since Negroes have been recipients of relief dispensed without discrimination; have held responsible office; and have participated in the deliberations of 802. But among Negro musicians there is a feeling, more or less wide-spread, that some of the opposition, some of the propaganda which they meet at every turn originates among their competitors who are fellow members of the union. If true, this would not be strange, for after all it is a highly competitive field.

The article quoted from the *Times* was inspired by the engagement of Count Basie's band in one of New York's famous night spots. This engagement, according to Mr. Gould, was brought about by the Music Corporation of America for the sole purpose "of affording a show case and radio outlet for Count Basie." Whoever is responsible for this courageous attempt to give the Negro musician his opportunity deserves the gratitude of the Negro, and certainly of those who are interested at least in the theory of a fair chance to every man. (Elmer Anderson Carter, "Swing" [editorial], *Opportunity*, July 1938)

By the way, the swing carnival was on May 29, 1938, and the night-club where Count Basie was booked was the Famous Door on Fifty-second Street. Several radio broadcasts from the summer of 1938 still survive and have been issued.

As Carter pointed out, New York had an integrated musicians' union, and still black musicians encountered many problems. The situation elsewhere was even worse, as composer and vocal coach Phil Moore reported. Born in 1918, Moore started as a jazz pianist and singer and went into the popular music field in the early 1950s. Although Moore's piece ran a few years after Carter's, I include it here for the sake of continuity.

Jim Crow on the Band Stand

PHIL MOORE

There are two musicians unions in practically every principal city in the country, except New York. One white and one colored. These two locals operate in the same jurisdiction and they get along just swell. That is, as long as the members stay in their own zones. These zones are set up more or less by the white locals.

There have been occasions when colored bands have been hired by large white spots with all the best wishes of the white union. On the first or second working nights, stink bombs were tossed into the establishments during the height of the evening's business, and shortly thereafter the Negro band was tossed out.

When a radio station that had an exclusive contract with a white local wanted to hire a Negro musician, the station had to clear the man through the white local. This condition exists in the motion picture industry, theatres, ballrooms and hotels.

Whenever a man wants to get a job that pays decent money he has to be okayed by the white local. . . .

. . . What can be done about all this?

Through organized propaganda Mr. Cigarette Company and Mr. Motion Picture Company should be boycotted and socked right in the moneybags. That's where they feel it most. (Phil Moore, "Jim Crow on the Bandstand," *Negro Digest,* September 1946, pp. 55–56)

Nevertheless, there were positive signs during the swing era that overall jazz was becoming more accepted by the classical establishment. The Juilliard School in Manhattan, then and now one of the world's leading music conservatories, invited Benny Goodman to lecture and to offer a master class for clarinetists (I think this began as early as 1939) while his African American colleague Teddy Wilson taught pianists there every summer from 1945 through 1952. Authors of music books also began to treat jazz as a serious genre.

Alain Locke (1886–1954), the aforementioned editor of the *New Negro* anthology, received his doctorate from Harvard and was a professor of philosophy at Howard University. In the following excerpt, he uses the word *par* to mean that swing music was being treated as an equal to other types of music; however, he also notes that the "stock"—that is, the monetary success of black musicians—was still below par. Locke insists that African Americans need to be more informed about their own music, a complaint that persists in the black community.

Negro Music Goes to Par

ALAIN LOCKE

The music season just closing has been one grand crescendo for Negro music, with almost too many events and too wide an up-swing to be adequately chronicled in a single article. In addition, three noteworthy books of serious musical criticism on jazz* have been issued and several notable documentations of Negro folk music made. But the predicament is a pleasant one, since it does vindicate our title as a fair and honest assessment of the musical situation. This year Negro music has really gone to par.

The main reason lies perhaps in this central fact, attested by a number of serious documentary concerts of Negro folk music: that instead of being sentimentalized extravagantly, Negro music is being intellectualized seriously, soberly, and in some cases controversially. Just as the swing era has marked something of a reaction from the dilution and commercialization of the Tin Pan Alley period, so now the faddist interest in Negro music is deepening into technical analysis and criticism. The public taste may still be undiscriminating and fickle, but inner circles, both amateur and professional, are swiftly becoming critical and technically expert. It is, incidentally, high time for the Negro audience to become itself more seriously critical and expertly informed about its own music, which it has tended to take too much for granted all along. And it is more than high time, too, for some of our Negro musicians to have their say. . . . Much has yet to be done to raise the status of the jazz musician: the dazzling success of an outstanding few must not blind us to the real conditions. As a matter of fact, there is a direct connection between any economic improvement in this field and the artistic quality of the product. In this respect certainly the stock of Negro music is still below par.

It is for this reason that the shifting patronage from the dance hall, vaudeville stage and casual motion picture spot to the concert stage, the non-commercial recording societies, and occasionally government patronage as in the Library of Congress and the Department of the Interior's music recording projects, represents something of great

---

* "American Jazz Music," by Wilder Hobson—W. W. Norton Co., New York—$2.50.
"Jazz: Hot and Hybrid," by Winthrop Sargeant—Arrow Editions. New York—$5.00.
"The Kingdom Of Swing," by Benny Goodman and I. Kolodin—Stackpole Sons. New York—$2.00.

value and promise to the future of Negro folk music and the musicians whose art derives directly from it. They are thereby offered their first real opportunity to play and be heard as "artists." Having survived by sheer luck in spite of commercial exploitation, they should now seize the hand of good management for the next step upwards. (Alain Locke, "Negro Music Goes to Par," *Opportunity*, July 1939)

Another controversial matter within the black community was the way in which performers presented themselves. The old styles of showmanship, coming out of minstrelsy and vaudeville, out of Broadway and the theater, were the norm right through the swing era, but by the 1940s the new generation of jazz musicians, the bebop generation, wanted simply to play the music. Louis Armstrong (born 1901—formerly thought to be 1900—and died 1971), because of his leadership role in the jazz field and his preeminence as an entertainer, was criticized by some parts of the African American community for sticking to his old ways. Their appraisal of Armstrong is the concern of the next selection. This piece, the most recent in this collection, will provide insights into the ways scholars currently look at how jazz raised racial and cultural issues. Krin Gabbard is a professor of comparative literature at the State University of New York in Stonybrook. His field is fascinating because it has exploded in the past thirty years to include comparisons not only of printed writings in different languages but of all kinds of cross-cultural products. Gabbard writes quite a bit about jazz and has published several books, including one devoted to jazz and film. In this short sample of Gabbard's approach, he looks not only at the ways people have responded to Armstrong, but also at how Armstrong himself responded to changing times.

Louis Armstrong and His Audiences

KRIN GABBARD

Seventy years after Louis Armstrong made his first commercially successful recordings, his voice was prominently featured over the final credits of *12 Monkeys*, the most well-attended film in the United States for several weeks early in 1996. In spite of his seemingly inexhaustible popularity, Louis Armstrong has seldom been attached to a stable set of meanings. His most enduring image—the widely grinning jester with the white handkerchief—has been read as the craven surrender to racist stereotypes. It has also been understood as the ironic under-mining of these same stereotypes, as the clever diversion of attention away from a flamboyant display of masculinity, and as the genuine expression of real enthusiasm and warmth. Disputes about his record-ing career have been equally dramatic.

But the most thoughtful writings on Armstrong as a cultural figure probably come from outside conventional jazz criticism. While researching a chapter on Armstrong's films for a book on jazz and the American cinema (Gabbard 1996), I was impressed by the eloquence with which African American writers have addressed Armstrong's career. Ralph Ellison, James Baldwin, Rex Stewart, Albert Murray, Amiri Baraka, Stanley Crouch, Michele Wallace, Cornel West, Dizzy Gillespie, and Henry Louis Gates, Jr., have all contributed substan-tially to our view of Armstrong. A thorough understanding of his role in American culture would bring together these and many other writ-ers and would require methods from literary theory, gender studies, anthropology, folklore, psychoanalysis, and African American studies. To do Armstrong justice, we would have to consider the discourses of carnival, the phenomenon of the trickster, the articulation of masculin-ity at different historical moments, the theories of humor, and the con-struction of concepts such as "high" and "low" culture.

If we disregard the large body of commentaries on the trumpeter's recorded solos and consider him as a complex cultural figure, three basic themes emerge in critical discussions of Armstrong's career: (1) attempts to place him somewhere on either side of (or above) a debate about art versus entertainment; (2) his sexuality and how it may or may not have been expressed in his performances; (3) arguments relating to his polysemous deportment on stage and ultimately to his significance for African American peoples. Although these issues are often interre-lated, they can provide an organizing structure for the arguments about Armstrong that appear in the popular press as well as in the works of artists and intellectuals. (Of course, the "popular" is often indistinguishable from the "intellectual" in such debates).

1. Artist or Entertainer?

Critics began bestowing lavish praise on Armstrong as early as 1928. For many writers in the jazz press, the trouble began in the late 1930s when Armstrong regularly worked with a conventional swing band and ventured beyond the vague boundaries of jazz by recording with the Mills Brothers, a gospel choir, and even a group called The Polynesians. Although some critics today express pleasure in records such as "To You, Sweetheart, Aloha" (1936) and "On a Little Bamboo Bridge" (1937), jazz purists felt betrayed. By the mid-1940s Armstrong was held in contempt by the New Orleans revivalists, who canonized his recordings of the 1920s and then rejected most of what followed, but also by the young beboppers who were born during the Harlem Renaissance. James Baldwin dramatized the disdain toward Armstrong among the boppers in his 1957 story "Sonny's Blues," in which a black World War II veteran confronts the desire of his younger brother to become a jazz musician. When his brother has trouble explaining the kind of musician he wants to become, the older man intervenes:

> I suggested helpfully: "You mean—like Louis Armstrong?"
> His face closed as though I'd struck him. "No. I'm not talking about none of that old-time, down home crap."

The younger brother eventually names Charlie Parker as the artist he aspires to imitate. In Baldwin's story the chasm between Armstrong and Parker becomes a metaphor for the cultural gap separating the brothers as well as for the revolution taking place among young African Americans during the postwar years.

A few years after Baldwin's "Sonny's Blues," Amiri Baraka took a different view in his *Blues People* of 1963, regarding Armstrong not as the played-out representative of an obsolete music nor even as a devoted artist but rather as the "honored priest of his culture." Baraka distinguished Armstrong from the seminal white jazz trumpeter Bix Beiderbecke, whose emotional life was "based on his conscious or unconscious disapproval of most of the sacraments of his culture." Armstrong, by contrast, "was not *rebelling* against anything with his music. In fact, his music was one of the most beautiful refinements of

Afro-American musical tradition, and it was immediately recognized as such by those Negroes who were not busy trying to pretend that they had issued from Beiderbecke's culture" (Baraka 1963, 154).

In my research on jazz and cinema, I discovered that Armstrong regularly appeared in films where questions of jazz and art were debated. In *New Orleans* in the 1940s, *High Society* in the 1950s, and both *Paris Blues* and *A Man Called Adam* in the 1960s, Armstrong played a crucial role in the films' debates about jazz as opposed to classical music or about the value of older jazz as opposed to more contemporary music. Armstrong probably held so much appeal for white audiences that he made these kinds of discussions palatable. If these films had associated Miles Davis, Thelonious Monk, or virtually any other modernist black musician with "art," the white audiences at whom these films were directed would surely have reacted differently.

2. Virile or Emasculated?

As I have argued in an essay on Spike Lee's *Mo' Better Blues* (Gabbard 1992), the jazz trumpet has always provided an especially powerful means for expressing male sexuality, and Armstrong is uniquely responsible for perfecting the codes of that expression. But when Virgil Thomson (1981) praised Armstrong in a 1936 review, he added a curious historical comparison, suggesting that Armstrong resembled "the great *castrati* of the eighteenth century." Theodor Adorno, in one of his several attacks on jazz and popular music, seized upon Thomson's remark to support his own claim that jazz brings about the castration of the listener, who ought to be listening to the more manly music of someone like Arnold Schoenberg (Adorno 1981, 130). For Adorno, the smiling buffoon with the trumpet was anything but virile.

And yet there is no denying the masculine intensity in Armstrong's demeanor as well as in his solos, especially during the early years of his career. More than any other popular artist in American musical history, Armstrong perfected the art of building an instrumental solo to a dramatic climax, often with what might even be called "foreplay." But

Armstrong does not seem to have updated the techniques he learned as a young man for expressing masculinity *without* threatening certain white men in his audiences. If, as commentators such as Gary Giddins (1988) have claimed, black audiences in the 1930s saw sexual power alongside Armstrong's clowning, few seemed to have recognized it later when images of black masculinity began to change.

3. Uncle Tom or Trickster?

Several specific episodes in Armstrong's life are relevant to this question. Gerald Early (1989) argues that Armstrong had been a hero in the black community for several decades but that he lost a large portion of this audience when he played the King of the Zulus in the New Orleans Mardi Gras parade of 1949. When pictures of the trumpeter in blackface and a grass skirt were widely published, according to Early, many African Americans felt that Armstrong was "holding the entire race up to scorn" (296). Albert Murray has defended Armstrong against those who attacked him for appearing as King of the Zulus, suggesting that critics outside of New Orleans confused Mardi Gras blackface with minstrelsy and that the specific ritual function of the King of the Zulus was "to ridicule the whole idea of Mardi Gras and the lenten season" (Murray 1976, 190). For Murray, Armstrong was simply playing the trickster.

If Armstrong was sending an ambiguous message as King of the Zulus, he was much more straightforward when he publicly denounced President Dwight Eisenhower and Arkansas governor Orval Faubus during the struggle to integrate Little Rock's public schools in 1957. Armstrong was widely criticized after he said that the American government could "go to hell" and that Eisenhower had "no guts." In fact, the *Kaiser Index,* the guide to articles in African American newspapers, shows more entries on Armstrong during this period than at any other moment in his career. In the white press, columnist Jim Bishop suggested that Armstrong's subsequent apology to Eisenhower may have been the result of a drop in ticket sales and "some empty tables at the Copacabana" (*New York Journal-American,* 2 January 1958:17). Bishop did not acknowledge, however, that Armstrong only apologized *after* Eisenhower took action by sending federal troops to Little Rock to enforce court-ordered integration. Although Charles Mingus gave Orval Faubus a permanent and negative role in jazz history with his 1959 composition "Fables of Faubus," I am still seeking evidence that Mingus or any other bopper or jazz modernist publicly supported Armstrong when he denounced official racism.

Ralph Ellison (1964) has been most eloquent in placing Armstrong within the traditions of the trickster: "Armstrong's clownish license and intoxicating powers are almost Elizabethan; he takes liberties with kings, queens and presidents; emphasizes the physicality of his music with sweat, spittle and facial contortions; he performs the magical feat of making romantic melody issue from a throat of gravel; and some few years ago was recommending to all and sundry his personal physic, 'Pluto Water,' as a purging way to health, happiness and international peace" (Ellison 1964, 67).

In the literature on tricksters, most of it by folklorists and comparative anthropologists, there is a consensus that tricksters are liminal figures, identified with creative powers and the violation of taboos, especially sexual ones. As Henry Louis Gates, Jr., and others have written, the trickster stands apart from the action, "signifyin(g)" on events rather than effecting them, making everyday life seem comic on the spot. Barbara Babcock-Abrahams (1975) makes a useful distinction between volitional and nonvolitional liminality (151). As a black American growing up in the early years of this century, Armstrong had his marginality forced upon him. Part of what makes Armstrong so interesting is how he coded his sexuality, surrounding it with highly unthreatening display in his singing and mugging. In this sense he is most like the trickster whose often hyperphallic behavior is balanced by conduct that tends to deny sexuality.

When Ellison compares Armstrong to a Shakespearean character, he is of course invoking a fictional figure to define a real one. Ellison may have based this comparison on an Armstrong who took on a life of his own as a fictional character. We see this trickster Armstrong in many of his films, most prominently when he parodies the potent gangster in the "Public Melody Number One" sequence in *Artists & Models* (1937). Armstrong was also claimed as a trickster in MGM's "Swing Wedding," a remarkable cartoon feature of 1937 in which a frog bearing a strong likeness to Armstrong starts a wild party that soon turns into chaos. Like both the Elizabethan fool and Bugs Bunny, the Armstrong frog disrupts from the sidelines, dissolving the action rather than focusing it. Armstrong's image was readily available, as here, when a trickster was needed for a *fictional* text, just as he was available three decades later when James Baldwin needed a symbol for a generational crisis in his "Sonny's Blues." Michele Wallace (1990) has written of Armstrong in a somewhat different but relevant context in an article about Michael Jackson.

> My mother, who is a total fan of Jackson's, says he makes up words. But isn't that what black singers have always done? Ella Fitzgerald and Louis Armstrong simply made "scatting" official. Henry Louis Gates calls this aspect of black culture "critical signification." It is a process in which black culture "signifies" on white culture through imitating and then reversing its formal strategies and preconditions, thus formulating a masked and surreptitious critique. The perfect example is the relationship of "jazz" to white mainstream music. But what I'm beginning to wonder is: how "critical" is it? (86)

For many young black people in the United States today, the answer is probably "not much." Wallace makes a much stronger case for the "cultural signification" of Michael Jackson. But of course Jackson was born into an entertainment industry that resembles Armstrong's as much as a player piano today resembles a synthesizer.

Wallace is right that Armstrong's critiques of dominant culture may seem a little too "masked and surreptitious" today. Still, Armstrong probably ought to be read outside narrow notions of what today constitutes a positive role model. And as Stanley Crouch (1978) has argued, Armstrong played on traditions of American humor that are not easily separated into strictly white and black strands or effortlessly classified as demeaning or resisting. There are legitimate questions about how Armstrong functioned within discourses of race, art, and sexuality, and the answers must be complex, if in fact there are answers.

Bibliography

Adorno. Theodor. 1981. "Perennial Fashion—Jazz." In *Prisms.* Trans. Samuel and Shierry Weber. Cambridge: M.I.T. Press.

Babcock-Abrahams, Barbara. 1975. " 'A Tolerated Margin of Mess': The Trickster and His Tales Reconsidered." *Journal of the Folklore Institute* 11:147–86.

Baldwin, James. [1957] 1990. "Sonny's Blues." In *From Blues to Bop,* ed. Richard N. Albert, 174–206. Baton Rouge: Louisiana State Univ. Press.

Baraka, Amiri (as LeRoi Jones). 1963. *Blues People: Negro Music in White America.* New York: Morrow.

Crouch, Stanley. 1978. "Laughin' Louis." *The Village Voice,* August 14:45.

Early, Gerald. 1989. *Tuxedo Junction: Essays on American Culture.* New York: Ecco Press.

Ellison, Ralph. 1964. "Change the Joke and Slip the Yoke." In *Shadow and Act,* 61–73. New York: Random.

Gabbard, Krin. 1992. "Signifyin(g) the Phallus: Mo' Better Blues and Representations of the Jazz Trumpet." *Cinema Journal* 32, no. 1:43–62.

———. 1996. *Jammin' at the Margins: Jazz and the American Cinema.* Chicago: Univ. of Chicago Press.

Gates, Henry Louis, Jr. 1988. *The Signifying Monkey: A Theory of Afro-American Literary Criticism.* New York: Oxford Univ. Press.

Giddins, Gary. 1988. *Satchmo.* New York: Doubleday.

Gillespie, Dizzy, with Al Fraser. 1979. *To Be or Not to Bop.* Garden City, N.J.: Doubleday.

Gleason, Ralph J. 1975. "Louis Armstrong." In *Celebrating The Duke and Louis, Bessie, Billie, Bird, Carmen, Miles, Dizzy and, Other Heroes,* 33–61. Boston: Little, Brown.

Murray, Albert. 1976. *Stomping the Blues.* New York: McGraw Hill.

Stewart, Rex. 1972. *Jazz Masters of the 30s.* New York: Macmillan.

Thomson, Virgil. 1981. "Swing Music." *A Virgil Thomson Reader,* 28–32. New York: Dutton.

Wallace, Michele. 1990. "Michael Jackson, Black Modernisms and 'The Ecstasy of Communication.'" In *Invisibility Blues: From Pop to Theory,* 77–90. New York: Verso.

West, Cornel. 1990. "New Cultural Politics of Difference." *October* 53:93–109.

For further reading, see Gabbard's extensive treatment of Armstrong's films in chapter 6 of his book *Jammin' at the Margins* (cited in full in the Bibliography above).

7

Reactions to Bebop

Jazz has been constantly evolving, and with each change has come controversy. The music called "bebop," which came to light in the mid-1940s, was castigated and spurned. In a humorous response, beboppers called those who defended older jazz "moldy figs," particularly if they favored Dixieland music, which had been superseded by swing but was enjoying a revival. Some of the beboppers criticized Louis Armstrong and others who pre- sented their art as good, old-fashioned entertainment. A feel- ing for the controversy is provided by a feature article from *Collier's,* which was a widely read, general-interest magazine, not a music journal.

> Generally speaking, you can't sing it and you can't dance it. It is, to use the expression of a bewildered jazz man, "head music." These abstract and intellectual qualities make bebop squalling anarchy in dance-hall circles. "These birds," said one dance-hall manager, "are killing the goose that laid the golden egg."
>
> Partisanship over the question: To be or not to bop, as Music World termed it, is intense and louder than any brass section in the world. The anti-bop school says it's a fad; the boppers say it is the music of the future. . . .

Bebop represents a revolt, not only from the monumental corn of big band arrangements but from the rigidity of tradition. Consequently, the boppers have cast aside many traditional jazz ideas and forms and introduced new effects. The melody, for example, doesn't linger on. It's gone—or is only occasionally perceptible. Instead the boppers strive for dissonance, or as many boppers put it, "new interesting sounds." There are swift changes of key and the simple danceable rhythms are gone. You have to be an extremely accomplished musician to attempt bop. It helps too if you happen to be more than slightly neurotic. . . .

It is music, the boppers are insisting, and they now claim to have won over the majority of young musicians and young jazz fans. Its nonplaying addicts follow it chiefly through records and concerts, such as the one Dizzy Gillespie gave at Carnegie Hall last fall and those staged by Norman Granz under the general title Jazz at the Philharmonic. These concerts have now reached such a peak of popularity that Variety, theatrical trade paper, speaks of them as "Wham Coin for Jazz Long-hairs." . . .

Whether bop is here to stay or is merely a fad is a question which is not going to be settled here. But the tremendous enthusiasm of the public for Stan Kenton's band, which has gone in heavily for the dissonant effects of bop, seems to indicate the public at large can take a modified bop and like it. Reports from Paris indicate that the music of Gillespie and Parker has become tremendously popular there. Gillespie has just left for a grand tour of Europe. Jazz historians view this as a very important factor in calculating bebop's long-range effects, for Parisians were followers of Dixieland when it was hardly known here. (Harry Henderson and Sam Shaw, "And Now We Go Bebop!" *Collier's*, March 20, 1948)

"To Be Or Not To Bop," the expression attributed to *Music World* in the above excerpt, was later the title of Dizzy Gillespie's autobiography (Garden City, N.Y.: Doubleday, 1979).

In a more sober appraisal below, Bill Gottlieb does a good job, with the help of Dizzy Gillespie, of clarifying some of the differences between swing and bop styles.

The Anatomy of Bebop

BILL GOTTLIEB

No doubt about it, "Bebop" is replacing swing. Ask any musician under twenty to name his favorite instrumentalists. If he's aiming any higher, musically, than a bread-and-butter existence, chances are better than even he'll name Dizzy Gillespie, Yardbird Parker, Thelonious Monk or one of the other revered members of bebop's Mt. Olympus.

When last spring I visited Metropolitan Vocational High School in New York, [the] only public school where you can "major" in popular music, I spoke to teacher Irving Lash, who summarized what I'd heard from the students and from young musicians everywhere:

"I'm a Benny Goodman man myself," explained Lash. "But I find that in their minds the students have relegated Goodman, Armstrong and the entire swing tradition to the moldy museums previously inhabited only by the Dixielanders. Their gods are beboppers like Diz and Bird or orchestral modernists like Stan Kenton or Boyd Raeburn. Practically no others mean a thing."

To outsiders bebop comes as an unpleasant jolt, with most new listeners attempting to shut off the cacophony by planting their hands over their ears. But open ears backed by open minds leave such listeners fascinated by the complexity of the form and thrilled by the virtuosity of the executors.

First thing in bebop to strike the listeners is its unabashed power and the breath-taking abundance of its notes, which are generally played at breakneck speed. Dizzy's arranger, Tadd Dameron, claims he can write passages for the jazz genius containing up to twenty notes a second (even more for Parker), each of which can be heard loudly and distinctly, not lost in a glissando. (Though I clocked his record of *Things to Come* at half speed, I was still unable to count fast enough to follow the number of notes in Dizzy's solos!) Sheer virtuosity isn't good music. In Dizzy's case, however, it so happens that even his most rapid phrases come out as figures of burning beauty.

Another characteristic of bebop is the flowing (legato) movement of its notes, rather than the jumpy movement of typical swing. "Also," as Dizzy explains, "the accents in bebop tend to fall on the up beat, while in swing it falls more on the down beat. Coupling this with its legato characteristic, you might get a phrase like ooBAHooBAHooBAH, while in swing it would be OO-bah, OO-bah, OO-bah."

The name bebop itself came, onomatopoetically, from a two-noted BEEbop tag that recurrently ends many of the music's phrases.

Apparent in bebop are its dissonant chords and passages; its avoidance of simple oom-cha rhythmic backgrounds and its frequent key changes. The old-fashioned, sweet ballad *How High the Moon* was adopted as the bebop anthem solely because it happens to make five major and minor key changes in the first ten bars. *Whispering,* a sentimental favorite of the 1920s, also became a bebop favorite not only because of the key changes in the melody but because the harmony was singularly adapted to bop treatment. Since the tune wasn't recognizable from its harmony, especially when bopped, the name *Whispering* was finally dropped for *Groovin' High!*

As many innovations take place "beneath" the music as on top. For example, instead of having the guitar repeat the same chord for four consecutive beats, with frequent returns to that identical chord, the bebop guitar makes frequent chord "changes" within each bar and from measure to measure.

The above explanation is only fragmentary. Let it merely indicate that the music, in spite of its name, is not nonsense, any more than its seeming harshness is noise. Bebop is modern progressive music, harmonically suited to the times.

It's a difficult music to play and understand. That's why our young musicians, better schooled than yesterday's swing men, are turning to it once they find that swing is a pushover. (Bill Gottlieb, "The Anatomy of Bebop," originally in *New York Herald Tribune,* September 26, 1947)

I would add that "Whispering" was not renamed "Groovin' High" (a title that suggests drugs) just because it was no longer recognizable, but because Gillespie had written a totally new melody to the chords of the older song, and this effort deserved a new title. For two songs to share the same chords is not really that unusual; certain chord progressions occur repeatedly in the songs of the 1920s and 1930s—the chords in "Tiger Rag" were a particular favorite. Perhaps too much has been made of the beboppers' writing new melodies to the old chords. What is truly significant is their emphasis on new melodies. Where the repertory of such swing artists as Armstrong and Goodman—always with the exception of Ellington—often contained a high percentage of well-known popular songs, the boppers played relatively fewer well-known melodies and a much higher percentage of their own compositions. Even though the music was still based on familiar chord progressions, primarily thirty-two-bar pop progressions and twelve-bar blues—the audiences would naturally find it harder to follow since they didn't have a familiar melody to guide them through the progression.

One more point Gottlieb and Gillespie omitted: it is often said that bebop was played faster than swing, but in fact it was often played much more slowly as well. In becoming less tied to dancing, jazz also freed itself of the need to play everything within a general danceable range from medium-slow to fast. Boppers would play at extremely fast and extremely slow tempos. In short, they expanded the expressive range of the music.

To be fair to bop's detractors, not all bebop was on the level of Parker and Gillespie, pianist Bud Powell, and drummer Max Roach. In the mid-1940s the solos of pianist Argonne Thornton (later known as Sadik Hakim) and even of trumpeters Kenny Dorham and Miles Davis (both of whom really improved later on, of course) are sometimes painfully awkward, and to swing fans some bop must have paled beside the elegant perfection of such swing masters as Armstrong, trumpeter Bunny Berigan, or Teddy Wilson. Gillespie himself addresses this in the following piece.

Here Gillespie is set against Tex Beneke, the saxophonist (and vocalist) on such Glenn Miller hit records as "In the Mood" (1939). Gillespie and Beneke don't entirely disagree with each other; really, they are just coming from different angles. Gillespie notes that *Life* magazine had recently featured an article on bop ("Bebop: New Jazz School Is Led by Trumpeter Who Is Hot, Cool, and Gone," 11 October 1948: 138–42), showing how accepted it had become. He also points out that some musicians were playing loud or fast without substance, which hurt the bop cause. Beneke takes a moderate stance, acknowledging the musical validity of bop and recognizing that Gillespie, as one of its leaders, should concentrate on it. Beneke, however, feels that most bands should include bop as a minor part of their repertory, put in for variety and for "spice" but not emphasized.

To Bop . . .

DIZZY GILLESPIE

I'm not saying that there's going to come a day when every band in the business is going to be playing bop and nothing else. That would be wrong.

What I am saying though is that just about every band has to play some bop, even if the people don't recognize it as such. There are little strains in almost everybody's records these days that smack of bop and that's the best evidence I can think of.

That certainly wasn't so three or even two years ago. Then it was all up hill. At first we had a lot of bad language thrown at us and there's even some right now, but when a magazine like *Life* does a big spread on a certain kind of music you can be pretty sure that that kind of music is here, and for good.

About the worst thing for our music are these kids without all of the background they ought to have, trying to outblow everybody. They make bop a joke, even though I'm sure they want to play good. Ask any musician and you'll find out that you've got to have all the rudiments down cold before you can bop.

You know, they even play bop on the radio, on live commercial shows. I heard Fred Waring try it on his show and it sounded all right. That's a real help. Remember when Benny was trying to get what they called swing started? He had a real fight to make it stick and it took a lot longer than three years too!

All these bands are beginning to play real crazy stuff and they're getting bookings with it too. Remember we're really just getting started. There's all this vocal bop too that boys like Charlie Ventura and Buddy Stewart are doing and that's almost a field in itself.

The people are taking to bop and they're showing that that's what they want so I say to the bands that are just getting started, you've got to play bop if you want to make it.

. . . Or Not to Bop

TEX BENEKE

The surest way to alienate dancers, fans, record buyers, and the other assorted clientele which go to pay a band's meal ticket is to play nothing but be-bop.

I'm not a longhair, a wet blanket, or a die-hard reactionary. I think that Dizzy Gillespie through the medium of what he calls be-bop has made a major contribution to the world of music. His extraordinary style has forced the public to develop a more educated ear and to accept sounds which would have been considered discordant before the advent of be-bop.

Be-bop has allowed us to use many figures in our arrangements which we were never able to use before, figures which give us music colors which we need to express the mood of a song. We use be-bop figures in our own scores very often, but we don't use them to the excess they are used in a be-bop band.

Here is [where] the be-bop boys make their mistake.

Be-bop is a musical spice, a musical tang and color which must be used justly and sparingly. You don't sit down to dinner and eat nothing but salt or pepper . . . and you shouldn't sit down to an evening of music and play nothing but be-bop. The fact that bands shatter this basic rule is what causes the big complaint against be-bop and dance bands in general.

Too many bands and bandleaders take a single phase of musical development and worry it to death. Bop is a good influence, but use it sparingly. As for you, Diz, you are the originator, the proud pappa of boppa, play it silly. I get my kicks from your Bopera . . . but, as for the rest of you guys . . . if I'm not being presumptive . . . give it to me easy.

Throw a little over your shoulder. You've been spilling the salt. (Dizzy Gillespie and Tex Beneke, "To Bop or Not to Bop," originally in *Record Review*, September 1949)

Some of the modernity and spice of the new jazz was the result of harmonies inspired by modern classical composers. Igor Stravinsky and Béla Bartók were avowed favorites of Charlie Parker, John Coltrane, Jimmy Heath, and other young artists. Parker even liked to inject a little phrase from Stravinsky's "Petrouchka" into his improvisations. Eddie Finckel wrote "Boyd Meets Stravinsky" for Boyd Raeburn's band in 1944; the bandleader Woody Herman recorded "Igor," by Shorty Rogers and Red Norvo, in 1946; and clarinetist Buddy DeFranco recorded George Russell's "A Bird in Igor's Yard" in 1949. (As we will see in chapter 12, jazz continues to draw from the classical world, and vice versa.)

Al Rose, a New Orleans native who promoted that city's legacy through his concerts, books, and radio programs, criticizes the trend toward drawing from modern classics in the following article. He is unwittingly condescending, and quite typical, in his assumption that black musicians are controlled by white attitudes. Rose argues that as soon as blacks began to incorporate classical influences, they were simply serving the interests of white audiences instead of remaining true to themselves. He is so wrong that I hardly know where to begin. For one thing, beboppers did use classical harmonies, but that's about all—their music still swung mightily and was rooted in the blues and popular songs. For another, white audiences in general were mystified by modern classics (they still are) and would hardly have requested them. Finally, Rose disrespects the intellectual breadth of the bop generation by not allowing that African Americans might be interested in classical music by their own choice.

The Negro has rejected his great musical artists. Magnificent interpretive singers like Bessie Smith and Chippie [Hill] have given way to sexy, technically facile nowhere chicks like Billie Holiday and Sarah Vaughan. Sincerity and originality have resigned in favor of cleverness and acrobatics. The voiceless, no-piano playing, insipid stylings of Nellie Lutcher take the jukeboxes by storm in Negro spots. It's the era of the saloon singer, the aimless horn. Last week the trumpet held the spotlight, today the tenor sax, and on tomorrow's horizon the bouncing baritone. What kind of nonsense is that? Great music depends on the artist, not the instrument.

A sterile, essentially insipid work like Gillespie's "Emanon" has the same kind of appeal as a song by Sinatra. It's superficial, has no lasting qualities and will be forgotten as soon as some other joker comes along with something more weird. True jazz, on the other hand, is timeless and deathless. Listen to Louis' "West End Blues" or Hines' "Monday Date" if you don't believe me.

So, when I say the Negro has made no progress in music recently, I mean it! That's from a standpoint of the audience even more than the musician. There's no reason why the Negro has to be a faddist. There's no reason why he has to like something because somebody tells him it's supposed to be good.

It's time for the Negro to get back on the high road to real progress in music. That means the playing and appreciating of straightforward, legitimate jazz, unencumbered by Debussy scales, the influence of Juilliard school graduates and commercial sound effects. (Al Rose, "Critic Raps False Interpretation of Music, Lauds Jazz as Only True Negro Music Form," *Philadelphia Tribune*, ca. March 16, 1948)

Black audiences had difficulty with bop as well. Eddie "Cleanhead" Vinson, Gillespie, and others have reported about engagements where black audiences demanded more accessible material. The *Philadelphia Tribune,* a black newspaper, noted on June 2, 1951 that "[saxophonist and composer] Jimmy Heath and his Bop All-Stars are still displaying their temperamental brand of Gillespying." On June 5 the paper acknowledged that "it was pleasing to the ear, and sporting a fine-thread of the melodic for a change." On February 10, 1953 a *Tribune* columnist noted, "Specs Wright and his smooth riding drums has developed a fine stylized brand of Boperooing. The group are smooth and rhythmic, and not bad on the listeners, despite the difficulty of boppers being commercial riders"—that is to say, despite the fact that bop is noncommercial. As late as August 27, 1955, the *Tribune's* weekly magazine section featured an article entitled "Has Bebop Killed Jazz?" but by then it answered to the contrary. Author Elliot Clarksdale concluded, "Today it looks as though bop is finally coming through. . . . Look out, you'll be singing and dancing to bop and like it before you know it."

Many among the older generation of black musicians had trouble getting used to bop. Leroy "Stuff" Smith, a marvelous, hard-swinging jazz violinist, spoke out against it:

Terming be-bop music an "illegitimate child of swing," Leroy (Stuff) Smith, famous hot fiddler, said this type of frantic music is ruining the musical foundation of many up-and-coming young instrumentalist[s].

Not only that, he added, but the lack of any definite melodic pattern in bebop will never cause it to replace swing as many of its supporters contend.

. . . [B]ebop will eventually die out, he asserted.

"During my thousands of appearances in dance halls, nite clubs, on the stage and radio I have discovered that the public only takes to forms of music that they are able to hum and whistle after hearing two or three times," he said. "Notwithstanding the fact that I am a musician myself, I find I am unable to detect any melody in bebop." ("War Rages Over 'Bebop' Music Style," *Philadelphia Afro-American,* November 15, 1947)

Because Louis Armstrong was a leader in the jazz field, his word was important, and the press sought him out for comments. In a short statement for *Esquire,* he was flattering:

Don't you know I'm crazy about that "Re Bop" stuff? I love to listen to it. I think it's very, very amusing. One thing, to play "Re Bop" one has to have mighty good, strong chops from what I've witnessed. I'm one cat that loves all kinds of music. ("Louis Armstrong on 'Re Bop,'" *Esquire's 1947 Jazz Book*)

Soon, however, in longer statements for the jazz magazines, Armstrong came out firmly against bop. He drew some criticism for his stance.

Writer Raps Armstrong for Criticism of Trend

Roy W. Stephens

Louis Armstrong, in the pages of a national music news sheet, took a blast at modern contemporary jazz (bebop) which left California jazz circles gasping for breath and which pointed a bluntly scornful finger at the musical brain-child of Dizzy Gillespie, Charlie Parker and Thelonious Monk.

Dwight Whitney, newsman for "Time" magazine, cornered Armstrong and obtained an interview from the "King" which quoted him as saying:

> "Them bebop boys are great technicians. Mistakes—that's all bebop is. Man, you've gotta be a technician to know when you make 'em. Them cats play too much music—a whole lot of notes nothing . . . You've got to carry a melody."

First Heard in 1918

"Some cats say Old Satchmo is old-fashioned, not modern enough. Why, man, most of that modern music I first heard in 1918. Ain't no music out of date as long as you play it perfect. . . . You give me the music. I'll figure out what to do with it."

Yep, that's what Armstrong, the Dean of Jazz, said about my good friend Bebop. He didn't pull his punches, on the contrary, he was entirely frank for which musicians should be grateful.

Nevertheless, in spite of Louis Armstrong's greatness (which we acknowledge without reservation), we modestly feel that the trumpet prototype was thinking of that old fable about the fox and the grapes, the sour grapes.

Satchmo Too Old?

Armstrong is 47 years old, possibly too old to jam dozens of notes into a couple of bars at a nerve-wrangling tempo, possibly too old to rip off cascades of rich full and resonant tones, and possibly too old to remember when his own wonderfully-phrased solos brought a few nods of discord from persons whose ears had [not] become accustomed to "progressive" music.

Unquestionably a master of his instrument and one of Jazz's most influential musicians, Louis Armstrong has somehow forgotten that his present stature in jazz could not have been established had he as Woody Herman said, "kept his ears closed to what in the old days was considered 'progressive' music and 'new' ideas."

Should Be Careful

Because of his position in music and because he has been—perhaps he still is—the glistening idol of countless youngsters, Armstrong should be wary of discouraging these creative young minds merely because he seems to think "them cats play too much music—a whole lot of notes, weird notes that don't mean nothing." The statement itself is absurd.

We admire Armstrong. We admire him because he had the courage to combat the few opposing factions which didn't understand his music the way he dragged the beat or the manner in which he played around it.

Armstrong played his way the way his heart wanted him to play, the way he loved to play, the way he HAD to play.

There's no getting around the fact that jazz in 1947 is vastly different from what it was in 1918—in spite of Louis' intimation that he heard bebop at the close of World War I.

Would Hit Purse

And, because the musicians of 1947—and the public of 1947—are trying to judge contemporary music more critically, musicians like Fletcher and Horace Henderson say things like "Louis's views should be published by the millions" (Fletcher) and "Bebop should be stored away with C-Melody saxophones" (Horace). Nonsense!

It's simple economic logic that if the public demands bebop the Hendersons are going to take a drastic cut in their pocketbook.

Armstrong's denunciation of bebop was harmful—not because of what he actually said, but because of the manner which the general public will interpret his diatribe. The King said only one thing with which we agree whole-heartedly. "Ain't no music out of date as long as you play it perfect." (Roy W. Stephens, "Writer Raps Armstrong for Criticism of Trend," *Philadelphia Afro-American,* November 15, 1947)

The fight over bop became bitter. By March 1948 Armstrong was reluctant to discuss the matter.

"They're always misquotin' me so I don't like to discuss it no more." He walked over to a stack of letters and pulled forth one of those four-page hot club bulletins. "Read this. I never said that. They're always addin' words. What do they want to do that for, anyway? You know, one trouble with the beboppers is that they can give it, but they can't take it! They tear you down, but if you say somethin' against them, they yell you're old fashioned and you don't know nothin' about jazz any more."

"I'd never play this bebop because I don't like it. Don't get me wrong; I think some of them cats who play it play real good, like Dizzy, especially. But bebop is the easy way out. Instead of holding notes the way they should be held, they just play a lot of little notes. They sorta fake out of it. You won't find many of them cats who can blow a straight lead. They never learned right. It's all just flash. It doesn't come from the heart the way real music should." (George Simon, "Bebop's the Easy Out, Claims Louis," *Metronome*, March 1948, pp. 14–15)

As late as 1961 (I estimate the date from Armstrong's reference to the film *Paris Blues*, released that year), Armstrong had not recanted. When discussing jazz in the following excerpt, he also brings up his love and respect for classical music (discussed further in Joshua Berrett, "Louis Armstrong and Opera," *Musical Quarterly*, summer 1992). But much of his problem with the newer jazz is clearly a simple case of older-generation values versus the new, a conflict that's been repeated throughout history.

Jazz Is a Language

BY LOUIS ARMSTRONG

People keep asking whether I think jazz "isn't what it used to be." I guess that's the kind of question they figure is going to stir up some argument. But I don't like to get into arguments, so I tell 'em two things: nothin's like it used to be—and jazz is *good* as long as people want it to be.

Sure, there's a lot of talk now about the modern music. It's a lot different from what we call jazz, which is what I grew up with. I don't like it too much. This new music has nothing to express, nothing to explain. You know what I mean?

Jazz is something else again. You never get tired of playing good jazz and you never get tired of listening to it. We were taught right from Beethoven and Bach in the old days. Beautiful things. We had that as a fundamental and we went on from there to play jazz. Some people don't understand that the basis of jazz is a kind of language. You use it to say all kinds of things and explain all kinds of moods. But it starts from good music—then goes on its own.

This new music—I call it jujitsu music. A youngster isn't going to learn anything from that but how to tear up his lip. It doesn't have as big a following as jazz. I guess they think that's because people don't understand it too well. I don't think that's it at all; I think the reason it doesn't have as big a following as jazz is that it doesn't have the same things to say.

But I'm not one of those cats that says modern music doesn't belong. I don't think you can say that about any kind of music. Each kind has a language of its own. All music has a place; some kinds are bigger and more universal than others, that's all.

Another thing. I don't think movies have done much to tell the real story of jazz. But *Paris Blues* does. At least, it tries to dig the real story of American jazz musicians in Paris. That's why I interrupted a State Department tour of Africa to spend a month in Paris on the film— that, *and* the chance to work with The Duke (Ellington) who did a new jazz score for the picture.

If there's any kind of a shortage of good jazz nowadays, maybe it's because there's a shortage of jazz musicians. In the old days, the youngsters had plenty of people to listen to and learn from. There aren't as many nowadays—and maybe some of these younger fellows don't pay as much attention as they should.

Whatever it is, there just isn't the place for the youngsters to get the experience like there was before. 'Course, that's true in many businesses today, but we notice it more. There aren't as many of us oldtimers around to tell 'em, not only about the music itself—but about the people that played it—people like Joe Oliver who gave me my breaks.

But when you find a youngster that listens, you know you got something. The ones that listen always turn out to be good musicians—and I don't care what kind of music they play. See what I mean? (Louis Armstrong, "Jazz Is a Language," *Music Journal*, 1961)

William "Count" Basie (1904–1984), the pianist and bandleader, did not share Armstrong's problems with the new music. During the 1950s he hired such key modern figures as Thad Jones, Frank Foster, and Eddie "Lockjaw" Davis. Reading his positive and open-minded comments below, one understands why he was beloved by the musicians who worked with him!

The Story of Jazz
COUNT BASIE

... Nearly every chapter of the story of jazz till now has seen a change in the style. In the 1910's the style was found in the playing of the New Orleans bands and Jelly Roll Morton, and in the '20s by the jazz of Armstrong's Hot Five, of Ellington and myself in the '30s, and in our own time the bebop jazz of Charlie Parker and Dizzy Gillespie.

It's only right that any new style is talked about and severely criticized in *any* field, and bebop is no exception. But we must all remember that the active musicians create jazz and authorize style changes. Perhaps the most intriguing aspect of bebop jazz is its rhythmic structure. Bebop is improvised jazz. Bebop *polyrhythmics* are actually revolutionary. To the new listener the old solid beat is not as evident but, actually, the bebop rhythm section is the most functional in history. It maintains the basic 4/4 beat on which all good jazz has been based and differs from swing rhythm emotionally and mechanically. Bebop drummers no longer keep time with the bass pedal. The top cymbal is the chief tool. Where the swing drummer used a staccato beat, the bebop drummer produces a legato sound. The practical progress achieved by a switch from bass pedal to top cymbal is an economy. In addition to adding tonal dynamics to rhythmic propulsion, his left hand, both feet—not to mention high-hat pedal, bass drum, snares and tom-toms—are left free for improvised effects never before made possible! Needless to say, a fresh approach to the instrument is needed.

Incidentally, the root of bebop rhythmics, it has been said by several authorities, is simply a modification of my own section, with three changes: the section has been made leaner, the 4/4 basic moved from bass drum to cymbals and the section sound has become more legato and vertical. This makes the modern rhythm section the simplest and most functional of all time.

Will the jazz of today show greater durability and be just as enjoyable to the next generation? I think so! And, if Cinderella's good Fairy Godmother will grant me just one more wish, I will be around to *enjoy it, too!* (Count Basie, "The Story of Jazz," *Music Journal,* ca. 1955–61)

Other established black artists embraced bop. Vibraphonist and bandleader Lionel Hampton said:

The New Movement is a product of the younger musicians who have been fortunate enough to obtain a musical training most of the old-timers lacked. These boys are now capable of expressing their basic feelings and ideas in a new and more relevant idiom. (C. B. "Bebop Called Music in Tune With the Times," *Philadelphia Afro-American,* July 3, 1948, p. 7)

Saxophonist Coleman Hawkins and pianist Mary Lou Williams were involved in bebop from the start, and they found the music a natural development from swing.

A remarkable publication on the new music was Leonard Feather's book *Inside Bebop* (later retitled *Inside Jazz*). It is impressive that Feather had the perspective as early as 1949 to write this perceptive history of the new music and to provide detailed musical examples, with explanation, and biographies of key figures. Feather was one of the few jazz critics who was also a musician, a pianist who wrote pieces for Benny Carter and Dinah Washington; a composer of one of the first jazz waltzes and of one of the first jazz pieces to employ the classical "twelve-tone" serial music technique; and a producer who put together all-women groups and groups that combined musicians from several countries. Feather was born in London in 1914, moved to New York in 1939, and died in California in 1994.

8

The Drug Problem

When I was getting involved in jazz during the 1960s, my elders often warned me that "jazz musicians are all drug addicts." Unfortunately there was some truth to this assertion in the postwar period, when highly addictive heroin became the drug of choice. Previously, marijuana use had been common among musicians, common enough to be immortalized in Louis Armstrong's 1928 recording "Muggles" (slang for marijuana cigarettes, later known as "joints"), which was basically an untitled blues looking for a name, and in Don Redman's theme song, "Chant of the Weed," which he used on radio broadcasts. I'd guess many listeners and producers were aware of these references, but I'll bet some naive radio executives thought of Redman, "Isn't that lovely—he's into gardening." Drug connections and users were called "vipers," and when saxophonist Budd Johnson spoke "pig Latin" on Armstrong's 1933 recording of "Sweet Sue," the band leader introduced him by saying he'd do some "viper" talk. (Laws controlling marijuana in the U.S. were enacted in 1937.)

Cab Calloway made his fortune singing about drugs. In the 1933 film *International House*, Calloway prefaces "Reefer Man" ("reefer" is marijuana) by looking at the bassist and asking, "Why, what's the matter with that cat here?" The band members yell, "He's high!" Calloway responds, "Whaddaya mean, 'He's high'?" The band yells,

"Full of weed!" In the 1932 film *The Big Broadcast,* Calloway sings about "Smokey Joe," who went down to Chinatown where "all the cokeys [cocaine addicts] laid around; some were high and some were mighty low." Joe was in search of "Minnie the Moocher" (the mooch was a popular dance, but I think a moocher, like Charlie Parker's friend "Moose the Mooche," was also a drug connection) because "all his junk ran out." Joe says he'd probably find Minnie "kicking the gong around" (partaking in Asian opium or its derivative, morphine, represented by Asian gongs; a gong introduces this piece). At this point Calloway, in filmed performance, mimics sniffing up some morphine or cocaine from the back of his hand.

Jazz musicians drank alcohol, and many became alcoholics— Bunny Berigan, Lester Young, and Coleman Hawkins toward the end of his life. In a profession where one is constantly performing in venues that serve alcohol, where free drinks are often counted as a "bonus," and where fans offer to buy you a drink, overindulgence is a perennial danger. Although doctors have determined recently that small amounts of wine are invigorating and healthy, clearly alcohol can be as dangerous as any drug, and that is why it was the first substance to have been outlawed. Prohibition lasted from 1919 (earlier in some states) through the end of 1933, but it would have to be counted as a failure in that its legacy includes international gangster organizations built up through the sale of illegal spirits.

Are jazz musicians more likely to be involved with alcohol and drugs than the general population? I believe so, but the percentages are probably about the same as for other performers who work in nightclubs or who expend high energy for each show. Certainly rock musicians and film actors have had as many publicized cases of substance abuse as members of the jazz community.

Things took a turn for the worse when heroin arrived on the scene. It became common knowledge that heroin had hold of Billie Holiday (whose 1947 arrest was front-page news in the black press) and of Charlie Parker (who was sent for about six months to a state hospital in Camarillo, California, beginning in August 1946). Tragically, this news didn't scare away the younger musicians; instead it convinced them that heroin must be the secret to success in jazz. The peer pressure to try heroin at least once became so enormous that even the most clean-cut musicians I've met from the generation born between about 1920 and 1935 had tried heroin at least once. Many, of course, became addicted and spent much of their lives chasing it, all while trying to manage a performing career and to lead a semblance of a personal life.

As early as 1947, the black press was aware of a drug problem among jazz musicians, as indicated in the following article.

Anything for a Thrill
Marijuana, Zoot Suits: All Products of the Jazz Craze
RALPH MATTHEWS

"Will you take it wet or dry?" That query from the house man at one of the intimate apartments where performers, musicians and those who hang around the underworld fringe gather, means only one thing to the initiated.

It means, do you want a drink (wet) or do you want a brace of reefers (dry).

If you are just a teetotaler, you might order a drink, just to be sociable and do your best to pour down the concoction the host serves up, telling you that it is a popular high-priced brand—it seldom is.

And if you haven't "got your boots on," meaning "hep to the jive," which in turn means worldly wise, you'll be stuck not only with the check for your drink, but for a round for the house.

Square If You Squawk

If you raise too much of a squawk you are marked down as a "square," and are blackballed the next time you try to gain admittance.

Places like the "cabbage patch," a reefer pad, cannot afford to have squares around. Not only are they poor spenders, but they might stool to the police and queer the racket.

The "cabbage patch" type of speakeasy is a practically new creation coming into being in the wake of the jazz craze, which really began to catch its stride around 1934 when swing music and jam sessions swept the country like wild fire, bringing bobby soxers, jitterbugs, hep cats and zoot suiters in their wake.

Musicians Depend on It

Musicians, forced to fantastic demands on their nervous systems by the increasing screams, cat calls and near-riots of uninhibited youngsters who went into the same frenzies over swing music that their elders did over a revival meeting, sought outside stimulants to keep up the maddening pace.

Some tried drinking, but alcohol deadened the senses and brought on either dullness or the drinker became immune to its effects.

A drinker was little good to a top-flight band in which thousands of dollars were at stake if his musicianship was faulty due to lack of coordination due to over-imbibing. Most big bands put a ban on drinking during working hours and enforced the rule with heavy fines.

Had to "Send Themselves"

But the music makers had to "send themselves" in order to reach the heights demanded by their new generation of teenagers.

Slowly but surely the reefer began to find its way into the music world, and from there it drifted to habitues of dance halls and into gathering places of jazz addicts.

The "cabbage patch" type of speakeasy sprang up all over the country, and today reefers are even sold to school children by unscrupulous vendors willing to turn a dollar at the price of spreading juvenile delinquency throughout the land.

"Snuffy Snow"

Many a person who would shrink from horror at the thought of cultivating the dope habit in the traditional form known as "banging" or "sniffing snow" will accept a puff on a reefer just for the thrill.

The "banger" is the type who uses a needle, and becomes so violent when once addicted to the habit that he will even commit murder to obtain the drug.

There are few doctors who have not experienced one or the other of the thousands of tricks and subterfuges which these victims have devised to obtain doses legally—illegally if necessary.

Morphine Addict

The morphine addict is commonly called a "snow bird" because he puts the snow white powder on the back of his hand and sniffs it like snuff.

This is accompanied by a nervous twitch which has become a stereotyped impersonation for the dope addict in theatre portrayals.

Lowest Smokes Opium

Probably the lowest type of dope fiend, if there is such a thing as degrees of depravity, is the opium smoker.

The devastation wreaked in China and in the Chinatowns around the world is far too familiar for elaboration.

To connect dope with the jazz age we need but recall that one of the greatest band leaders of modern times, Cab Calloway, an actor as well as a musician, practically mushroomed to fame with his famous song, "Minnie the Moocher," in which he essayed the role of a dope addict "Cokey Joe."

"Chant of the Weed"

Don Redm[a]n also penned a weird and mystic tune which is still in demand on juke boxes and dawn patrol programs, titled "The Chant of the Weed." Many other composers have used this theme.

The reason for the rise of the reefer craze in addition to the practical applications cited above, is that different from the vicious opium pipe it used the accepted and popular appeal of the cigarette.

Many youngsters think it smart to smoke reefers who would shy from other forms of dope.

Cigarettes Help

They do not frighten easily because they have already been pounded with the theory that cigarette smoking itself is harmful, but they not only fail to see anybody dropping dead from the habit, but hear the virtues of competing brands praised to high heaven over the radio.

So, even reefers, they conclude, cannot be half as bad as people claim.

Another appeal is the thrill that humans get from doing anything unlawful. People do not enjoy night clubs half as much today as they did when it was necessary to say "Joe sent me" to get into a dive under prohibition.

Did you ever walk into a room of joysters and smell a sickening odor, half sweet, half nauseating? Prick up your nose and take a good sniff. There are reefers around.

For more tell-tale evidence, glance about the room. See if there are bottles of coca cola around. Reefer smokers drink a lot of coke. It does something to them; and also look for fruit.

Avoid Heavy Food

Reefer bugs love to munch on fruit—oranges, grapes, soda crackers. They disdain heavy foods like cakes or sandwiches.

Two reefers can serve a group of from four to ten. They like to puff the fumes up their nostrils and pass the weed from lip to lip.

Don't worry too much about the sex angle. Most reefer smokers are not amorous. When a wolf wants to do some serious necking he buys liquor, not reefers. The effects are almost contrary.

Affects Mind

Alcohol affects the physical being and makes the person either overly sensuous or overly pugnacious. They want to love or fight.

Reefers affect the mental and spiritual side.

The victim thinks lofty thoughts, and under its influence an unlettered moron may try to explain the nebular hypothesis and clarify all you do not understand about atomic energy or the Einstein theory of relativity.

It is under the influence of reefers that famous modern musicians produce those tedious variations accepted today as music, and it is under the same influence that many jitterbugs believe that the noise they are making actually is music.

Circumspect people who steer clear of the "cabbage patch" and who like a little melody with their instrumentation are left as orphans in the storm as the jazz craze rumbles on. (Ralph Matthews, "Anything for a Thrill," *Philadelphia Afro-American,* February 22, 1947)

By the early 1950s, jazz magazines had run news stories about the short-term drug-related arrests of Stan Getz (caught robbing a drugstore), Miles Davis, Art Pepper, and others. Charlie Parker talked openly about it, saying, "Any musician who says he is playing better either on tea [marijuana], the needle, or when he is juiced, is a plain, straight liar" (Michael Levin and John S. Wilson, "No Bop Roots in Jazz: Parker," *Down Beat*, September 4, 1949).

Even Calloway, who despite his songs insisted on having clean-cut people in his band, wrote "Is Dope Killing Our Musicians?" for *Ebony* (February 1951), in which he spoke out against drug use in jazz and called for musicians to fight the trend. Although Calloway didn't refer to addicted musicians by name, the article was accompanied by photos with captions that clearly identified the culprits. For example, Calloway wrote, "One young trumpeter, recently picked up on the West Coast for possession of heroin, happens to be one of the most brilliant minds in contemporary jazz." Nearby was a photo with the caption, "Miles Davis, top trumpet player, was picked up by Los Angeles police recently, charged with having dope in possession." Gene Krupa (who had been arrested in 1943 when his bandboy was caught with marijuana and was also found to be underage and a draft dodger) and Dexter Gordon are similarly fingered. There are additional photos of Billie Holiday, bassist John Simmons, pianist Eddie Heywood, trumpeters Fats Navarro and Howard McGhee, and drummer Art Blakey, each with a caption about their involvement with drugs. In a radio interview with Leonard Feather in spring 1951, Parker said that Calloway's article was "poorly written, poorly expressed and poorly meant. It was just poor . . . And in case an investigation should be conducted, it should be done in the right way, instead of trying to destroy musicians and their names." (See Carl Woideck's carefully researched study, *Charlie Parker: His Music and Life* [Ann Arbor: University of Michigan Press, 1996], pp. 43–44.)

By 1955 the drug problem in the jazz community was national news. That year, Frank Sinatra starred as a heroin-addicted jazz drummer in the Hollywood film *The Man with the Golden Arm*. During 1954 and 1955, Charles Winick interviewed 357 musicians about drug use, and he published the results a few years later as "The Use of Drugs by Jazz Musicians" (*Social Problems* 7, no. 3 [winter 1959–60]). Winick promised the musicians complete anonymity and asked them to talk about the drug habits, if any, of their band mates. He concluded that cocaine use was rare, probably because of its high cost, and marijuana use was common—54 percent were occasional users, 23 percent were regular users. As for heroin, 53 percent had tried it at least once, 24 percent were occasional users, and 16 percent were hard-core addicts. Heroin accounted for most of the illegal drug traffic in the U.S., and it was directly outlawed by the Narcotic Control Act of 1956, which made its sale to minors punishable by life imprisonment or even death.

The heroin crisis in the jazz community was devastating. So many died and so many had their careers interrupted or destroyed that the generation who grew up in the 1960s began to steer clear of it. In the mid-1990s there is very little heroin use in the jazz community, but it continues to surface. Pianist Brad Meldhau, a marvelous young talent, had a publicized brush with it and, thankfully, a recovery. Cocaine and alcohol are still problems, and marijuana remains popular in certain circles.

9

Race Politics and Jazz
in the 1950s and 1960s

The classification of race is a meaningless human invention, according to anthropologist Ashley Montagu (for example, in his book *Man's Most Dangerous Myth: The Fallacy of Race*) and numerous other scientists. We people are all of one species, and the fact that we come in different sizes and shapes is no more significant than the ways that any other species may vary, though none varies in nature as much as we do. Yet there is no eliminating race from human perception. Since the beginning of time humans have displayed a tribalism, a loyalty to their own group rather than to the species as a whole. Racism, it seems clear to me, is a part of the general condition of human tribalism. One could call it "ethnocentrism," but that label seems too tame for this violent force.

Tribalism is obviously innate. It practically defines our species' history, whose major dates signify wars of one kind or another. As soon as human populations were large enough to come into contact with one another, the question has almost always been, "Who will dominate?" not "How do we combine forces?" Tribalism is clearly evident in the animal kingdom, where one pride of lions will aggressively compete with and attack another and where one group of chimpanzees (once thought to be peaceful creatures) will beat a member of another troop to a bloody death. While human males engage in the violence, the tribalism is just as much a part of females' attitudes. Happily, in the past two hundred years or so, we have seen a major movement toward world cooperation and world peace.

In jazz ever-present problems of tribalism are incredibly complicated. Jazz is, after all, the creation of African descendants in America, drawing upon the African American culture that developed during contact with European peoples and, to some extent, Native Americans. Then, out of this tribal mix, from the very beginning of jazz European Americans got involved. (White Americans are barely aware of it, but Native American culture had a major impact on them as well, as evidenced, for example, in the many Native American names that dot our national map.) Some, like the Original Dixieland Jazz Band (ODJB) and Paul Whiteman, used self-serving publicity that credited themselves for it all, and naturally black artists resented their success.

In chapter 6 you read about the music industry practices that make success difficult for black bands. In addition, even the most well-meaning white artist would make more money than most black artists as a simple result of demographics. Benny Goodman, a Jewish American, was not only respected among blacks but, with the support of his producer John Hammond, insisted on touring with such black colleagues as Teddy Wilson, Lionel Hampton, and later Charlie Christian. In his 1939 autobiography, *The Kingdom of Swing* (written with Irving Kolodin, published by Frederick Ungar, New York), Goodman devotes pages 156–157 and 161–162 to black arranger and composer Fletcher Henderson, crediting the success of the band to Henderson's music. Goodman paid Henderson well at a time when Henderson needed the money—his own band was doing poorly—and on radio broadcasts Goodman can sometimes be heard crediting Henderson when he introduces one of Henderson's pieces. So why, as many black musicians have often bitterly noted, did Goodman make much more money than Henderson made as a band leader? It was partly a result of demographics. Until roughly the 1980s, white people listened to white musicians more than to black ones. Since blacks have remained at one seventh or less (12 percent in the 1990 census) of the population, a white musician automatically had a larger audience.

As the music became more recognized and accepted, some African American jazz fans and professionals were concerned that, unless blacks were especially active in supporting jazz, it would lose its powerful tie with the black community. They felt ripped off, and felt as if the nonblacks who were so enthusiastically researching, teaching, and performing jazz had in effect stolen it from black America. This bitter feeling disturbed the already delicate relationship between the black and white "tribes" within jazz. These spokespersons were not satisfied with the demographic argument—even though blacks are a minority, they felt that their people had a special role in supporting and documenting jazz, and that the proportion of African Americans involved in jazz should be much greater than for other cultural groups.

In 1955, black author Guy Booker wrote an article stressing the need for African Americans to take control of the music and the way it is presented in written works. He charges that the few trained black American scholars at that time may have also accepted white cultural values as part of their education; therefore, they may have felt that jazz was not a seemly subject for their research.

Colored Historians Too Lazy
To Write Own History of Jazz; Let Whites Do It
Vast Field of Race's Contribution to Music Badly Neglected As "Let Whites Do It" Feeling Prevails
GUY BOOKER

One of the most chronic of all complaints by Negroes is the one in which they seem always to say, "the white folks are stealing our music." One hears it everywhere the topic of jazz music is discussed. It's the theme of today's conversations on rhythm and blues and the current rock and roll craze. One heard it back in the days of the Original Dixieland Kings from New Orleans, through Paul Whiteman, Benny Goodman and down to Woody Herman.

Over the decades since jazz came out of New Orleans to become America's No. 1 contribution to world music, charges of tune piracy, stealing by white singers of the best features of the top Negro vocalists' styles and nearly everything else has been talked about and written up in the colored newspapers and magazines, but nothing has come of any of it.

Today the alarming and disheartening fact is that the white folks own jazz, control it completely and dictate what it should and shall be. Negroes have little or nothing to say or do about it at all. Although they create and play it, sing it and dance to it, the fact is that jazz as the black man's heritage has just about been taken from him.

This situation is largely due to the plain dumbness and laziness of Negroes who are in a position to do something about it and in this case, the finger points to the colored historian.

While white musicologists like Alan Lomax, Charles Edward Smith, Frederic Ramsey, Jr., Rudi Blesh, Dave Dexter and John Hammond, Jr. have gone ahead and written the history of jazz the way they wanted to, the colored historians have spent most if not all their time hanging around intellectual cocktail parties or rejoicing in their presence at some "interracial" gathering of jazz enthusiasts where a premium is placed on rubbing shoulders with whites.

Actually, colored historians are afraid of some aspects of the real story of the race. So anxious are they to show how much Negroes "are just like white folks" that they shun the sordid, wretched, often vile background of jazz: its beginnings in houses of ill fame, borderellos [sic], gin joints, work camps, cotton patches and the like.

They don't want the contact necessary for any real research with the relatives or friends who knew them of the Jelly Roll Mortons, the Bessie Smiths, the Tampa Reds, the Blind Lemon Jeffersons, the Ida Coxes, the Buddy Boldens, the Pinetop Smiths, the Billie Holidays, the King Joe Olivers, the Thelonious Monks, the Dinah Washingtons, the Jimmy Yanceys and the thousand and one Negro musicians and singers whose contributions to jazz all the world seems to rave over except their own people.

Today there are just a handful of Negro writers who profess to write or lecture on jazz. They are Prof. Sterling Brown of Howard University, pinup cartoonist E. Simms Campbell, Prof. Lawrence Riddick, former curator at the Atlanta University, W. C. Handy,

"Father of the Blues," and the poet, Langston Hughes . . . Of the group, only Mr. Handy and Langston Hughes are known to have written any books on jazz.

The late James Welden Johnson, poet and onetime NAACP executive secretary, wrote incidentally of jazz in his book, "Black Manhattan." Roi Ottley merely named some names of jazzmen in "New World A-Comin'." The late Dr. Carter G. Woodson, eminent historian, paid little attention to the subject.

Hughes did a very good job on his "The First Book of Jazz" (Franklin Watts, $1.95) published last February. It at least showed he was thinking of the situation in which the hundreds of so-called Negro writers skip one of the most significant aspects of Negro history and folklore mainly because they are too lazy or are afraid of writing something their friends at the corner bar might sneer at as being "low brow stuff" or "things we are trying to get away from."

The famous poet evidently realizes that there are enough biographies around right now to fill several hundred books if only some of the Negro writers would put down their cocktail glasses and got busy researching the lives of contemporary singers and musicians.

Meanwhile, the white musicologists are going into Negro neighborhoods, homes, and back alleys digging up the story of jazz from those who created it who are considered in such a bad light by their own people that they have no one else to impart their precious information to but the whites.

The writers who would like to do something on the subject, get lost in worrying about who will publish it. Without writing a line, they spend their time worrying about a publisher which should be the last problem instead of the first. One of these days, Negroes are going to wake up but it'll be too late for the horse will have already been stolen and the barn door shut. (Guy Booker, "Colored Historians Too Lazy to Write Own History of Jazz; Let Whites Do It," *Philadelphia Tribune,* weekly magazine section, August 13, 1955)

Billy Taylor heated up the debate in 1957 with the following essay. As the producer of occasional jazz profiles for CBS-TV's "Sunday Morning," as an important voice (literally) in jazz radio since the early 1960s (I grew up with his programs), as the director of jazz events at the Kennedy Center, and as a guest of honor at numerous conferences, Taylor is one of the most visible figures in jazz. With all this activity, one tends to forget that he is also a significant and accomplished jazz pianist who has worked with Dizzy Gillespie, Charlie Parker and virtually every other jazz great, including Stuff Smith, by the way. One of his groundbreaking contributions that signaled Taylor would be more than just a performer was his outspoken article below. He notes with appreciation white fans' and critics' support of jazz, but he loudly protests the lack of support for the music from black audiences and the near absence of black experts on jazz history. In the process, he also provides a good overview of the jazz scene at that time.

Negroes Don't Know Anything About Jazz

Billy Taylor

Strange as it sounds, American Negroes who created jazz music, today hardly know anything about it. You'll find this just as true among the musicians who play jazz in order to earn a living as you will among those who play just for kicks. Only a handful are well enough informed on the subject to discuss it intelligently with anyone except other musicians in their own narrow circles.

It is just amazing how uninformed many top performers are about the historical background of the music they use as a medium of expression.

Semantics has become a fashionable word of late. And nowhere is the word more overworked than in jazz circles, where all kinds of semantic acrobatics are being performed by self-styled experts, critics and other writers on jazz. Frankly, the semantics of jazz annoy me! Such words as "hot," "bop," "progressive," "funky," "East Coast" and "West Coast" mean one thing to one person and something else to another. Actually, these labels have done much to confuse the public about jazz. Much of the public is puzzled and is asking: "Is jazz really good music and do the musicians who play it have anything really important to say?"

Certainly, the men who created jazz had much to say. They were Negroes who found it impossible to voice their opinions verbally, so they devised their own way of playing to get the freedom of expression they were otherwise denied.

Today, however, jazz is no longer the exclusive medium of expression of the Negro.

As the Negro has become more articulate and outspoken, his music has reflected his growth. And in each stage of its development, jazz has become more and more the medium of expression of all types of Americans and, to a surprising degree, musicians from other lands and other cultures.

Contrary to popular conception, most of the popular jazzmen of today are serious-minded, creative artists who are trying to contribute something worth-while to the society in which they live. Men like John Lewis, Dave Brubeck, Quincy Jones and Shorty Rogers are typical of this kind of musician. But there are countless others who are also making very significant, though less publicized, contributions to jazz and to our culture. All of these musicians deserve recognition. They should be written about and listened to. They should be presented in concerts by Negro schools and other organizations who loudly proclaim their interest in enlightening our people. They should be accorded the dignity their stature as artists calls for.

Negro newspapers and magazines could be a big help in this respect, but it seems to me that most of the ones which do offer so many pictorial and written examples of the cultural achievements of Negroes in other fields, just cannot seem to find any jazz musicians to write about except the ones who use dope, drink excessively, have been arrested or have otherwise had trouble with the society in which they live.

And it also seems to me that our periodicals sometimes deliberately go out of their way to play up the personal failings of certain jazz musicians, thus continuing the ancient stereotype that jazz is bad music because of its past association with "vice," and since it is bad, everyone associated with it must consequently be bad. Writers who become livid with rage when this kind of thinking is applied to Negroes as a race, think nothing of going along with the "they're all alike, those jazz musicians" way of thinking in their own writings.

To me, this attitude by Negro editors seems completely unreasonable. To continue blasting against the old moving-picture stereotype of

Negroes stealing chickens, toting razors, grinning and shuffling about and acting like "Uncle Toms" is standard procedure in most Negro periodicals, and I for one would like to see the same efforts extended to the music Negroes originated. By not doing this, I think these editors are shirking their responsibility as molders of the public opinion.

Today's Negro should at least be given a clear-cut idea of the importance of jazz as a contribution to American culture. There seem to be only a very few Negroes interested enough to write seriously on jazz topics. Library shelves are almost bare of books authored by Negroes on jazz. Langston Hughes, with his *Primer of Jazz,* has made a start in this direction, but there is a world of material not yet touched. At least some of this documentation should be done by Negroes.

Classes in jazz appreciation and jazz technique have long been conducted in many major U.S. colleges and universities, but I haven't heard of any such courses being even mentioned in our Negro institutions of higher learning.

Negro high schools and colleges which could do much to make promising young jazz musicians aware of their potential aren't doing it and haven't even tried! They could show these budding players the achievements of their predecessors in the field and offer them encouragement and guidance instead of, as in too many instances, treating such students as odd characters and putting them on the defensive by frustrating their attempts to practice and perform for their fellow students.

As a jazz musician with a personal stake in the future of the music I play, I would like to see the musicians who come along after me well trained and well prepared for the life and career they expect to follow.

They could get this training and guidance if schools of the caliber of Virginia State College, Howard University, Tuskegee and Hampton Institutes, Texas Southern University, Morgan State College and Atlanta University would introduce courses on jazz into their curricula. These courses should, of course, be taught by musicians who have not only been trained to teach, but who also have had practical experience playing jazz.

This suggestion isn't as far-fetched as it may sound. There are thousands of well-trained musicians who have played with top-flight jazz units who would welcome the opportunity to work at a first-rate school training and giving these youngsters the benefit of their experiences and a clear-cut insight into their musical heritage.

Somehow, we've got to make Negroes more aware and appreciative of what jazz has meant and still means to the advancement of the race. Writers like Hugues Panassie, Robert Goffin, Alan Lomax, Leonard Feather, Rudi Blesh, Charles E. Smith, Mike Levin, Barry Ulanov and Sidney Finklestein have done much to start the ball rolling in this direction, and, of course, others too numerous to mention also have written much on the subject—but where are the Negro writers who could be writing about not only yesterday's greats but today's greats as well? Will Negro writers be content to let writers like Nat Hentoff, Bill Coss, Marshall Stearns, Whitney Balliett, Orrin Keepnews and the other interested and talented white writers tell the whole story of jazz? Don't they have anything to say as Negroes?

What needs to be done right now is to instill in more Negroes a sense of pride in the accomplishments of their own music. In many ways, jazz has done more to break down the color line between the white and colored races, I would say, than religion, and it was way ahead of sports in blazing the path to firmer friendships and understanding between the races. Where are the Negro priests and ministers who could take an active part in showing the good that jazz has done? Where are the Negro counterparts to Father Norman O'Connor and Reverend Alvin Kershaw [ministers who promoted jazz]?

The startling discovery way back in the early days of jazz that good music knows no color line has worked for the better ever since. Today in recording studios across the country, colored and white musicians put on tape for posterity the best efforts of their combined talents. Negro and white musicians tour all over the country in jazz shows and even perform side by side in the South.

But it is surprising to note that the percentage of white jazz fans is considerably higher than the percentage of Negro jazz fans. Surely a musician like Duke Ellington, with his great compositions and his great orchestras, has done enough to advance the cause of Negroes as a race to warrant the same enthusiasm and support which we give to Jackie Robinson and our other great athletes.

It is an accepted fact that jazz is more popular today than it has ever been. It is possible for more people to hear it, and today, more than ever before, it is being presented as an art form in concerts and in supper clubs designed for listening. Even the U.S. State Department is sending jazz groups all over the world to give concerts under its auspices and is presenting a daily jazz program on the *Voice of America*.

Jazz festivals, forums and seminars are being organized on a larger scale than ever before. Jazz is being analyzed, studied and played at such famous resorts as the Music Inn at Lenox, Mass., and at Newport, Rhode Island. Concerts are regularly scheduled at such temples of music as New York's Carnegie Hall, Philadelphia's Academy of Music, Chicago's Ravinia Park, the Hollywood Bowl in Los Angeles, the Civic Opera House in Chicago, and elsewhere. A pitifully few of those concerts are sponsored by Negroes and Negro organizations.

Most Negro school kids respond to jazz. They dance to it, listen to it, argue about it and collect it on records. But their knowledge of the music is much too incomplete. One reason for this lack of knowledge is the fact that they can't hear many of the best jazz musicians perform in person. Negro theaters, like New York's Apollo, rarely offer a show composed solidly of top jazz talent, and they say that this is because there is no demand for such a show. Negro night clubs offer the same answer when asked why they don't present jazz to their clientele.

I have lectured to groups and spoken privately to many Negroes who could learn to understand and love the music which some of their not-so-distant relatives helped bring into being. These are intelligent and mature individuals as well as excited kids who are listening for more in the music they enjoy than the frenzy of a drum beat and a twanging guitar. And because their interest has been aroused they are being given a better idea of the tremendous impact jazz has made, not only in this country, but all over the world.

It would indeed be wonderful if the American public could be made aware through every medium possible that jazz is a contribution to American culture of which we can be justly proud.

Most of us who are active in jazz circles today are sincerely trying to express through our music our emotions, attitudes and thoughts on many varied subjects. Some of us raise our voices in protest over problems and situations which disturb us, while others among us are more concerned with the age-old search for truth and beauty. If we are to be heard, we must be supported by people who understand and love our music. I, for one, sincerely believe that more of this support should come from members of my race. (Billy Taylor, "Negroes Don't know Anything about Jazz," originally in *Duke Magazine*, August 1957)

As a follow-up to Taylor's piece, let's look briefly at a report in *Ebony* some thirty years later.

During his last visit to a large Mid-western city, legendary drummer Max Roach made a personal appearance at a downtown record store to promote his latest release. The place was packed with fans, most of them White. However, when he appeared at three record stores in the city's Black community, only about 10 people showed up.

For Roach, who has been a major figure in jazz for more than 40 years, such incidents may be disheartening, but they aren't really surprising. For more than a decade, Black jazz artists and aficionados alike have been concerned about the apparent lack of appreciation of the art among some Blacks. They cite the predominantly White audiences, the inadequate airplay on Black radio stations, the low record sales compared to other forms of music, and the general underexposure to jazz, particularly among younger Blacks. . . .

Though jazz studies programs, concerts and jazz bands and orchestras are now common on many college campuses, some of the largest, best-funded programs are at predominantly White institutions.

Jazz is rarely given equal time on Black-oriented radio stations. There are also stations that confuse the issue by erroneously labeling pop instrumentals as jazz. Ms. [Betty] Carter says, "A lot of young disc jockeys don't know what jazz is themselves. They play what they call 'fusion' and 'new-age' jazz, eliminating a lot of good, hard-working jazz artists." (Marilyn Marshall, "Are Blacks Giving Away Jazz?" *Ebony*, February 1988)

Although such new forms of jazz as "fusion" had evolved, the perceived problem of blacks' insufficient support of jazz persisted, as the reader can see. In my opinion, African American support for jazz is slightly greater than that of the nonblack population. For one thing, young black artists continue to emerge into the national consciousness. In addition, there are bars and nightclubs in most black neighborhoods that feature local artists who do not have a national following. Although there are fewer such venues than there used to be, they do exist, and every African American community has its local jazz legends. But patronage of local artists does not count in surveys of jazz audiences. Conversely, the nightclubs and concert halls that feature national stars are so expensive that they may be out of reach for many black fans.

Surveys conducted by the National Endowment for the Arts in 1982 and 1985 showed that blacks were more likely to describe themselves as jazz fans than were nonblacks. Unfortunately these surveys didn't ask respondents to name the artists they liked. One of the complaints voiced above is that blacks who do like jazz may only be familiar with contemporary pop-oriented jazz—the controversial "fusion" that we'll discuss in the next chapter. And it is certainly true that most young blacks, like most young whites, prefer popular music to any kind of jazz—it's called "popular" music because it's what most people prefer. But black support of jazz is a bit greater than is generally recognized. Still, among jazz aficionados, the debate continues: Do African Americans have a special mission, an obligation, to support jazz in higher percentages because it is an important part of their culture and history?

There was little debate among African Americans about the need for civil rights, increasingly a concern of the black press since World War II. By the 1960s, dialogue between blacks and whites in U.S. society had become heated and burst into the media. This exchange happened in the jazz field as well and spilled over into the pages of the music magazines. In 1962 *Down Beat's* editor decided to focus on the race issue after Ira Gitler gave a negative review for vocalist Abbey Lincoln's album *Straight Ahead* because he felt she was pushing a political message too stridently. As Gitler put it, "I dislike propaganda in art when it is a device. . . . The notes state that part of her liberation as a singer 'has come from renewed and urgent pride in herself as a Negro.' The only trouble is that she has become a 'professional Negro.' . . . She is involved in African nationalism without realizing that the African Negro doesn't give a fig for the American Negro. . . . Pride in one's heritage is one thing, but we don't need the Elijah Muhammad type of thinking in jazz. . . . Now that Abbey Lincoln has found herself as a Negro, I hope she can find herself as a militant but less one-sided *American* Negro" (*Down Beat*, November 9, 1961, pp. 35–36). This review prompted a freewheeling discussion that got into the whole topic of prejudice in and outside jazz. Some excerpts follow.

The growth of ill feeling—based on racial differences—between Negro and white jazzmen has become distasteful to most, alarming to some. A few self-proclaimed oracles have warned that ill feeling would lead to strict separateness and eventually kill jazz. But these are the few; the many recognize the situation as one that will be resolved with understanding on both sides.

Down Beat invited [singer] Abbey Lincoln, [drummer] Max Roach, [critic] Ira Gitler, [trumpeter] Don Ellis, [pianist] Lalo Schifrin and [critic-producer] Nat Hentoff to meet with [*Down Beat's*] Bill Coss and Don DeMicheal to air the situation. Much of the ensuing conversation revolved around Gitler's review of Miss Lincoln's Candid album *Straight Ahead*. . . .

Hentoff: . . . I think the key thing in your review that I'd like to know how you can defend is the term "professional Negro." This really is the worst kind of epithet because it immediately implies falseness, dishonesty. I think you really have to have your facts before you can say this about anybody. I think there are professional Negroes—there are professional Jews, there are professional civil libertarians, there are professional Goldwaterites. But it's a rough charge.

Gitler: I felt she was leaning too much on her Negritude in this album. . . .

Miss Lincoln: How could you have listened to it that objectively since you had come to the conclusion that I was a racist? You automatically could not possibly have listened to the music objectively.

Gitler: I don't think you are a racist.

Miss Lincoln: You did say that in essence.

Gitler: I said Elijah Muhammad type of thinking and only implied by that that I don't want a separation of black and white. I want to keep the two together in jazz.

Miss Lincoln: Well, that's your problem, not mine.

Gitler: That's my opinion, not a problem.

Roach: It's the social problem of this country. . . .

Miss Lincoln: . . . And I'll tell you something. You know when I *was* a professional Negro nobody seemed to mind. . . . There was a time when I was *really* a professional Negro. I was capitalizing on the fact that I was a Negro, and I looked the way Western people expect you to look. I wore ridiculous dresses, and I sang the songs that were expected. I was a professional Negro. I was not an artist. I had nothing to say. I used innane, stupid material on the stage. And as soon as I said, "I don't want to do this anymore; I want to give the best that I have to the public," they came down on me with all four feet.

. . . I'm not that idiotic that I'd dislike people because of the color of their skin. I dislike what white people have done to my people. Intensely.

DeMicheal: This brings up a point that has bothered me for some time. We might as well use the term Crow Jim [reverse racism]. To me, a lot of the Negro jazzmen have limited the people that they say swing—the people they will hire—to Negroes. They will say white guys don't swing, don't play jazz, and they have stolen our music.

Miss Lincoln: And they have.

DeMicheal: They haven't. I don't agree with you there. . . .

Roach: . . . That's a social subject, this Crow Jim, and everybody has such a wrong attitude about it. They think the guys are shutting them out, but if a guy wants a *good* jazz player, nine times out of 10 he stands a better chance of getting him from the black population than from the white population because of exposure.

DeMicheal: You're saying we are products of our social environment; therefore jazz is learned. Why would a Negro boy learn jazz better than a white boy?

Roach: My son—he listens to records all day. From before he was born—in his mother's belly—that's all he's been hearing.

DeMicheal: So has my son.

Roach: All right. Then he stands a chance.

. . . .

Miss Lincoln: Don, I don't believe there's such a thing as Crow Jim. You know what Jim Crow is? Jim Crow makes it impossible for the black man to function in this country to the capacity that he should. Now you cannot possibly tell me that because certain Negro musicians hire the few . . . First, there's not that much work. A white musician can always get a job. . . .

DeMicheal: Wait a minute. Let me say something about Ira [Sullivan] [trumpeter and a saxophonist]. Ira has not been able to work much in the last two years because he has always worked with Negro musicians, mostly on the south side of Chicago, and now those guys won't hire him because he's white. Now, you explain that. . . .

Roach: It's not just toward Ira. It's toward all white people . . . It's directed. So Ira now becomes an outsider, even though they realize who Ira is . . . Now, this is the time for Ira to get all white musicians, because now there is just too much hostility over there for him to enjoy himself, not against him personally, but against the white settlement now. That's what's happening in Chicago. Don't you know the ferment of the people? Do you feel it? The black people of this country have taken on a different role as far as the social scene is concerned. . . .

Miss Lincoln: . . . [W]e are not the ones who have done this. The black man is so eager to integrate that it makes me sick. He's eager for anything he can integrate into. It's the white man who doesn't want to integrate. Do I want to integrate? Not necessarily. Integrate into what? Why do I necessarily have to want to integrate? I have been refused all this time. Maybe I have decided I like being with my own people. Do you believe you have the right to tell me I must integrate with people who have always abused me and looked at me askance . . .? ("Racial Prejudice in Jazz," panel discussion, *Down Beat*, March 15, 1962)

By 1965 Archie Shepp had angrily entered the debate. Shepp, born in 1937, has been on the music faculty at the University of Massachusetts in Amherst since the 1970s, but he had to push through plenty of resistance to get there. A respected saxophonist, composer, and playwright, Shepp's work has always had a warmth, lyricism, and humor not always associated with the avant-garde, so in a way it is surprising that he had such a hard time getting recognized. John Coltrane helped promote Shepp's career in 1965, but the critics continued to be tough on Shepp. By the end of that year he wrote a defiant and poetic piece about how he felt.

An Artist Speaks Bluntly

ARCHIE SHEPP

I address myself to bigots—those who are so inadvertently, those who are cold and premeditated with it. I address myself to those "in" white hipsters who think niggers never had it so good (Crow Jim) and that it's time something was done about restoring the traditional privileges that have always accrued to the whites exclusively (Jim Crow). I address myself to sensitive chauvinists—the greater part of the white intelligentsia—and the insensitive, with whom the former have this in common: the uneasy awareness that "Jass" is an ofay's word for a nigger's music (*viz.* Duke and Pulitzer). [Ellington was denied a Pulitzer.]

I address myself to George Russell, a man whose work I have always respected and admired, who in an inopportune moment with an ill-chosen phrase threw himself squarely into the enemy camp. I address myself to Leonard Feather, who was quick to exploit that phrase and a few others, and who has asked me to be in his *Encyclopedia of Jazz* (I prefer to be in *Who's Who;* they at least know that reference works are about men and not the reverse). I address myself to Buck Walmsley, to Don DeMicheal and Dan Morgenstern, in short, to that entire "critical community" that has had far more access to this and other media of communication than I and fellows of my sort.

Allow me to say that I am—with men of other complexions, dispositions, etc.—about Art. I have about 15 years of dues-paying—others have spent more—which permits me to speak with some authority about the crude stables (clubs) where black men are groomed and paced like thoroughbreds to run till they bleed or else are hacked up outright for Lepage's glue. I am about 28 years in these United States, which, in my estimation is one of the most vicious, racist social systems in the world—with the possible exceptions of Northern Rhodesia, South Africa, and South Viet Nam.

I am, for the moment, a helpless witness to the bloody massacre of my people on streets that run from Hayneville through Harlem. I watch them die. I pray that I don't die. I've seen the once children—now men of my youth get down on scag, shoot it in the fingers, and then expire on frozen tenement roofs or in solitary basements, where all our frantic thoughts raced to the same desperate conclusion: "I'm sorry it was him; glad it wasn't me."

I have seen the tragedy of perennially starving families, my own. I am that tragedy. I am the host of the dead: Bird, Billie, Ernie, Sonny, whom you, white America, murdered out of a systematic and unloving disregard. I am a nigger shooting heroin at 15 and dead at 35 with hog's head cheeses for arms and horse for blood.

But I am more than the images you superimpose on me, the despair that you inflict. I am the persistent insistence of the human heart to be free. I wish to regain that cherished dignity that was always mine. My esthetic answer to your lies about me is a simple one: you can no longer defer my dream. I'm gonna sing it. Dance it. Scream it. And if need be, I'll steal it from this very earth.

Get down with me, white folks. Go where I go. But think this: injustice is rife. Fear of the truth will out. The murder of James Powell, the slaughter of 30 Negroes in Watts, the wake of Chu-Lai are crimes that would make God's left eye jump. That establishment that owns the pitifully little that is left of me can absolve itself only through the creation of equitable relationships among all men, or else the world will create for itself new relationships that exclude the entrepreneur and the procurer.

Some of you are becoming a little frightened that we—niggers— ain't keepin' this thing simple enough. "The sound of surprise"? Man, you don't want no surprises from me.

How do I know that?

Give me leave to state this unequivocal fact: jazz is the product of the whites—the ofays—too often my enemy. It is the progeny of the blacks—my kinsmen. By this I mean: you own the music, and we make it. By definition, then, you own the people who make the music.

You own us in whole chunks of flesh. When you dig deep inside our already disemboweled corpses and come up with a solitary diamond—because you don't want to flood the market—how different are you from the DeBeers of South Africa or the profligates who fleeced the Gold Coast? All right, there are niggers with a million dollars but ain't no nigger got a *billion* dollars.

I give you, then, my brains back, America. You have had them before, as you had my father's, as you took my mother's: in outhouses, under the back porch, next to black snakes who should have bitten you then.

I ask only: don't you ever wonder just what my collective rage will—as it surely must—be like, when it is—as it inevitably will be—unleashed? Our vindication will be black as the color of suffering is black, as Fidel is black, as Ho Chi Minh is black. It is thus that I offer my right hand across the worlds of suffering to black compatriots everywhere. When they fall victim to war, disease, poverty—all systematically enforced—I fall with them, and I am a yellow skin, and they are black like me or even white. For them and me I offer this prayer, that this 28th year of mine will never again find us all so poor, nor the rapine forces of the world in such sanguinary circumstances.

And you can tell Ira Gitler that he is a fool. "Repelled flies" indeed! What a thing it is to play God, snuff out yet born professional lives with impunity—worse, ignorance.

To Walmsley: one of the most thrilling musical experiences of my life was to play for the people of Chicago. You know it was amid cries of "MORE" that we were reluctantly allowed to leave that stage that night. You didn't seem to be able to muster the journalistic honesty to report that, though. Perhaps the jeers you heard were produced in that crabbed, frightened illogicality of your own post-R&B consciousness. Your patent opinions were predictable, your tastes alarmingly similar: Stanley, Woody, and Gary.

I leave you with this for what it's worth. I am an antifascist artist. My music is functional. I play about the death of me by you. I exult in the life of me in spite of you. I give some of that life to you whenever you listen to me, which right now is never. My music is for the people. If you are a bourgeois, then you must listen to it on my terms. I will not let you misconstrue me. That era is over. If my music doesn't suffice, I will write you a poem, a play. I will say to you in every instance, "Strike the Ghetto. Let my people go." (Archie Shepp, "An Artist Speaks Bluntly," *Down Beat*, December 16, 1965)

In the same issue as Shepp's piece, Leonard Feather wrote a column about an ongoing exchange about race among critics in another magazine, *Jazz*. His wide-ranging response compares the volleys over race to the debates surrounding bebop in the 1940s, and Feather admits that as an advocate of bop he was guilty then of overreacting, by defending bebop at the expense of earlier jazz.

A Plea for Less Critical Infighting, More Attention to the Music Itself
LEONARD FEATHER

There has been a resurgence in recent months of a brand of literary wrangling that should have been extinguished permanently with the moldy figs-vs.-beboppers nonsense of the 1940s.

Jazz criticism, at best, like all forms of criticism, is a parasitical and totally dependent occupation. Without the powerful engine of art, the caboose of criticism would grind to an immediate halt. Yet one finds constantly that several of the better-known jazz writers, or at least those among them who are concerned more with abstractions than with the realities of the music itself, use their time not so much to listen to jazz as to turn the art into a literary soapbox.

Lately, in the pages of another jazz magazine, I found a rather pathetic series of endless tirades in the letters-to-the-editor department. I am not singling out the magazine for any blame in the matter; as you know, the same sort of nonsense has been going on in this magazine, but with at least a modicum of moderation and rationality.

The letters all bore such headlines as "Frank Kofsky to Ira Gitler," "Martin Williams to Frank Kofsky," and they accomplished about as much for the advancement of jazz as an evening with Lawrence Welk. The tone was generally abusive, petty, pretentious, and, of course, nitpicking. It would have been funny if it had not all been so deadly serious in intent.

Many readers of *Down Beat* are too young to recall that when jazz made a major step forward with the arrival of bebop, this same sort of thing was going on. While I was using the pages of *Metronome* for feature stories on Dizzy Gillespie, Boyd Raeburn, and their contemporaries, Nat Hentoff in Boston was on the air denouncing Gillespie, Raeburn, et al., as cold, unemotional, and harmful to the future of jazz.

But the argument did not end there. Both sides were on the offensive as well as the defensive; both camps were slinging as much mud as they were receiving, thereby canceling out the value of whatever arguments they were trying to promulgate.

While Ralph Gleason and George Avakian were jumping on me for daring to claim that Charlie Parker and Gillespie were even jazzmen at all, let alone great jazzmen, I was wasting time needlessly denouncing as charlatans some innocuous and ineffectual old men of New Orleans whom the moldy figs had resurrected and who, to them, represented the only true jazz.

All of us were equally guilty of senselessly using up print with these silly squabbles; we should have realized that only time would determine the value of Dizzy's contribution and of Bunk Johnson's. All that came of the disputes was that a great deal of ill will was engendered.

Today the arguments tend to revolve around racial matters. Two or three white critics are trying desperately to prove, to Negro musicians, that they are totally in sympathy with the separationist theory. They want to show that they think just like soul brothers, that to all intents and purposes they *are* soul brothers. I do not believe that Negro musicians are naive enough to fall for such flagrant sycophancy. They are more likely to trust a man with whom they can agree on some points, disagree during a mutually stimulating polemic on others, and wind up shaking hands.

Note to all you white critics who want to identify with the Negro:

It isn't going to help to rail and rant about the white power structure. It isn't enough to show your sympathy by shedding crocodile tears for Malcolm X. Protest all you like concerning your disaffection from the white world and all its twisted values, there is still only one qualification that will get you by: be born black. Aren't you a little late for that?

Some of the critics who today are embroiled in angry debate over the social revolution of our decade are beginning to lose sight of the central reality out of which their entire racial postures took shape: the love and beauty and brotherhood inherent in the music itself.

The same argument applies to other forms of childishly pseudo-intellectual divagations along nonracial lines (in one of those letters I saw a reference to "the hypothesis of Heliocentricism"). All this is a million light-years away from the actual notes and chords and modes and rhythms of jazz.

I never yet have met a musician who takes these brawls seriously; I am not sure I have even met one who has read any of these diatribes. If he were ever to be caught helpless in a bus between one-nighters with nothing else to read, his reaction probably could be boiled down to that classic phrase that has been used as a squelcher ever since jazz (and the digressions from it) began:

"Play the music, man!" (Leonard Feather, "A Plea for Less Critical Infighting . . . ," *Down Beat,* December 16, 1965)

10

Avant-garde and Fusion: Two Opposites? 1960 to the Present

Both *avant-garde* and *fusion* are still controversial within the jazz community. A notorious case in point is Wynton Marsalis's policy for Lincoln Center's jazz program: he usually excludes both. Both types of music push the boundaries of jazz, forcing us to reconsider the question, "What is *jazz?*" Let's take each term in turn, making an effort to define each and to understand the debate that each inspires.

The current jazz avant-garde originated in the works that Ornette Coleman, John Coltrane, pianist Cecil Taylor, and others were creating around 1960. Each musician develops his own approach, but they all break out of the common preconceptions of jazz. They may perform without relying on a given chord progression, or without the steady beat provided by a walking bass. There really is no perfect term for this music. The term *avant-garde* is related historically to the advance guard or front rank of an army, and to the word *vanguard*. It is often applied to artists of all genres, and suggests that if these are the front rank, everyone else will eventually follow suit. But time has proven that, unlike the revolutions of Louis Armstrong (which was not contentious) or Charlie Parker (which was hotly disputed), this 1960s revolution never became the norm, nor will it ever be. *Experimental* suggests something unfinished, possibly unsuccessful; *new* no longer applies; and so on. So avant-garde will have to do, for now at least.

Billy Taylor and vocalist and composer Betty Carter felt that avant-garde jazz had turned off black listeners.

In the '50s and '60s, the music form continued to move in other directions, most notably toward "free" jazz, which took improvisation to the highest degree with its loosely structured rhythms. Some jazz devotees say that period was when the problem began. "Many musicians were experimenting with abstract techniques," says Billy Taylor, "and they played music that was not accessible."

Ms. Carter agrees. "Some of the music turned off Black listeners, because it had no beat or pulse," she says. "But this is what Black people love: to pat their feet and move their heads. I can't blame this [the movement away from jazz] on the audience. I blame it on the music, which didn't have any Black rhythms." She adds, "We had people thinking they had to be intellectuals to understand the music, and that's not true. We understood Charlie Parker's music, and Duke's music and Monk's music." (Marilyn Marshall, "Are Blacks Giving Away Jazz?" *Ebony*, February 1988)

Imamu Amiri Baraka, then known as LeRoi Jones, recognized the existence of a jazz avant-garde as early as September 1961. Baraka is a vital force in literature as a poet, dramatist, and essayist, and he often performs (and has recorded) with jazz musicians. In this essay he helps the reader think about the need for an avant-garde and to focus on the elements that make these players sound different from the norm.

The Jazz Avant Garde

LEROI JONES

There is definitely an "avant garde" in jazz today. A burgeoning group of young men who are beginning to utilize not only the most important ideas in "formal" contemporary music, but more important, young musicians who have started to utilize the most important ideas contained in that startling music called BeBop. (Of course I realize that to some of my learned colleagues almost anything that came after 1940 is BeBop, but that's not exactly what I meant.) And I think this last idea, the use of Bop, is the most significant aspect of the particular avantgarde I'm referring to, since almost any so called modern musicians can tell you all about Stravinsky, Schoenberg, Bartók, etc., or at least they think they can. I say *particular* avant garde since I realize that there is also another so called "new music," called by some of my more serious colleagues, *Third Stream,* which seeks to invest jazz with as much "classical" music as blatantly as possible. But for jazzmen now to have come to the beautiful and logical conclusion that BeBop was perhaps the most legitimately complex, emotionally rich music to come out of this country, is, for me, a brilliant beginning for a "new" music.

BeBop is roots, now, just as much as blues is. "Classical" music is not. But "classical" music, and I mean now contemporary Euro-American "art" music, definitely can and should be "milked" for as many *definitions* as possible, i.e., *solutions* to engineering problems the contemporary jazz musician's life is sure to raise. I mean, more simply, Ornette Coleman has had to live with the attitudes responsible for Anton Webern's music whether he knows that music or not. They were handed to him along with the whole history of formal Western music, and the musics that have come to characterize the Negro in the United States came to exist as they do today only through the acculturation of this entire history. And actually knowing that history, or those formal Euro-American musics, only adds to the indoctrination. But jazz and blues *are* Western musics; products of a Euro-American culture.

We are, all of us, *moderns,* whether we like it or not. Ruby Braff is *responsible,* finally, to the same ideas and attitudes that have shaped our world as Ornette Coleman. (Ideas are things that must drench everyone, whether directly or obliquely). The same history has elapsed in the world for both of them, and what has gone before has settled on both of them just as surely as if they were the same man. For Ornette Coleman, as it was for Charlie Parker *or* James Joyce, the relationship between their actual lives and their work seems direct. For Braff or for Charlie Parker and Bud Powell imitators or Senator Goldwater, the relationship, the meaning, of all the ideas that history has stacked so wearily in front of them, and some utilization in their own lives, is less direct. But if an atomic bomb is dropped on Manhattan, moldy figs will die as well as modernists, and just because some cornet player looks out his window and says "what's going on" does not mean that he will not be in on things. He goes too. (I am trying to explain "avant garde." Men for whom history exists to be *utilized* in their lives, their art, to make something for themselves and not as an overpowering reminder that people and their ideas did live before us). And I am merely trying to stress the fact that I believe the formal music of Europe can be used by modern jazz musicians to solve *technical* problems. "How to play exactly what I feel," is what one of these musicians told me. How?

Before I go further, I want to explain "technical" so as not to be confused with people who think that Thelonious Monk is "a fine pianist, but limited technically" (which sounds like Roger Fry praising Giotto, above the Byzantines, for his "faithfulness to living features and incidents." Norman Rockwell is probably more "faithful" than Giotto ever was). But by *technical,* I mean more specifically being able to use what important ideas are contained in the residue of history. For instance, to be able to doubletime Liszt piano pieces might help one to become a musician, but it will not make a man aware of the fact that Bartók was a greater composer than Liszt. And it is the consciousness, on whatever level, of facts, ideas, etc., like this that are *the* most important part of technique. Knowing how to play an instrument is the barest superficiality if one is thinking of becoming a musician. It is the ideas that one utilizes *instinctively* that determine the degree of profundity any artist reaches. To know, in some way, that it is better to pay attention to Beethoven than to Aaron Copland is part of it. (And it is exactly because of his lack of instinctive profundity that someone like Oscar Peterson's technique *is* glibness. That he can play the piano rather handily just makes him easier to identify. There is no serious instinct working at all).

To my mind, *technique* is inseparable from what is finally played as content. A *bad* solo, no matter how "well" it is played is still *bad.*

APHORISMS: "Form can never be more than an extension of content." (Robert Creely). "Form is determined by the nature of matter. . . . Rightly viewed, order is nothing objective; it exists only relatively to the mind." (Psalidas). "No one who can finally be said to be a 'mediocre' musician can be said to possess any *technique*." (Jones).

"Formal" music, for the jazz musician, should be *ideas*. Ideas that can make it easier for this modern jazz player to get at his roots. And as I have said, the strongest of these roots are blues and what was called BeBop. They sit autonomous. (And I know BeBop couldn't have existed without Artie Shaw or the ODJB, but I don't think that's the point). Blues and BeBop are *musics*. They are understandable, emotionally, as they sit: without the barest discussion of their origins. And the reason I think for this is that they *are* origins, themselves. Blues is a beginning. BeBop, a beginning. They define other varieties of music that come after them. If a man had not heard blues there is no reason to assume that he would be even slightly interested in, say, Joe Oliver (except perhaps as a curio or from some obscure social conviction). Cannonball Adderley is *only* interesting because of BeBop. And not because he plays BeBop, but because he will occasionally repeat an idea that Bop once represented as profound. An idea that we love, no matter what the subsequent disfigurement.

The *roots,* blues and Bop, are emotion. The *technique* (issuing from life, which should include Europe's ruined minds and music lessons), the ideas. And this does not leave out the consideration that certainly there is pure intellect that can come out of the emotional experience and the rawest emotions that can proceed from the ideal apprehension of any hypothesis. The point is that such displacement must exist as instinct.

To go further towards a general delineation of the musicians I will cite later as part of a growing jazz avant garde, I think first I should furnish at least two more definitions, or distinctions.

Using, or implementing an idea or concept is not necessarily imitation, and, of course, the converse is true; imitation is not necessarily use. I will say first that use is proper, as well as *basic*. Use means that some idea or system is employed, but in order to reach or understand quite separate and dissimilar systems. Imitation means simply *reproduction* (of a concept), for its own sake. Someone who sings exactly like Billie

Holiday or someone who plays exactly like Charlie Parker (or as close as they can manage) *produce* nothing. Essentially there is nothing added to the universe. It is as if these performers stood on a stage and did nothing at all. Much of Lou Donaldson's work is the attempted reproduction of Charlie Parker's more accessible ideas. Ornette Coleman uses Parker only as a hypothesis; his (Coleman's) conclusions are quite separate and unique. Sonny Rollins has certainly listened quite a bit to Gene Ammons, but Rollins' conclusions are insistently his own, and are certainly more profound than Ammons'. A man who rides the IND to work doesn't necessarily have to think he's a subway. (And a man who thinks he's a subway is usually just crazy. It will not help him get to work either).

> **REEDS: Ornette Coleman, Eric Dolphy,** Wayne Shorter, Oliver Nelson, Archie Shepp.
>
> **BRASS: Don Cherry, Freddie Hubbard.**
>
> **PERCUSSION: Billy Higgins, Ed Blackwell,** Dennis Charles (drums); Earl Griffith (vibraharp).
>
> **BASS: Wilbur Ware, Charlie Haden,** Scott LaFaro, Buell Neidlinger, Chuck Israels, George Tucker, others.
>
> **PIANO: Cecil Taylor.**
>
> **COMPOSITION: Ornette Coleman, Eric Dolphy, Wayne Shorter,** Cecil Taylor.

These are most of the people this essay intends to hamper with the *nom de guerre* avant garde. (There are a few others like Ken McIntyre whom I think, from the reports I've received, also belong in the group, but I've not had a chance to listen yet). The names in boldface are intended to serve as further delineation as far as the quality and quantity of these players' innovations. Hence, Ornette Coleman sits by himself in the reeds, Dolphy in his groove, and Shorter, Nelson and Shepp in theirs. (There are more bass players than anything else simply because the chief innovator on that instrument, Wilbur Ware, has been around longer and more people have had a chance to pick up).

But actually, this naming of names is not meant as a strict categorizing of "styles." Each of these men have their *own* way of playing, but they represent, as a group, at least to me, a definite line of departure.

Melodically and rhythmically each of these players use BeBop extensively. Coleman's *Ramblin'* possesses a melodic line the spatial tensions
of which seem firmly rooted in 1940's Gillespie-Parker composition
and extemporization. The very jaggedness and abruptness of the
melodic fabric itself suggest the boppers' seemingly endless need for
deliberate and agitated rhythmical contrast, most of the melodies
being almost extensions of the dominating rhythmical patterns.
Whistle *Ramblin',* then any early Monk, e.g., *Four In One* or *Humph,*
or Bird's *Cheryl* or *Confirmation,* and the basic *physical* similarities of
the melodic lines should be immediately apparent. There seems to be
an endless changing of direction; stops and starts; variations of impetus; a "jaggedness" that reaches out of the rhythmic bases of the music.
(It seems to me that only Jackie McLean, of the post-bop "traditionalists," has as much linear contrast and rhythmic modulation in his compositions and playing as the boppers, e.g., *Dr. Jackle, Condition Blue,
etc.).* In fact, in bop and avant garde compositions it seems as if the
rhythmic portion of the music is inserted directly into the melodic portion. The melody of *Ramblin'* is almost a rhythmic pattern itself. Its
accents are almost identical to the rhythmic underpinnings of the
music. The same was true in Bop. The very name BeBop comes from
an onomatopoetic attempt to reproduce the new rhythms that had
engendered this music, hence; *BeBop,* and with that ReBop. (While it
is true that "scat" singing came into use in the early days of jazz, "bop-
ping," the kind of scat singing (scatting) that became popular during
the 40's was more intent on reproducing rhythmic effects and as such
making a melody out of them, e.g., *OoShubeeDobee Oo Oo* or
OoBopsh'bam-a-keukumop, etc. But even in the incunabula of jazz and
blues, something like the chants and field hollers were little more than
highly rhythmical lyrics).

One result of this "insertion" of rhythm into the melodic fabric of
Bop as well as the music of the avant garde is the subsequent freedom
allowed to instruments that are normally supposed to carry the entire
rhythmic impetus of the music. Drum and bass lines are literally
"sprung" . . . away from the simple, cloying 4/4 that characterized the
musics that came immediately before and after Bop. And while it is
true that the post-boppers took their impetus from Bop, I think the
development of the *Cool School* served to obscure the really valuable

legacies of Bop. Rhythmic diversity and freedom were the really valuable legacies. The cool tended to regularize the rhythms and make the melodic line smoother, less "jagged," relying more on "formal" variation of the line in the strict theme and variation sense. More and more emphasis was put on "charts" and written parts. Formal European music began to be canonized not only as a means but as some kind of *model*. The insistence of Brubeck, Shorty Rogers, Mulligan, John Lewis, that they could write fugues and rondoes or even improvise them was one instance. The almost legitimate harmonies that were used in Cool or West Coast Jazz reminded one of the part singing tradition of Europe. And groups like Shorty Rogers' Giants made a music that sounded like it came out of an organ grinder, the variations and improvisations as regular and static as a piano roll.

The "Hard Boppers" sought to revitalize jazz but they did not go far enough. Somehow, they had lost sight of the important items to be gotten from Bop and substituted largeness of timbre and the recent insistence on quasi-gospel influences for actual rhythmic diversity. The usual rhythms of the post-cool Hard Bopper of the 50's are amazingly static and smooth compared to the jazz of the 40's and the 60's. The rhythmic freedom of the 40's is lost in the 50's only to be rediscovered in the 60's. Because rhythm and melody complement each other so closely in the "new" music, both bass player and drummer also can play "melodically." They need no longer be strictly concerned with thumping along, merely carrying the beat. The melody itself contains enough rhythmic accent to propel and stabilize the horizontal movement of the music, giving both direction and impetus. The rhythm instruments can then serve to elaborate on the melody itself. Wilbur Ware's playing is a perfect example of this. And so it is that drummers like Blackwell, Higgins and Charles can roam around the melody, giving accent here, inferring actual melody elsewhere. Elvin Jones, in his recent work with John Coltrane, also shows that he understands the difference between playing melody and "elegant" elaboration around a static rhythm.

So if the heavily accented melody springs the rhythm section, it also gives the other soloists more room to swing. The strict 4/4 is missing, and the horn men can even improvise on the melodic efforts of the rhythm section. This is one reason why in a group like Coleman's it seems as if they have gone back to the concept of collective improvisations. No one's role in the group is as *fixed* as in the "part singers" of the 50's. Everyone has a chance to play melody or rhythm. Cecil Taylor's left hand is used as much as a purely rhythmic insistence as it is for the melodic-harmonic placement of chords. The left hand constantly varies the rhythms his music is hinged on. Both Taylor and Coleman constantly utilize melodic variations based on rhythmic figures. BeBop proved that so called "changes," i.e., the repeated occurrence of certain chords basic to the melodic and harmonic structure of a tune, are almost arbitrary. That is, that they need not be *stated,* and that since certain chords infer certain improvisatory uses of them, why not improvise on what the chords infer rather than playing the inference itself.

The greater part of the avant garde's contribution is melodic and rhythmic; only a few have made any notable moves harmonically, though Coleman and Dolphy tend to utilize certain ideas that are also in use in contemporary "European" music, notably, timbre as a harmonic principle. That is, where the actual sound of the horn, regardless of the note, contributes *unmeasured* harmonic diversity. (John Coltrane has done some marvelous work in harmonics as well). Nelson, Shepp and Shorter also, to a lesser degree, utilize this concept, and even stranger, Shorter and Nelson have learned to utilize the so called "honking" sounds of the rhythm and blues bands to great effect. Nothing was wrong with honking in the first place, except that most of the R&B people who honked did little else.

It is also important that all of the reed players I have named are intrigued by the sound of the human voice. And it is my idea that jazz cannot be removed too far from the voice, since the whole concept of Afro-American music is hinged on vocal references. Earlier, I mentioned my belief that BeBop and blues are almost autonomous musics. To add some weight, or at least provide a measure of clarification, I'd add that not only are blues and BeBop the two facets of Afro-American music that utilize the rhythmic potentials of the music most directly, but also they are the two musics in which the vocal traditions of African music are most apparent. Purely instrumental blues is still the closest western instruments can come to sounding like the human voice, and the horns of Charlie Parker, Sonny Rollins, John Coltrane, and most of the reed players of the new avant garde maintain this tradition as well. The timbres of these horns suggest the human voice much more than the legitimate "instrumental" sound of swing or the staid, relatively cool timbres that were in evidence post-bop.

I mention these general aspects of what I have termed the avant garde, i.e., their rhythmic and melodic concepts and the use of timbral effects to evoke the vocal beginnings of jazz, but only to show a line of demarcation. There are certainly a great many "new" features individual players possess that are not common to the group as a whole, individual discoveries and/or idiosyncracies that give each player his easily identifiable style. To name a few: the unusual harmonies that Wayne Shorter employs in his writing and his integration of Rollins' use of space and John Coltrane's disdain for it; (Shorter's main trouble, it now seems, is The Jazz Messengers). Vibist Earl Griffith's lovely discovery that one can play the vibes like Lester Young, instead of continuing to imitate Milt Jackson's appropriation of Coleman Hawkins; Griffith's light, gauzy tone, and behind-the-beat placement of his line all point to Pres and a fresh approach to vibes. Charlie Haden's guitar player approach to the bass, even going as far, sometimes, as *strumming* the big instrument; Don Cherry's fantastic melodic sense (I think that Cherry is the only *real* innovator on his instrument). Archie Shepp's refusal to admit most of the time that there is a melody or Oliver Nelson's use of R&B and so called "Mickey Mouse" timbres to beautiful effect. All these are separate facets of this new music, an amassing of talent and ideas that indicate a fresh road for jazz.

The first music Negroes made in this country had to be African; its subsequent transmutation into what we know as blues and the parallel development of jazz demonstrated the amazing flexibility of the basic character of the music. But to move as far away from the parent music as popular Swing, or so called West Coast jazz, or even into the artificially exciting, comparatively staid regular rhythms of hard bop traditionalism demonstrates how the African elements of the music can be rendered almost to neutrality. Blues was the initial Afro-American music, and BeBop the re-emphasis of the non-western tradition. And if the latter saved us from the vapid wastes of Swing, singlehandedly, the new avant garde (and John Coltrane) are saving us from the comparatively vapid 50's. And they both utilized the same general methods: getting the music back to its initial rhythmic impetuses, and away from the attempts at rhythmic regularity and melodic predictability that the 30's and the 50's had laid on it. (LeRoi Jones [Imamu Amiri Baraka], "The Jazz Avant-Garde," *Metronome*, September 1961)

The end of the preceding piece is a highly condensed preview of an important book that Baraka/Jones would publish in 1963. Entitled *Blues People* (New York: William Morrow), it was more about jazz than blues, but this was built on the idea he states above, that blues was the first truly African American music that was distinct from African music. In that last paragaph he also states his preference for a jazz that draws heavily on African American traditions and not as much from the classical traditions.

Down Beat used to publish a yearbook (the last was the 1980 edition), and *Down Beat Music '66* included a conversation about the avant-garde entitled "Point of Contact: A Discussion." The moderator, Dan Morgenstern (born in 1929), is a leading authority on jazz, a prolific author, and the director of the world's largest jazz archive, the Institute of Jazz Studies, at the Rutgers University campus in Newark, New Jersey. The panel he organized in 1966 included leading avant-gardists Cecil Taylor (pianist), Sonny Murray (drummer, associated with Taylor and others), and Archie Shepp, along with Roland Kirk, a wildly creative reedman who played in many contexts; Cannonball Adderley, one of the leading soloists of hard-driving jazz as well as an early pioneer in fusion; and finally, representing the business side of music, Art D'Lugoff, the respected owner of New York's Village Gate (now moved from its original location). The following excerpts begin with Roland Kirk commenting that "avant-garde," far from indicating defiance, has become just another marketing label in the music business, or another artifical way of separating one musician from another.

Kirk: . . . My words will be very simple, because I don't have the background or anything. We all talk about prejudice and black and white, but when I was back home in the Middle West, I never knew anything about the avant-garde or swing or . . . Only thing I knew about there was Dixieland and modern jazz. It sort of disgusts me that so many people are making it off the name "avant-garde musician." Because the thing is when I was in school, I wasn't taught by the white man that avant-garde was classical; I *heard* that avant-garde was classical when I heard Varèse, Stockhausen, and people like this. I can accept it that it would be a new kind of music to jazz, but to put the title "avant-garde" on it takes us into another area.

We shouldn't separate ourselves. For me to say Archie is better than me because he's "avant-garde" is wrong. Cecil cut a record around '59 with Coltrane and Kenny Dorham and a rhythm section that was playing 4/4. I don't know why he cut it, but he cut it. He played his same style, but I didn't look on him as an avant-garde musician; I looked on him as another piano player who was contributing. For us to hang ourselves up on this kind of thing, I think we're killing what we're trying to present. We're separating ourselves. We're doing what the white man wants us to do—separating ourselves from the music. Instead of all of us getting together and playing and accepting each other, we're getting farther away. I would like to play with Cannonball, and I'd like to play with Cecil. But if I come to Cecil, he would say, "You don't know my arrangements."

Everybody says, "It's freedom." If it's freedom, then I should be able to get up and play what I feel. So we're defeating our cause when we take this music we call jazz and say you have to be a certain kind of musician to play with each other. Like I'm conducting sessions down at the Village Vanguard on Mondays, and everybody comes with a group; nobody wants to play with each other. Like I say, "Man, let's play some things in B natural." And it's, "No, baby, I've got my group I want to play with."

What I'm saying is that we should all get together.

Later on, Shepp speaks out about the politics of class and race in the jazz business.

. . . I think that it has been too long the nature of such conversations that questions of class—economic, social classes, educational differences—have divided black men. Black men have been divided along class lines, and that's precisely what happened here—the question that Roland raised when he said you cats talked like the white man. But we don't mean to talk like the white man. Cecil's point was quite cogent when he said we were all fundamentally a product of white culture. Perhaps some of us talk more like the white man than others. . . . I want to answer a few things about what my neo-black bourgeois, middle-class thing may be—which is certainly not much, which is something I don't believe in, which I don't try to propagate, but which is rather something that's been handed to me. It certainly shouldn't be something to separate us now. I think the suggestions that Cecil raised are excellent ones, and I think the things he has suggested as the reasons for our oppression are precisely the point. That is—and I think Ball [Cannonball Adderly] mentioned the same things—that it is not musical differences but social and economic differences that separate us. This has been done, I think, by a class of people very much like Art. . . . I don't think that should be misconstrued. When I say this I don't mean that all white men are—as Cecil pointed out very clearly—a drag, or that all white men are my oppressors or that they *mean* to be my oppressors. I don't mean to say, Art, that you're the same man Max Gordon is or that Joe Termini is or that they are the same as you. Rather we are forced by dint of circumstance—you are a clubowner, I am a musician. Somehow there is this terrifying fact: you don't hire me—as much as you talk. And I'm going to ask you point blank, and I don't want an answer right now, I want a gig; my price is $850 a week, and I'm asking you for a job right now; I want to know when you are available, when you can hire me, and so on. Because I think any argument you make must be commensurate with that, that you hire people who are not known, and that if you believe so profoundly in jazz, that you work to see that other artists are heard from.

To Cannonball, let me say this: you're a man whose work I've followed, before I considered myself knowing how to play the saxophone. I remember when you played *The Song Is You* and *Willow, Weep for Me*. I own some of your records; I'm not just talking in a vacuum. But I don't think that you're being quite fair to Cecil when you make those separations. The outstanding thing that came out in the discussion between you and Cecil and Roland were the regional differences. They were the differences of class, of North and South, of differences in educational standards, of differences in money, of the black bourgeois vs. the country boy. . . .

Finally D'Lugoff defends himself, saying that he hires anybody he likes, black or white, but that he has to be mindful of the financial concerns:

D'Lugoff: To Archie Shepp and Cecil Taylor, I say . . . I feel that many of the artists have a right to be heard. I think, though, that they're barking up the wrong tree. I think they are accusing the wrong people. I think— not that they're untalented, because they are talented; not just because they're black, because there are many black people who work, unless they're willing to say the black people who do work have sold out. . . . What can I say when my club hires 80 percent colored? . . . I don't hire them because they're colored. I hire them because they have something to say, and they reach an audience. I don't say the audience is right. I don't say my taste is impeccable. All I say to you is I try to make a living and do a creative act. I don't say that I don't make mistakes. I don't say the people who work sometimes don't make mistakes; I'm willing to take them back. But one thing: am I entitled to make a living for myself and the people who work there? Well, people can say, "Of course." But I think in view of the fact that many clubs are failing, am I entitled to ask that? . . . I'm talking not as a nice white guy but as a nice human being. We're all born and we don't choose our parents. And white racists and black racists better learn that.

Shepp: There are no black racists.

D'Lugoff: There are black racists and there are yellow racists and there are white racists. And I want to tell you something. . . .

Taylor: And the white racists have most of the money.

D'Lugoff: That's right. But I'm not one of them, baby. ("Point of Contact: A Discussion," moderated by Dan Morgenstern, *Down Beat Music '66,* 1966)

Financial concerns were becoming a major issue in jazz in the mid-1960s. Concurrent with the avant-garde movement in jazz was the beginning of a new kind of fusion of jazz with popular music. (Fusion was often called "jazz-rock," but these musicians drew more from such soul artists as James Brown and Sly Stone than they did from rock.) In fact, a number of prominent jazz artists went from the avant-garde almost directly into fusion, a move that caused great consternation. In 1970 and 1971, just before he formed his fusion band Return to Forever, Chick Corea toured with Anthony Braxton, Dave Holland, and Barry Altschul in Circle, performing free improvisations. Herbie Hancock's sextet of the early 1970s was performing long, dreamy excursions based on several themes, with freely improvised segments, just before he released his funky hit "Chameleon" at the beginning of 1973. Even Miles Davis, the mentor of them all, had been producing more and more challenging music—on *Sorcerer* and *Miles in the Sky*—before he began using rock and soul rhythms. Columbia Records even began promoting Davis's works as "Directions in Music" rather than jazz.

Davis's sales went from, I believe, about fifty thousand copies of *Miles in the Sky* and perhaps eighty-five thousand copies of *In a Silent Way* to five hundred thousand copies of *Bitches Brew*, his groundbreaking double album recorded in 1969 and issued in 1970. Hancock's combined sales for *Headhunters* and its hit single "Chameleon" soared to one million, making it the best-selling jazz record in history up to that time. Corea's sales jumped as well, and understandably, purists among musicians and fans felt certain that money was the musicians' only motivation for switching to fusion. Yet *Bitches Brew* was an eerie, challenging album, with much dissonance over its accessible beat; and Hancock's *Headhunters* and Corea's *Return to Forever* albums benefited from marvelous writing. All of these works involved quite a bit of musical creativity.

We return to Leonard Feather for a review of the music heard in the 1970s. He begins with a discussion of fusion and touches on other events in avant-garde, mainstream, and big band jazz. In conclusion he presents some musicians' comments about the pressures in the jazz business as of 1980, specifically the pressure to perform in more commercial styles.

The Decade of 'What Is Jazz?'

LEONARD FEATHER

The 1970s will be remembered, at least among many of us who have lived through them in the role of chroniclers, as the decade of the irresolvable dilemma. The question "What is jazz?" has become more than ever before incapable of a firm answer.

Can the slickly packaged fusion sounds of Bob James and Earl Klugh be defined as jazz? Does Herb Alpert's "Rise" album define the term jazz as it is understood today? Can Angela Bofill qualify as a jazz singer?

Virtually every jazz critic the world over would answer all three questions in a resounding negative; yet in mid-December these artists occupied the top three slots in Billboard's list of best selling jazz LPs.

The paradox is even more complicated than that. The latter half of the 1970s saw the emergence of a new breed of music, much of it on the Oslo-based ECM Records label, most of it involving a strong improvisational element. The groups or artists have included Oregon, the guitarists Pat Metheny and John Abercrombie, and the pianist Keith Jarrett, who may have earned a future place in the Guinness Book of Records with the release of his "Sun Bear Concerts." Composed of five complete solo piano recitals given by Jarrett in Kyoto, Osaka, Nagoya, Tokyo and Sapporo, it ran to a record-breaking ten albums and was issued in a boxed set priced at $50.

Jarrett and the other ECM artists have established a growing retinue of admirers, particularly in Europe and Japan, and to some extent in the United States. Are they playing jazz? Leading experts disagree. The musicians themselves are not particularly anxious to be so categorized.

Another movement that began to gather strength during the 1960s and has since become a major force can be observed in the work of players who emerged from the Chicago-born AACM (Association for the Advancement of Creative Music) and its spinoff units such as the Art Ensemble of Chicago and Air. Many of the black progenitors of these organizations have moved to New York. Some, particularly the trombonist George Lewis and the saxophonist Black Arthur Blythe, are musicians of extraordinary talent.

But are they playing jazz?

Again the point is moot. Most of these artists have expressed a reluctance to be stigmatized as jazz musicians; they prefer the word to be bruited about that they are creating black classical music. In Germany, where their avant garde manifestations have enjoyed special attention, the term "free jazz" has been applied to this phenomenon. Still, the characteristics long associated with jazz—a swinging, rhythmic pulse, a steady beat, tonality—are often totally and deliberately excluded.

Moreover, some of the exponents, particularly the multi-reed virtuoso and composer Anthony Braxton, have worked extensively with American and European whites; so even the "black classical" definition may be just as inapplicable as the word jazz.

As you can see, we have a problem. If jazz was ever definable—and in retrospect it seems that the music of earlier decades was far more easily classified than that of the 1970s—it has certainly reached a point at which there is almost no agreement on where the borderline lies that separates it from the records on the charts, the ECM sounds, or the AACM Manifestations. The debates that went on during the 1940s, when advocates of bebop were locked in a holy war against the diehard "Moldy Figs" with their advocacy of the New Orleans traditions, seem like ladies' tea party chatter compared to the arguments now raging with respect to the various fusion forms.

There were a few events during the '70s about which no disagreement exists concerning their jazz validity. Without doubt, bebop or hard bop, a music associated with the '40s and '50s, came back in full force, enabling such expatriates as the saxophonists Dexter Gordon and Johnny Griffin to make triumphant returns to their homeland. Dizzy Gillespie lives; Art Blakey's Jazz Messengers, some of whose members were not born when bebop drew its first breath, are bringing essentially the same message today as when their original incarnation was organized.

There has been a small but significant group of young musicians playing in styles inspired by an earlier generation. Instead of being sucked into the fusion or free-music vortex, they reflect the tonal, swinging values of their swing or bop era predecessors. Typical of this trend are the fiery trumpeter Jon Faddis, who joined the Thad Jones–Mel Lewis orchestra at 18; Tom Harrell, a trumpeter discovered by Horace Silver; the saxophonists Scott Hamilton, Ted Nash, Dave Schnitter and [Ricky] Ford, and the guitarist Cal Collins.

Another carryover from earlier years, though with a decidedly contemporary touch, is the big band. The Toshiko Akiyoshi–Lew Tabackin orchestra leads the field.

Along with all the new concepts, the past few years have seen their share of Welcome revivals: a new career, in her 80s, for Alberta Hunter, and in his 90s for Eubie Blake. Fats Waller and Eubie were adopted by the Broadway stage with shows dedicated to their music.

Given the broad range of genres now known in some quarters, rightly or wrongly, as jazz, is it reasonable to claim that jazz musicians today enjoy more artistic freedom? When this question was posed to some 24 leading artists, the responses showed eight claiming there is less freedom; 12 believe that the new proliferation of contrasted idioms has let freedom ring; two replies were qualified; one was noncommital; one musician had no response.

On the positive side, pianist JoAnne Brackeen commented: "They are freer to be more free or less free—whichever fulfills them most." Guitarist Joe Pass said: "More free—but they don't use the freedom properly; they are too busy trying to get a hit." From saxophonist Lew Tabackin. "Today in America we have the choice to be true to our convictions; but we have to be prepared to suffer the economic and social consequences. Pressure is great to give in, and there are many rationalizations; still, we do have a choice." Others who hear more freedom are Dave Brubeck, Art Farmer, the Swiss pianist George Gruntz, the German composer Joachim Kühn, trombonist Albert Mangelsdorff, saxophonist Sonny Rollins, Sarah Vaughan and Joe Williams.

On the negative side Gerry Mulligan observed: "There's a lot of talk about freedom but precious little understanding of the responsibilities it entails—politically as well as musically." According to trombonist Bill Watrous, "We are free artistically in our own attitudes toward what we do; however, as far as the rank and file, which includes the record company executives as well as the masses they serve we are in a temporary chastity belt." Composer-pianist Horace Silver complained: "They are either propelled into a certain direction by record people, or they follow what the masses are doing, in order to make more money. Few have the courage to stand by what they believe in."

"New talents," said pianist Bill Evans, "don't find the freedom that new talents did in the 1950s or even the '60s, unless they are established, and very independent and strong." Also voting on [the] "less free" side were Toshiko Akiyoshi, Hubert Laws, Airto Moreira and Mike Nock.

Straddling the fence was Elvin Jones, who noted: "The answer depends on the integrity of the artist and his economic alternatives." Herbie Hancock was equivocal: "We are freer in having larger budgets to work with, better recording techniques, more time to spend in the studios. When I was with Blue Note I was not too much concerned with sales. Today, with Warner Brothers, it's a bigger ball game, and in a sense that's less free; however, it has brought me to the attention of a far greater audience."

What developments can be expected in the jazz of the 1980s?

Many replies pointed to the imminence of new forms of amalgamation; however, they disagreed on whether or not this is a happy prospect.

Comments Herbie Hancock: "Look at the crossovers—Joni Mitchell getting into jazz with her Mingus album, even Dolly Parton going from country to rock. I went from jazz to fusion to disco and r&b; my next album will touch rock and Latin bases.

"The 1980s will bring a real renaissance," Hancock added. "New areas, new forms, more use of computers in music, yet at the same time more interest in acoustic sounds, a back-to-nature movement parallel to the ecology movement."

"Musicians will continue to incorporate other idioms," said Horace Silver, "but will weed out the commercial tripe and bring back the sense of depth that has been missing."

JoAnne Brackeen expects "new instrumentations—a musician will play many instruments excellently; I hope a deep creativity will increase. Perhaps this country will look into more rhythmic subtleties and pitch variances—and communication with the public, let's hope, will expand tremendously. Uplift the planet!" (Leonard Feather, "The Decade of 'What is Jazz?'" *Boston Globe,* January 1, 1980, reprinted from the *Los Angeles Times*)

Fifteen years later, Peter Watrous, a jazz critic for the *New York Times,* argued that the pressure to perform fusion has left a disappointing legacy. Although Miles Davis was not the first artist to get involved in fusion, his entrance had a profound impact, partly because of his leadership in the field and partly because his early fusion records had a freewheeling improvisational style that showed many jazz musicians how to enter that arena without losing their edge. As Watrous notes, however, by the 1980s Davis and his many sidemen, including Wayne Shorter and Herbie Hancock, faltered. And they seem to be caught up in a fusion bind that is no longer even successful commercially.

A Jazz Generation and the Miles Davis Curse

Peter Watrous

The arrival of the saxophonist Wayne Shorter's "High Life," his first record in seven years, makes jazz fans tremble with fear. Mr. Shorter, 62, is arguably the most influential living jazz composer. Like his peers who inhabit jazz's loftier realms—Herbie Hancock, Ornette Coleman, Chick Corea, Sonny Rollins—he has spent the last quarter century flashing bits of his grand talent, then finding the nearest drain down which to dump the rest.

And his "High Life," which will be released on Tuesday, turns out to be a pastel failure and a waste of his enormous talent; it is as if Picasso had given up painting to design greeting cards. Mr. Shorter was a composer who, 30 years ago, brought to jazz an entirely new harmonic vocabulary, one that is still the training ground for young musicians.

"High Life" shows none of that vision; simply, it's an eager-to-please instrumental pop album, with only a vestigial relationship to mainstream jazz and virtually no connection to Mr. Shorter's glory years. But it is a fascinating document, one whose esthetic explains much about a generation of musicians and the idiom called fusion, and ultimately about the curse of Miles Davis.

Fusion, which Mr. Shorter helped define, first as part of Miles Davis's group and then as a founder of Weather Report, was a mule idiom, a bastardization of jazz and pop. It was a marriage of funk and black music in Mr. Davis's hands, and rock and world music in those of others. Its first real statement of intent appeared on Mr. Davis's

"Filles de Kilimanjaro" (1968), which was notable in its use of electric keyboards. Fusion was meant to be the great black and white hope, and it enabled its practitioners to make money: Mr. Davis and his pianist, Herbie Hancock, had real pop hits.

It would be easy to dismiss what Miles Davis, who died in 1991, wrought as commercialism. (There are plenty of examples of everyone from Mr. Hancock to Mr. Coleman, in print, selling short the jazz tradition that allowed their brilliance to flourish.) Yet the context that produced such abrupt changes of esthetic and sensibility was clearly all powerful. In four years Mr. Davis and his band moved from the acoustic music exemplified by "Live at the Plugged Nickel," a recently released collection of recordings from 1965 that is one of the great examples of group and formal improvisation found in 20th-century music, to the hyper-electric "Bitches Brew" and rock audiences.

But culturally and politically, everything had changed around the musicians during those four years. The Vietnam War dominated the public consciousness. The civil-rights movement, the Chicago Democratic convention, the assassinations of Robert Kennedy and the Rev. Dr. Martin Luther King Jr.; the list went on.

Rock was in its ascendance and offered plenty of examples of performers making money and being creative at the same time. Jazz musicians, regularly reminded of their music's pre-eminence only 25 years earlier and feeling progressively left out of popular culture's turmoil and excitement, wanted a way back to relevance. In retrospect, the means they chose was shockingly ephemeral.

Jazz audiences had been growing whiter, in an era of intense racial divisions. The vanguard of jazz had abandoned dance-based rhythms and, in so doing, had alienated fans. Early fusion, in its commercialism, was a way to regain jazz's lost audience, particularly black listeners who had drifted away. The appeal of fusion was irresistible, especially when neglect and privation were seemingly the options. Even Duke Ellington toyed with pop music during this time.

While the early attempts at fusion were often musically sophisticated, the music quickly faltered, losing its complexity and experimental vigor, and by the late 1970's it barely existed. Within a handful of years, jazz fusion became a sort of instrumental pop music, using pop's melodic ideas, rhythms, instruments and textures. And with that, a dream vanished; like any mule idiom, it was barren.

But let's back up. Wayne Shorter may be the most important living jazz musician. His sensibility permeates the work of virtually every musician under the age of 30 playing mainstream jazz, and plenty who are older. In his early work, his improvising—restrained and precisely colored—suggests that he completely understood the saxophone tradition from which he sprang. (Oddly, his work on soprano saxophone leads directly to Kenny G.) But his most durable influence has been compositional: he introduced a completely new harmonic vocabulary, one that gave jazz a new sense of languor and urgency.

The recordings Mr. Shorter made between 1964 and 1967 for Blue Note—"Night Dreamer," "Juju," "Speak No Evil," "The All Seeing Eye," "Adam's Apple" and "Schizophrenia"—reduce many of today's young musicians to outright exploitation. His compositions are staples of jazz studies—the perfect practice ground for young musicians exploring ambiguous, post-be-bop harmonies.

While Mr. Shorter was recording masterpieces, Mr. Davis was changing directions. In 1969 he entered the studio to record the sessions that become "Bitches Brew," which sold 500,000 copies. In contrast, Mr. Shorter's albums on Blue Note were selling roughly 5,000 copies.

That year Mr. Davis began touring with his band, opening rock concerts for Santana. He performed at the Isle of Wight Pop Festival, in front of a crowd estimated at 400,000. Only five years earlier, at the peak of his creative energies, he was still often playing three or four sets a night at hole-in-the-wall clubs. Accompanied by Mr. Shorter, Mr. Davis went on to open shows for Crosby, Stills, Nash and Young, the Band, Laura Nyro and others. He performed at the home of rock, the Fillmore, and even recorded a live album there. Mr. Shorter still hadn't led a band in public [except for occasional gigs].

It's impossible to overestimate Mr. Davis's influence, and not just on Mr. Shorter. While Mr. Davis's sidemen and followers may not have taken his precise musical formula, they certainly benefited from the battles he won as the advance guard. The drummer Tony Williams and his group, Lifetime, recorded "Emergency" in 1969. The pianist

Joe Zawinul and Mr. Shorter formed Weather Report and released their first fusion album in 1971. That year, the guitarist John McLaughlin formed the Mahavishnu Orchestra. (The name was suggested by his guru, Sri Chinmoy.) Mr. Corea formed Return to Forever in 1972. Two years later, Mr. Shorter recorded "Native Dancer," a Brazilian jazz fusion album, and Herbie Hancock released "Headhunters," which quickly sold half a million copies, reaching No. 13 on Billboard's album chart.

This flurry of activity was noticed by musicians outside Davis's circle. Ornette Coleman hired the avant-garde guitarist James (Blood) Ulmer the same year "Headhunters" is released and issued his first fusion album, "Dancing in Your Head," a year later. In 1973, Joe Henderson recorded a fusion album, "Multiple." All the while, the pop-jazz label CTI Records, founded by the producer Creed Taylor, was taking jazz veterans like Stanley Turrentine, Freddie Hubbard and Milt Jackson into the studio to make some of the worst recordings of their careers.

Clearly, the esthetic success achieved by jazz musicians through years of practice and bandstand battles could be lost; jazz, improvisation and the forward momentum of innovations are muscles that wither when not used. There are few examples of jazz musicians who took an extended break from the music and reappeared playing better. And virtually every important member of the fusion generation has spent time moving between instrumental pop music and mainstream jazz. None of them, whether it be Chick Corea, Herbie Hancock or Wayne Shorter, have ever matched their earlier efforts.

So it has to be imagined: What would jazz look like today if Mr. Shorter, Mr. Hancock, Mr. Corea and others had maintained their nerve and kept moving in the mainstream of jazz, taking on its problems and amplifying their breakthroughs? What would have happened if the innovations of the Miles Davis quintet had been built on instead of abandoned?

One thing is sure. The legions of young people playing jazz now, picking up the broken pieces left by their elders of two generations earlier, sometimes to great effect and sometimes to the point of imitation, would not exist in the form they do today. As good as it is, would one of the best-selling albums of 1991 have been Joe Henderson's acoustic album "Lush Life: The Music of Billy Strayhorn"? Would historicism, instead of progressivism, be the vocabulary of the present?

Mr. Shorter's "High Life," with its reliance on the most obvious pop back beats and its sentimentalism, is quite likely a commercial mistake. The real money nowadays is in acoustic music with intellectual weight. Mr. Henderson, Mr. Shorter's label mate, sold 74,000 copies of "Lush Life." Mr. Shorter's three albums, electric and ostensibly commercial, recorded for Columbia during the 1980's never sold more than 20,000 copies apiece.

Yet that's one of the enduring legacies of Miles Davis: not only did he wipe out the serious aspirations of a generation but when the time is ripe for a Mr. Shorter to return to mainstream jazz, the place of his greatest achievements, he's blind to see it. And he's losing money too. (Peter Watrous, "A Jazz Generation and the Miles Davis Curse," *New York Times*, October 15, 1995)

Many of my musician friends hated Watrous's article, basically out of respect—Shorter, Hancock and Corea are still so respected among musicians that they (and I) are always ready to give them the benefit of the doubt. In a prominent editorial in *Down Beat* (November 1996), John Ephland called Watrous's piece "perhaps the worst" critical broadside "leveled at Shorter." Ephland noted that "the importance of Wayne Shorter was a constant throughout the '70s and into the '80s," and he defended Shorter's *High Life* album as a deceptively complex work, especially in terms of chord progressions. Yet to dispute Watrous's main points would be difficult. (The historicism whose origin he explains is a main concern of Chapter 11.)

By the late 1960s jazz artists who did not switch to fusion were in dire straits. Young audiences were not interested in the newer events in jazz. Instead, they were following the developments in rock and other popular music. Older listeners were, I suppose, loyal to the established jazz players they had grown up with, but only to a small number of big names. Around 1969, I was one of only six people in the audience for an exciting quartet led by pianist McCoy Tyner with Gary Bartz on saxophone, Calvin Hill on bass, and Freddie Waits on drums. Reflecting on jazz's dwindling audiences, *Down*

Beat and the *Chicago Tribune* critic Larry Kart announced "the death of jazz," at least as we knew it. (A recurring trend in jazz sees the popular press periodically heralding "Jazz is back," and at other times its critics pronouncing its death.)

Older black swing artists were hit especially hard. As John S. Wilson reported in the *New York Times* ("The Old Black Jazzmen: Where Are They Now?" July 21, 1969):

> Most of the big band musicians of the twenties and thirties have retired to day jobs, limiting their playing to occasional weekend gigs. Russell Bowles, who played trombone for Jimmie Lunceford, is a salesman at Macy's. Greeley Walton, a saxophonist with Cab Calloway and Louis Armstrong, is a departmental manager for E. F. Hutton. Sandy Williams, a trombonist with Fletcher Henderson and Chick Webb, runs an elevator in a building at 106th Street and Manhattan Avenue. Julian Dash, a saxophonist featured by Erskine Hawkins, and Tommy Benford, who played drums for Coleman Hawkins and Jelly Roll Morton, are both with Merrill, Lynch, Pierce, Fenner and Smith, the brokerage house. Mr. Dash is in charge of receptionists on the 10th floor of the firm's main office, 70 Pine Street. Mr. Benford is a messenger.

Fusion remains the most divisive issue within the jazz community. Get a group of jazz musicians together, say "Kenny G"—you needn't bother to complete a sentence—and you'll hear a heated debate. The difficulty with fusion will always be that it is impossible to be objective about it. On the one hand, some say pursuing fusion is selling out. With the huge jumps in record sales for fusion—tenfold and more for many artists—and certainly similar increases in audiences and concert fees, how could financial success not be an attractive consideration? On the other hand, how could any artist be successful in that medium unless he is also expressing creative ideas? I remember seeing trumpeter Freddie Hubbard on a New York television jazz program hosted by vocalist Joe Williams one Sunday morning around 1966. When Williams held up Hubbard's new album, *A Soul Experiment,* for the obligatory promotional, the trumpeter interrupted him, saying, "That's not really very good. It's basically a commercial thing." Bless Hubbard for his honesty, but the fact that musicians like him could make albums they didn't even like, just for money, fueled the critics who cried, "You're selling out!"

Finally, fusion has been controversial among musicians because its second generation, unlike the first, were not proven jazz musicians. Davis, Hancock, Shorter, Corea, and Joe Zawinul were not only established jazz players, but leading masters of the art, whereas Kenny G (actually Gorelick), Jeff Lorber, and any number of younger players came up within a self-contained fusion world. They never "proved themselves" in mainstream jazz bands, at least not well-known ones; thus they lack credibility within the jazz world. Of course, outside the jazz world, this issue of credibility counts for naught. People buy the records because they like them. But when Kenny G earns huge amounts of money and, say, the burning saxophonist Kenny Garrett does not (though he's doing well by jazz standards), musicians grumble about the disparity in pay, and in recognition, since Garrett is a far superior jazz player.

On a positive note, fusion artists have accomplished what skeptics denied: they really did bring young people back to jazz, maybe not in huge numbers, but in enough numbers that jazz is once again on the charts. McCoy Tyner and others now play to large audiences in America and abroad.

Fusion artists' second accomplishment was in revitalizing jazz composition. Fusion pieces typically involve electronic sounds and an eclectic mix of influences, often from Latin American and African sources. Their forms are unusual, too. Ellington and Strayhorn had opened up formal possibilities by writing many pieces with ten-bar sections and other unusual touches, as did Monk in the postwar era ("Criss Cross," "Boo Boo's Birthday") and Wayne Shorter and others in the 1960s. Fusion pieces are often through-composed—that is, they lead from the beginning to the end without repeating the beginning—or use long forms with several sections and themes. (Of course, twelve and thirty-two bars are still the rule in acoustic jazz.)

11

Traditionalism, Revivalism, and the "Young Lions," 1980 to the Present

"Jazz is back," the papers started to announce in the early 1980s (I read it in Boston in 1978), but within the field there is much controversy about the *way* it has come back. My students are constantly surprised about some of the things that are controversial among jazz professionals. For example, they can't imagine any kind of heated debate revolving around such a relatively cool and soothing trend as fusion. Similarly, they don't understand all the fuss about the "young traditionalists," many of them black, who have become prominent since the early 1980s. After all, their movement has helped attract listeners, both black and white, who were turned off by avant-garde jazz and had no interest in fusion. As Marilyn Marshall noted:

> These days, jazz is attempting to overcome its image as an elitist art form, and a number of younger artists are returning to traditional jazz roots. Perhaps the best known is trumpet virtuoso Wynton Marsalis. Other highly-touted young jazz artists include saxophonists Branford Marsalis and Donald Harrison, trumpet player Terence Blanchard, pianists Kenny Kirkland and Mulgrew Miller, and female drummer Terri Lyne Carrington.
>
> Jazz is also finding a home on more and more Black college campuses, which artists and educators say is essential if young Blacks are to

learn the art. In addition to Clark, such schools as Howard University, Southern University and Texas Southern University have strong jazz programs. Jazz artists are also visible on college campuses as instructors and visiting artists. (Marilyn Marshall, "Are Blacks Giving Away Jazz?" *Ebony,* February 1988)

Part of the traditionalists' efforts has been an ever-increasing emphasis on re-creating the older styles. In itself, revisiting the past is fine, but doing so has certain drawbacks, as Peter Watrous points out.

They're everywhere: tribute concerts, tribute groups, tribute records, repertory groups, floods of reissued records. This year's JVC festival, programmed by George Wein and as good an indication of official jazz culture as can be found, was more than ever laden with homages to past masters, from Mingus to Ellington, from Buddy Rich to Billie Holiday. Lincoln Center, which has started a long overdue jazz series, calls it Classical Jazz, with emphasis on the word classical. Of the eight jazz shows they've produced over the last two years, five have been tributes. The American Jazz Orchestra, a fine repertory group working out of Cooper Union, exists to perform classic big-band jazz in concert.

Jazz is awash with its past, and that's a mixed blessing. As much as the constant revivals of past glories make for satisfying, historically important listening, the danger is that if looking backward becomes jazz's prime activity, the music becomes embalmed, lifeless. (Peter Watrous, "Jazz Moves Fast Forward into Its Past," *New York Times,* September 18, 1988)

Re-creations are rife with musical problems. At any one concert a clear consensus about how to approach recorded music is rare, especially when the live players present are capable of improvising new music of their own. John Rockwell, another *Times* critic who writes about all kinds of music, is one of the few to have considered this problem. He was inspired to comment after attending concerts of the American Jazz Orchestra, a big band active in New York between 1986 and the early 1990s that specialized in jazz "repertory"—that

is, in the re-creation of famous recordings, along with commissions
of new music.

> A more interesting question is strictly esthetic: to what extent is jazz
> inherently improvisatory, and how should the performances of the
> American Jazz Orchestra (or any similar attempt at recreation, small-
> scale or large-scale) be balanced between fidelity and freedom?
>
> Clearly, jazz contains a crucial improvisatory element. Some jazz
> performances were and still are strictly notated (or memorized) and
> others are purely improvisational (like free jazz). But most jazz falls
> between those extremes, drawing sustenance from both sides. (John
> Rockwell, "Can Jazz Survive 'Classical' Treatment?" *New York Times,*
> September 14, 1986, section II, pp. 19, 26)

Speaking of improvisation, among the younger generation the
emphasis is on learning to improvise in the styles that predate John
Coltrane's and Ornette Coleman's breaking the boundaries in the
1960s. Peter Watrous notes the inherent dangers in this trend.

> In jazz, an entire generation of young musicians is rejecting, with a
> surety only Freud could have predicted, their immediate musical par-
> ents—the avant-gardists of the 60's and 70's—in favor of the 40-year-
> old rules of be-bop.
>
> A visit to almost any jazz club will find a band with a young Philly
> Joe Jones or young John Coltrane, well dressed, on the bandstand, liv-
> ing tributes to past masters. Celebrating their predecessors is a neces-
> sary step in the learning process. But taken to an extreme, as it often
> has been recently, this celebration comes at the cost of submerging the
> individualism that defines great jazz. Though half an hour with a
> John Coltrane facsimile, his style learned from records, is intriguing, it
> also seems empty and a bit perverse.
>
> Ultimately, that slavishness to the past subverts progress, and the
> new ideas that are implied in an individual style, that jazz needs to sur-
> vive. As with tributes, the young conservative jazz musicians often
> seem as if they're passive, with no musical voice of their own and
> defined and limited by the conservatism of their times, rather than

actively making sense of the present for themselves. (Peter Watrous, "Jazz Moves Fast Forward into Its Past," *New York Times*, September 18, 1988)

Jon Pareles wrote a long piece about this new traditionalism in 1984. Pareles focused, quite rightly, on trumpeter Wynton Marsalis, a key figure in jazz as of this writing. Born in 1961, Marsalis is from a jazz family in New Orleans—not a Dixieland family, but a modern jazz family. His father, Ellis, is one of the leading pianists in the city; he was featured on trumpeter Nat Adderley's album *In the Bag*, along with Nat's brother, Cannonball, back in 1962. Marsalis's older brother, Branford, is renowned for his saxophone work in jazz, in pop with singer and songwriter Sting, and in television for a while, beginning in May 1992, as the bandleader on NBC's "Tonight Show". Of Wynton's four other siblings, two are also jazz musicians—trombonist Delfeayo, who has chosen to concentrate on producing, and drummer Jason, the youngest. Wynton (the Irish name was given in tribute to the great black American pianist Wynton Kelly) has become a leader in the jazz field, and he wears this hat comfortably, proudly, and boldly. His trumpet style has changed dramatically over the years, as he has molded it, rather self-consciously, to reflect his changing philosophy. When he first recorded with Art Blakey in 1980 and then with Herbie Hancock, he was flashy and modern, darting in unexpected directions. Today, he pays tribute to such past masters as Louis Armstrong and Duke Ellington's mute specialist, Cootie Williams, in solos that sometimes sound, to these ears, like patchworks rather than coherent personal statements. His work is always technically astounding, however, and he is known for his peerless performances of classical music. Wynton is the only person to have won Grammies in both jazz and classical categories. He was also honored with the 1997 Pulitzer Prize in music composition.

Pareles also explores the avant-garde work of David Murray and Anthony Davis, among others, which would seem to be antithetical to Marsalis's traditional stance. Optimistically, Pareles concludes that the two camps are moving closer together.

Jazz Swings Back to Tradition

JON PARELES

The crowd outside Sweet Basil, on a Monday not long ago, is so large and so eager that even jaded Greenwich Village strollers stop to ask who's playing inside the jazz club. David Murray and Wynton Marsalis, they are told; that's why the place is packed.

That made several Mondays in a row that the David Murray Big Band drew full houses, playing a stack of new compositions that cut exultantly across the history of jazz. In the richly voiced chords and leisurely ballads, one can hear echoes of Duke Ellington; in the jumping call-and-response between saxophones and brasses, there's a whiff of Count Basie. Charles Mingus would have been proud of the band's gutsy, raw-boned swing.

David Murray, 29, sits at stage left, cradling his tenor saxophone, his ear cocked to the music. He rises for a solo that arcs upward from a sultry melody to harmony-defying squeals and squawks. The music he composes is designed to be shuffled and reshuffled, and it's likely that it will never be performed in the same order twice. That's one reason for the full house.

There are curiosity seekers in tonight's audience, since word has spread that the guest soloist is Wynton Marsalis, the widely praised 22-year-old trumpeter from New Orleans. In a few weeks, the young musician would go on to win Grammy Awards for his performances as both a jazz *and* a classical artist. Marsalis, who invariably performs in jacket and tie, has championed jazz's legacy as swinging, harmonically sophisticated music; what's more, he has denounced some avant-gardists as "charlatans."

Yet he's right at home in Murray's trumpet section, studiously concentrating on his parts and waiting for his chance to play a solo. When he gets the nod, he looses high, poised blue notes, then growls with gusto as the band digs into something like a New Orleans stomp. It's not a battle of styles—it's an embrace.

That gleeful moment reflects the new priorities of 1980's jazz: reclaiming jazz tradition from a modern perspective, shifting the balance from the soloist to the group and, more often than not, swinging with a vengeance.

It also marks yet another shift in the role of the jazz composer. Jazz might be defined as music created from the friction between planning and spontaneity, or between written and improvised music. A written score is only the outline of any musical performance, but especially so in jazz, where swinging rhythms defy exact transcription and where improvisation continually changes the balance of a piece. In the big bands of the 1930's, precise orchestral scores were laced with short and long solos; in the small-group jazz that prevailed after World War II, a composition was likely to be just a quick tune whose chords became a springboard for extended improvisation, repeatedly cycling through the sequence of chords that make up the form of a song. As improvisers broke away from standard harmony during the 1960's, jazz compositions grew less and less restrictive, and they became almost abstract in the 1970's, when a composer like Anthony Braxton might specify a register and a rhythm, but leave melody and harmony to be improvised. Now, after the upheavals of the 1960's and the fragmentation and experimentation of the 1970's, jazz composers face a historical question. What should they do now that everything is permitted?

It's a question with no simple answer. Jazz has evolved as a distinctly American mixture of art music, folk music and entertainment—a complex, classic tradition that supports itself primarily in nightclubs. Many of the pioneers who defined jazz while gaining worldwide popularity—among them Louis Armstrong, Ellington and Basie—are now dead. At this point in jazz history, it's impossible to point to one vanguard style or musician, such as John Coltrane, Ornette Coleman and "free jazz" in the late 1960's or Charlie Parker and Dizzy Gillespie and be-bop in the 1940's. And the jazz audience has dwindled, turning to rock and pop music or to the light, pop-styled instrumentals that the music business categorizes as "jazz-fusion." But because the music can be recorded live and inexpensively, jazz has not disappeared from the market. Indeed, this Friday will kick off the 1984 Kool Jazz Festival, a 10-day, 50-concert extravaganza in New York which will feature, among many others, Wynton Marsalis.

While most of the best jazz continues to be made by black musicians, and the lexicon of jazz—its blue notes, its swinging rhythms and the way improvisation and composition meld together—is

Afro-American, most of the audience for new jazz is still white, as it has been since the 1960's.

"I think that the black community, if they get a chance to hear my music, they appreciate it," says David Murray. "But my music doesn't have the opportunity to reach the total black populace." Murray is referring to the fact that jazz clubs are expensive places to hear music, and also that radio stations seeking black audiences are far more likely to play pop hits than jazz: "Black people don't get a chance to hear their own music on the radio," he says. But there is some question whether jazz is still "their own music." Many young people, black and white, simply prefer music they can dance to and pop songs—idioms less committed to innovation—and would continue to do so even if radio exposed them to jazz.

The 1960's avant-garde gave new jazz a fearsome, fire-breathing image. Leading jazz musicians claimed an affinity between their music and radical politics; even the labels placed on the music—"new thing," "free jazz," "energy music"—suggested revolutionary hopes. The rage expressed by such black spokesmen as Malcolm X and Eldridge Cleaver found an explicit parallel in the intense, expressionistic blowing of saxophonists like Pharoah Sanders and Archie Shepp—who were also working out new musical ideas by breaking down song forms and expanding their sonic palettes.

Younger jazz musicians today are not without their own frustrations. "Jazz is still put down into a lower class of economics and of acceptance," says Murray, in a quieter voice than one would expect after hearing his broad-shouldered saxophone tone. "I think the music should be uplifted. Instead, it's treated as a kind of slave music."

However, Murray adds, "I didn't start a bigger band for any political reason. I did it to hear more notes."

And so, after decades in which forms have been defied and shattered, a new generation of jazz composers have begun to rebuild. They are well-schooled, often in both jazz and the classics; they take virtuosity for granted. They organize bands that draw on not only the entire sweep of jazz—from African roots to swing to free-form improvisation—but the sonorities of folk music from around the world and the complex structures of classical music as well.

"It's still energy music." David Murray says. "It's just conforming to some things that were forgotten for a little while."

Such ambitious composers as David Murray, Anthony Davis, Henry Threadgill, Craig Harris, Douglas Ewart, David Holland, James Newton, Ronald Shannon Jackson, John Carter and Butch Morris are working their own transformations of older traditions.

"We are in a period of transition," says Albert Murray (no relation to David), the novelist and author of "Stomping the Blues," who is now adapting Count Basie's reminiscences into an autobiography. [published in 1985]. "There is a breakdown of certain conventions in society, and that doesn't send people looking in all directions. It sends them looking for fundamentals. It might be called postavant-gardism."

"There are going to be more people who can play everything," is the way David Murray puts it.

Both jazz and classical music were sidelights at the 26th annual Grammy Awards last February. After all, classical music and jazz each accounted for only 6 percent of record sales in 1983. New jazz, like contemporary classical music, represented only a fraction of that, and most of it was recorded by small, independent companies.

On the other hand, rock and pop account for more than half of all record sales—and for the bulk of the Grammy presentations. But on the awards broadcast, as Michael Jackson garnered Grammy after Grammy, something extraordinary happened when another young musician, Wynton Marsalis, in white tie and tails, went on camera.

Marsalis performed the finale of the Hummel trumpet concerto more smoothly than the Grammy orchestra, spitting out every triplet. Then he joined his jazz quintet for the daredevil stops and starts of his own tune "Knozz-Moe King" (a variant of "No Smoking," perhaps). Soon afterward, his second jazz album as a quintet leader, "Think of One," and his classical album of trumpet concertos by Haydn, Hummel and Leopold Mozart were respectively declared "Best Jazz Instrumental Performance, Soloist" and "Best Classical Performance—Instrumental Soloist (With Orchestra)." Marsalis is the first musician ever to win simultaneous jazz and classical Grammy awards.

Marsalis has risen more quickly than most young players. His first album, "Wynton Marsalis," sold 100,000 copies, a massive number for an album of jazz without electric instruments. His prowess befits the former first trumpeter of the New Orleans Civic Orchestra, a onetime student at the Juilliard School and the Berkshire Music Center at Tanglewood, and an alumnus of the Brooklyn Philharmonia and the "Sweeney Todd" pit band on Broadway. (He'll also be performing at the Mostly Mozart Festival this summer.) Yet classical music was barely half of his education. The rest came from his father—the pianist Ellis Marsalis, who has been teaching a generation of young New Orleans jazz musicians—and from playing in local rhythm-and-blues and jazz bands before carving out a national reputation.

In 1980, at 18, the trumpeter dropped out of Juilliard to join Art Blakey and the Jazz Messengers, a group that since the 1950's has been a springboard for young, aggressive jazz musicians. Marsalis's pure, pealing tone and mercurial solos caused the jazz press to declare him a prodigy. Then Marsalis joined the Herbie Hancock-V.S.O.P. quartet, with an even more demanding repertory. When he was barely 21, Marsalis began leading his own quintet, and became one of the few new jazz musicians signed directly to a major record label, Columbia.

In his Grammy acceptance speech, a slightly nervous Marsalis pointedly thanked "all the guys who set a precedent in Western art, and gave an art form to the American people that cannot be limited by enforced trends or bad taste."

Little by little, the history and performance of jazz have been accepted as an academic discipline, and a number of leading jazz musicians are teaching on college faculties: Archie Shepp and the drummer Max Roach at the University of Massachusetts; the saxophonist Jackie McLean at the University of Hartford; the bassist Richard Davis at the University of Wisconsin. Rutgers University has an Institute of Jazz Studies in Newark, and the music faculty at its New Brunswick campus includes the pianist Kenny Barron, the guitarist Ted Dunbar and the drummer Michael Carvin; the bassist Larry Ridley has tenure on the Rutgers faculty.

Outside the universities, such organizations as the Association for the Advancement of Creative Music in Chicago, the New Orleans Center for the Creative Arts and a creative-music workshop in

Woodstock, N.Y., have, in the last decade, fostered a new respect for the jazz tradition.

It is a climate in which, even as the inventors of the jazz tradition die out, younger musicians are exposed to all the history they want to hear, including reissued recordings. Marsalis, for one, has emerged from such training a vehement jazz traditionalist who believes in "swing, melodic invention and harmonic correctness." As he puts it, "Without chords and harmony and a rhythm—without the obstacles—improvisation is nothing."

Marsalis has been criticized for sounding like an encyclopedia of jazz trumpet styles, from Miles Davis's melancholy to Louis Armstrong's growls to Fats Navarro's liquid phrasing to Clifford Brown's clarity to Dizzy Gillespie's puckishness. "If you play trumpet and you *don't* sound like Miles or Dizzy or Clifford or Fats, you're probably not playing jazz," Marsalis argues. "If you don't sound like somebody else, you sound like nothing."

In much small-group jazz since the be-bop era, performances have taken the shape of theme-solo-theme. Marsalis's own quintet is up to something more, shifting keys and tempos from solo to solo, continually reorchestrating the themes. It is as if the late 1960's and 1970's, with their free-form experiments, never happened; Marsalis is grafting the complex forms of the 1980's onto the daring harmonies of the 1960's.

"The sincerity has to come back into music," Marsalis insists. "The 1960's let a lot of people in who were willing to be charlatans, some sort of noble-savage profundity. Each of our generations got weaker instead of stronger.

"To me, you definitely have to study be-bop," Marsalis continues. "It's like Beethoven having to know counterpoint. It's not enough for a guy to grow up in Texas and eat chicken and ham hocks, or whatever that 1970's social-critic view was. Music is precise; cats should know the chords and the theory. The old stuff has not been absorbed yet. Duke Ellington was writing hip arrangements in 1938, and they're still hip."

"The next thing is going to swing," he adds. "The key is in the rhythm. It's not in harmony or melody. The next innovation is going to be when somebody does something in the rhythm."

"I don't lose an hour of sleep worrying about whether my music 'swings,'" says pianist Anthony Davis, who has emerged from classical training with his own conclusions. Along with such other jazz composers as John Carter, George Lewis, Douglas Ewart and John Lindberg, the 33-year-old Davis has taken the postavant-garde direction of complex structures and extended pieces away from the bandstand toward the concert stage. He is probably the most abstract and classical-*sounding* composer among his peers: While improvisation threads through his pieces, the music's momentum comes not from a syncopated beat, but from the working out of compositional tensions, as it might in a piece by Schoenberg or Stockhausen.

Davis, the flutist James Newton and the cellist Abdul Wadud were invited to be part of the New York Philharmonic's Horizons '84 festival of new American music earlier this month as improvising soloists in Davis's "Still Waters."

Davis's Manhattan Plaza apartment shows the depredations of his 4-year-old son, yet around the piano things are orderly. A pencil is close at hand; Bach keyboard compositions top a stack of music on the piano itself; nearby shelves hold Davis's own scores, some in his own spidery handwriting, others bearing the clearer notations of professional copyists.

"I would be hard-pressed to tell you exactly what key this is in," he says, opening one of them to point out which parts are composed and which are improvised.

Davis, who studied classical music at Yale and the drumming of southern India at Wesleyan, played in jazz bands around New Haven. In New York, he worked his way up the jazz circuit, performing as a solo improviser and in groups led by David Murray, the trumpeter Leo Smith and others. Eventually, however, his ambitions as a composer led him away from the three-sets-a-night routine of club performance.

Davis writes pieces that are openly influenced by modern classical music, as earlier jazz was influenced by marches, hymns and pop tunes. In conversation, he is as likely to mention Steve Reich or Jacob Druckman—composers whose music uses no improvisation—as he is to cite Ellington. Davis's pieces are heady and atmospheric; they often use lush harmonies and intricate repeating patterns to create a sense of suspended time. The merits of Davis's music have been debated by classical critics as well as by jazz fans who want straightforward swing in their music.

"I don't think these traditions are as separate as some people would have you believe," Davis argues. "Afro-American music has always been American; Scott Joplin was obviously listening to a lot of music, including classical music, and I think that's true of Jelly Roll Morton, too. I came to the realization that I really wasn't concerned whether people looked at my music as jazz or not. I'm writing American music, and it draws on a whole spectrum of influences in all kinds of traditions. If somebody uses tradition as a way of limiting your choices, in a way that's as racist as saying you have to sit at the back of the bus. Ellington and Mingus are very important in the tradition of what I'm writing, but I have also studied Stravinsky, Messiaen and Takemitsu. What's so heinous about European influences? I think now there's an idea of finding common sensibilities rather than sticking to your own little community."

Davis has all but abandoned the usual jazz circuit in favor of places like the Brooklyn Academy of Music and an avant-garde performance loft in SoHo, the Kitchen, which recently sponsored him for a grant to write an opera based, intriguingly, on the life of Malcolm X. (A portion of "X" will receive a workshop performance in Philadelphia on June 29.) [It premiered at Lincoln Center in 1986.]

"I feel I'm liberated from the commercial function that this music had to perform before 1940," Davis says. "I don't feel it's my job to sell drinks. I'm writing art music, and I feel the responsibility to create the best music I can."

Only in recent years has jazz begun to get the kind of institutional help that American opera companies and symphony orchestras are used to receiving. The National Endowment for the Arts (which awards Federal grants for arts projects and, in its choices, signals a direction for private-foundation support) started a jazz pilot program in 1970, giving $20,050 to 30 individuals and organizations. By 1979, jazz grants to performers, organizations and educational programs had reached $1 million. In the past two years, N.E.A. jazz support has been approximately $1.3 million, out of a $13-million music budget.

Meet the Composer, an organization that awards grants to support live appearances by American composers, gave some 30 percent of its budget to jazz composers last year. Such support—and a new willingness by such classical-music presenters as the Carnegie Hall Corporation, which this year featured both jazz artists and composers at the Carnegie Recital Hall—allows composers to try out new forms that might not go over in a club setting.

"Government support is a very small part of what makes an art scene run," cautions Nancy Weiss, coordinator of the new-jazz program at New York's Public Theater. "In the long run, the survival of a kind of music has do with the marketplace; an art form is going to come and go on the basis of its audience."

Is it possible to reconcile the formal innovations that fascinate Davis and other chamber-jazz composers with the swing that traditionalists like Marsalis demand? A number of jazz composers are betting on it.

Some of the most exciting music anywhere is now being made by an axis of groups whose style might be called avant-gutbucket jazz—a loose rubric for the music of David Murray's big band and octet, the Henry Threadgill Sextet, Craig Harris's Aqua Band, Olu Dara's Okra Orchestra, Ronald Shannon Jackson and the Decoding Society, the Dave Holland Quintet, the Butch Morris Ensemble and other "little big bands," as they have been dubbed. At their best, these bands don't just look back; they offer a kaleidoscopic view of jazz from the roots up.

"If I can give somebody an inkling of how this part of the tradition links up with that part of the tradition," says Murray, "if they can hear that in my playing, that's wonderful."

Murray heard those connections as he was growing up, learning the saxophone as he listened to his mother play piano at the Berkeley, Calif., Missionary Church of God in Christ. "I was just down in Midland, Texas," he says, "at the church where my father is head deacon, playing a piece with the organ player. I put all the ingredients in that I'd put in a solo concert, all the squeals and squawks. All those sounds that are supposed to be new and avant-garde are also an expression of the blues in a religious form, speaking in tongues. I always feel like I've been a person who's playing the melody, and hooking that up with the rhythm. I come out of the church, and the church is all melody."

Murray is generous with his own melodies. In the Greenwich Village apartment where he lives with his wife, the photographer Ming Murray, he can lay his hands on some 130 original pieces, many of which intertwine three or four melody lines at a time. "Every part makes it work," Murray says. "It's not separate tunes, it's all one thing."

Among those pieces are arrangements for standard jazz quartet (piano, bass, drums, saxophone), for Murray's octet, for string orchestra, for the big band and for the World Saxophone Quartet (a new-jazz supergroup, with Murray, Julius Hemphill, Oliver Lake and Hamiet Bluiett on saxophones). Critics have compared this quartet without a rhythm section to a chamber-music group, while Murray likens it to street-corner doowop singing.

Because a sideman in one avant-gutbucket band may be the leader of another, the little big bands can trade ideas and may even build up a shared repertory—something that jazz hasn't enjoyed since the 1960s.

"There's getting to be a group of about 25 to 30 musicians that I associate with," says Murray, "and any one of those musicians knows my music. They may not know my newer music, but there's usually something that we can concur on and play. Or I may know some of their music."

Yet composers like Murray, as opposed to bandleaders of an earlier era like Ellington, seldom have a stable, working band to use as a compositional laboratory. To subsidize such occasional, large-scale projects as his big band or his string orchestra, David Murray writes theater and dance scores and tours the circuit of European summer jazz festivals.

In a briskly professional rehearsal on Sweet Basil's bandstand at noontime before a Monday night gig, Murray's big band whips through a dozen intricate tunes in two hours, pieces that pile melody on melody in counterpoint that would challenge Hindemith—although Hindemith never stomped like this. "Fire it up!" says Murray, urging the band to hit a tune harder. As that piece reaches its last chord, a few onlookers at the bar can't help applauding.

Such infectious, intelligent music seems destined to find its audience eventually. There appears to be something in it for everybody—free spirits, intellectual rigor, complex cross-references, old-fashioned melodies and an unstoppable beat.

The new jazz still has to overcome its image from recent decades—as music that is forbidding, incoherent or too complex for nonspecialists to understand. But with or without an increase in popularity, and with or without governmental support, the music itself has forged two invaluable connections: Jazz's past has become a respected resource; jazz's future—its young musicians—shows enthusiasm and tenacity.

"If you can play this music," says Wynton Marsalis, "you don't want to play anything else. You're always thinking that you're on the brink of something." (Jon Pareles, "Jazz Swings Back to Tradition," *New York Times Magazine*, June 17, 1984)

As I write this in 1997, several things have changed since Pareles made his observations. First of all, government support for the arts, jazz included, has decreased, even while respect for jazz is on the rise. Second, the avant-gardists and Marsalis continue to be at odds, and the promise suggested by the engagement with Murray was not fulfilled. In fact, Marsalis has become increasingly rigid in his definition of jazz. He and his colleague, critic and essayist Stanley Crouch, appear to believe that in order to be considered jazz, music must include the blues, improvisation, swing feeling, and what they call "the Latin tinge," after a statement made in one of Jelly Roll Morton's recorded interviews to the effect that the "Spanish tinge" is essential to jazz.

Marsalis's opinions would not be noteworthy except that he has gained more and more influence in the jazz community. He is artistic director of jazz at Lincoln Center and sets the programming and hiring policies there; has hosted a radio series and a television series designed to introduce audiences to various aspects of jazz, as he sees it; is a regular guest on television shows; and is routinely asked to put his imprimatur on all kinds of jazz projects around the United States. A number of critics and musicians feel that Marsalis is too close-minded in applying his influence. The following piece delineates some of their criticisms and offers Marsalis's detailed reponse.

Wynton Bites Back: Addresses His Critics

WILLARD JENKINS

> *"There are those people who are trying to protect (jazz) or say exactly what it is, and they're destroying it, because it grew from the mere fact that it embraced all the things that were available, from the Caribbean, from Spanish music, everything. It was all these things that allowed (jazz) to happen and it has been those types of ideas that have made it progress."*
> SAXOPHONIST-COMPOSER HENRY THREADGILL, JAZZ TIMES 3/94

> *"The jazz musician wields power that is neither melodramatic nor obnoxious, achieving individuality through the collective affirmation of the swinging band, now and again mediating on the moment at the piano keyboard and orchestrating the individual consciousness through the paces of blues and swing."*
> STANLEY CROUCH, 1994

"Jazz is, living high off nickels and dimes, tellin' folks 'bout what's on your mind. Jazz ain't nothin' but soul. For me, jazz is all the truth to be found, never mind who's puttin' it down. Jazz ain't nothin' but soul." So goes the partial lyric to a little ditty called "Jazz (Ain't Nothin' But Soul)," rendered most notably by Betty Carter and later Joe Lee Wilson. Or, to paraphrase a familiar refrain credited to Louis Armstrong and a host of others, if you don't know what jazz is, don't mess with it.

Seems Wynton Marsalis has expressed some very definite ideas about what jazz is, and perhaps more pointedly—what jazz isn't, or what isn't jazz. For this cardinal sin he's been summarily taken to task by a number of musicians and critics; a provocative example of the latter group's critical attitude coming from the sharp pen of Kevin Whitehead in the November 23 *Village Voice* Jazz Supplement. Titled "It's Jazz, Stupid" Whitehead's piece appears to be dealing with the notion of a constricted definition of jazz as the writer sees it, coming from the Lincoln Center Jazz Department, and most notably its Artistic Director Wynton Marsalis.

Whitehead intones: "According to said experts, we have to be vigilant, separating the frauds from musicians who really deal with swing and the blues—separating real jazz musicians from those who play not-jazz. In '93 a few local authorities—a Jazz at Lincoln Center honcho (presumably Marsalis or Jazz Director Rob Gibson) and a *Times* critic (presumably Peter Watrous) among them—tried their best to set me straight: William Parker, Albert Ayler, Muhal Richard Abrams, they don't swing, so they're out. Reggie Workman, Anthony Braxton, Cecil Taylor, that's "European music"—Taylor just comes from Messiaen. Jazz musicians can't come from Europe because jazz already has a European component, precluding further input from that quarter. Jazz needs standards, or people will think Kenny G is jazz, and the music will suffer. Jazz has its tradition-honed rules, and to be accepted you have to measure up."

Whitehead went on to criticize those who would narrow the boundaries of jazz, saying "Jazz has never been about one thing: no single criterion defines a music that can simultaneously encompass Bunk Johnson, Charlie Parker, and Billy Strayhorn." Earlier in the piece Whitehead suggests that "Narrow definitions of jazz in general rest on historical assumptions about the music, though exclusionists like to claim historical high ground. In jazz, one faction often tells another it's wrongheaded or not jazz; these were major 40s and 60s pastimes."

Kevin goes on to make a case for jazz being a music derived from a variety of sources. He relates how at various times in their careers such giants as Coleman Hawkins, Monk, Ornette, and others were thought to be out of the bounds of the jazz tradition of their day. Later in the piece Whitehead's take on the August 3 Lincoln Center Thelonious Monk concert, a sort of recreation of the big band Monk charts (a concert we referred to in our editorial last issue) suggests that "a mostly under-30 band led by Marcus Roberts" (most of them Marsalis associates or "Wyntonians" as Whitehead referred to them) didn't "really cut it technically;" continuing by suggesting that "patrons paid $35 to listen to on-the-job training, which raises the larger issue of why Jazz at Lincoln Center really exists: to educate the public about and expose it to quality jazz, or to subsidize Wynton's working groups, whose members are heavily featured uptown?"

Our editorial commentary on Jazz at Lincoln Center last issue (Vol. 4 No. 4) was met with some measure of interest from the jazz community. Telephone calls, letters, and assorted exclamations of support for our position—which we felt was an altogether reasonable and balanced one—arrived for several weeks thereafter. [In that editorial Jenkins basically maintained that the concerts, taken by themselves, were marvelous, but that they would be better, and it would be more responsible, to present a broader variety of musicians and styles.] The lone detractors appeared to be a few folks at the International Association of Jazz Educators Convention last January in Boston; and quite frankly those folks appeared not to have absorbed the piece in its entirety.

In response to Whitehead's piece in the *Voice*, and in what appears to be a "I'm mad as hell and I'm not gonna take it anymore" frame of mind, Wynton Marsalis wrote a rather lengthy letter to the editors of the *Voice* for publication. According to sources, when asked to edit the piece to standard *Voice* letter-to-the-editor length (which would have cut the letter by quite a bit less wordage) Wynton refused to do so. Just prior to the publication of our [*NJSO*] *JOURNAL* (Vol. 4, No. 4) editorial and days after publication of Whitehead's *Voice* piece, Jazz at Lincoln Center Director Rob Gibson sent *NJSO* the following letter from Wynton in hopes that we would consider publishing it.

To provide the *JOURNAL* reader with a bit of context we decided to quote the above passages from Kevin Whitehead's *Voice* article, as a prelude to publishing Marsalis' letter. One other point of interest related to at least one of Wynton's pronouncements in the letter is this from Whitehead's article: "Wynton's/Lincoln Center's most outspoken detractor is Lester Bowie (see the *Down Beat*, August 1993 interview Whitehead conducted with Bowie and Greg Osby), conspicuously an advocate of black musicians." This said in response to those who would attribute criticism of Jazz at Lincoln Center to a sort of reverse racism, presumably on the part of white critics. What follows is Marsalis specific response to Whitehead and general response to his critics everywhere, particularly those who would take the Jazz at Lincoln Center philosophy to task.

Wynton Speaks: "Who Actually Is Stupid"

As one reared in a tradition that greatly respects "playing the dozens," I have often enjoyed the twelve or thirteen years of insults posing as aesthetic insight from some segments of what masquerades as the jazz critical community. Normally, I take the position that nothing below me can hurt me, and nothing above me would, but a recent article by Kevin Whitehead in the *Voice*'s jazz supplement—"It's Jazz, Stupid"—was such a mixture of personal attack, attempted condescension, and disinformation that I have decided, finally, to step down into his arena, where arrogance and ignorance are served up in place of information. This must end. It is not the fact of criticism that disturbs me; criticism can easily lead to enlightenment for the musician and listener. I am disturbed, however, by our neophyte pundit's combination of inaccuracy and disrespect, which proves, under scrutiny, that if he thinks anyone is stupid, it must be our audiences, who have enthusiastically supported our efforts for the past seven years with sold-out concerts and standing ovations. Or perhaps he means the thousands of students who are constantly petitioning Jazz at Lincoln Center for more information and events.

I intend to deal with a number of erroneous propositions in his piece, but let me begin with the thing he knows absolutely nothing about—music. I was struck time and again by his misuse of musical terminology to support specious arguments. He discusses the repeated use of the minor third, which he calls "piano's basic blue note," as though it is an indication that someone is playing or alluding to the blues. Actually, it could be an indication that someone is in a minor key, in which case, the major third is the related blues interval. In fact, there is no one basic "blue note," but a series of notes in any given key that can be flatted or sharped to create blues intonations. For example, the major seventh against the dominant seventh; or the flat five against the fifth. There are many examples, but none takes precedence over the others.

He says that Earl Hines and Thelonious Monk are "out." What type of descriptive term is this in a piece of musical criticism? Given the fact that all jazz, from Buddy Bolden to Ornette Coleman, is "outside" of European conventions of instrumental technique and performance, while constituting twentieth century American conventions, what exactly is the writer saying? Whatever his meaning, he continues, later saying that the August 3rd Jazz at Lincoln Center concert of Thelonious Monk's music—which fortunately was taped!—was full of improvisations in which the players "ran blues changes, ignoring Monk's structural quirks and trap door silences—the out content." How does one "run blues changes?" Does he mean by playing on dominant seventh chords or superimposing the form of a blues on an unrelated song? Well, the majority of Monk's songs feature the dominant seventh chord with a flat five (a blues sound). So he can't mean that. As far as anyone imposing the 12-bar blues form on a 32-bar song like "Evidence," I can assure you—as will the tape—that this never happened.

By the way, what, exactly, is a blues change—in the context of a soloist "running it" on a song? I guarantee you we'll wait a long time for the answer to that, and if we get one, it will not be correct. And even this wrong answer will not be from the writer or his editor, Gary Giddins, a man whose position in the hierarchy of jazz criticism is far higher than the quality of his ideas, which are pedestrian when not self-serving. So far as the "structural quirks" and "trap door silences" are concerned, what did John Coltrane and Johnny Griffin, two musicians who were rightly celebrated for their work with Monk, do with "the out content," since neither of them used significant silences in their improvising[?]

Also, I would like to say that the late Charlie Rouse, who played with Monk for over ten years and toured with my band in 1987, was fond of saying that he played every Monk song with the sound of a blues. This is also what Charlie Parker said about his own playing of standard songs. None of these men, of course, understood the problems of jazz as well as the writer, who also claims that (the program's bassist) Reginald Veal and (pianist) Marcus Roberts were lost during features. Interestingly, the writer chooses not to say which Monk songs, and how they were lost. Were they playing the wrong chords, mutilating the form, playing in another key? We can always go to the tape, but I'm sure we won't have to—many so-called jazz critics have gotten used to abusing musical facts without fear of redress. After all, it's only jazz.

My integrity is then impugned by the insinuation that Jazz at Lincoln Center concerts are being used to subsidize my band members. My band members are on my annual payroll. We play about 120 concerts a year. The three or four concerts we play at Lincoln Center have negligible impact on our financial situation. To imply that an old boy system has to be in place for the public to want to hear Marcus Roberts (who won the 1st annual Thelonious Monk competition) or Herlin Riley or Wessel Anderson, is inappropriate and disrespectful.

Our freelance expert writes as though my opinions of what he considers "the vanguard" have a political basis that justifies the term "neo-conservative." I would like to clarify. I have been welcomed on the bandstands of such "vanguard artists" as Dewey Redman, Lester Bowie, and David Murray, and have played with Billy Higgins, Edward Blackwell, Elvin Jones, and Charlie Haden. None of these musicians had anything derogatory to say to me in person, musically or verbally. So my convictions are musical, not political, for I have also performed the musics of Jelly Roll Morton, King Oliver, Count Basie, Duke Ellington, Charlie Parker, Thelonious Monk, Miles Davis, Charles Mingus, the Modern Jazz Quartet, and John Coltrane with musicians who were integral to the development of these styles. I began with Art Blakey and have stood between Doc Cheatham and Harry Edison, next to Freddie Hubbard, Dizzy Gillespie, Art Farmer, Ruby Braff, Red Rodney, Jon Faddis, Sarah Vaughan, and Betty Carter. No matter the school, I have spent more time with musicians trying to share information than argue about what's right or wrong with their playing or mine. Who has this writer studied or played with, and what is the source of his authority other than poor editorial decisions?

If anything, the truly conservative vision is held by the writer and his ilk, all of whom have an investment in anarchic rebellion and sociological rhetoric as opposed to sophisticated affirmation and musical engagement. They pretend to be an oppressed intellectual minority, when, in fact, they sadly represent the overwhelming majority of critical opinions in jazz. If this were not true, the annual polls of jazz critics wouldn't always highly position the "out" musicians the writer pretends are unrecognized by the establishment. In case you didn't know it, my ever so eager to be rebellious friend, you and your editor are the establishment, although it is sinking fast under your watch.

In an attempt to pretend that our vision at Lincoln Center is narrow, Mr. Giddins allows the writer to state that, "Jazz has never been about one thing. No single criterion defines a music that can simultaneously encompass Bunk Johnson, Charlie Parker and Billy Strayhorn." Jazz at Lincoln Center has featured music either written by or associated with all of these musicians. No single criterion can define any art form, and, at Lincoln Center, we're not trying to provide any single criterion, which is why we've been able to present Harold Ashby as well as Dewey Redman, Doc Cheatham as well as Don Cherry, Jay McShann as well as McCoy Tyner, the music of Jelly Roll Morton as well as Randy Weston—to cite only a few examples. Because no single criterion applies doesn't mean that no criterion applies.

He says that Lester Bowie is Jazz at Lincoln Center's most outspoken critic. Bowie emphatically—and correctly—says he does not play jazz; he says he plays "Great Black Music." Well, we are *Jazz* (emphasis Mr. Marsalis) at Lincoln Center. We play jazz, jazz-blues, and we swing—as hard as possible, at different tempi—all night long. By swing, I don't mean a drum machine, but the rhythmic sensibility that allows for continued thematic development in the context of a jazz groove. If this writer—or any of the other would be taste-makers who want to hear "some hip black musicians"—would like me to illustrate what constitutes a jazz groove, I would be glad to. I do it all the time in jazz classes.

The writer further implies that I have a deficient knowledge of what "new" jazz is made of, that I have disdain for European influences. That is not the case. I'm concerned with degrees of influence and the true redefinition of material. Jazz musicians have reinterpreted and utilized European instruments, harmony, and form with such originality that a new music was born. Now we are supposed to believe that very small percentages of actual jazz make something jazz. Is anything with strings on it a piece of European concert music? Is any music using bass and drums jazz music? Does improvisation or call-and-response make something jazz? Obviously, no. Just because this writer is incapable of understanding what constitutes a piece of jazz, must we follow his example? As a professional musician, I have performed many pieces of avant garde "classical" music by composers as diverse as Berio, Stockhausen, Shapey, Schuller and Zwilich, to name a few. Therefore, I have a working musician's familiarity with that vocabulary, a familiarity that the writer obviously lacks since he mistakes those who do poor improvised versions of that music, with a few jazz smatterings, for jazz musicians—even when those same musicians make it clear that they aren't playing jazz.

Apparently, this writer has never taken it upon himself to achieve the real job of a critic, which is to illuminate what constitutes artistic success. He claims to be influenced by the thinking of Albert Murray. Well, he didn't read Mr. Murray closely enough. If he had, he wouldn't abuse the function of critical language, which is to communicate specific information or substantial aesthetic ideas. The real problem in jazz is not narrow definitions of it but the dominance of arrogant and incompetent writers who believe their underdeveloped taste constitutes the truth. I have done hundreds of master classes for students of jazz. If I stand before a class of students and tell them "Anything could be jazz and anything could be swinging," what and how would I tell them to practice? Students don't need vague generalities but specifics, like what King Oliver gave Louis Armstrong.

Finally, let me issue a wake-up call to the writer and his like-minded colleagues. Do not deceive yourselves. Through personal invective and misinformation, veiled paranoia and envy, you will not determine the context in which serious musicians will develop and are developing. You represent an unfortunate intellectual tradition that has burdened this art with varying degrees of paternalism and little actual concern for those musicians dedicated to meeting the extremely high standards set by the masters of jazz, all of whom *swing* (emphasis Mr. Marsalis). By attempting to impose aesthetic criteria far beyond what your knowledge allows, you wish to con the public into believing that you possess an intellectual superiority to jazz and to the musicians who play it. This has always been the case with jazz criticism of the lowest school. But this is the new day that you always are searching for. The "sound of surprise" that you all so often claim to want to hear will be the sound of accuracy.

Henceforth, I want to make it clear that I will no longer silently tolerate your willful disrespect of the skills required to play jazz music. I will be responding to inaccuracies in your reporting when I am made aware of it. My intention is not just to expose you for the charlatans that you are, but to supply the public with another opinion. If you wish to expose me publicly anywhere in any forum, please waste no time contacting me at Lincoln Center. I am always ready to discuss the specifics of *music* (emphasis Mr. Marsalis), not sociology or race politics. But no matter how often you are publicly exposed, I don't expect you all to change. As the great African proverb goes, "A log may lie forever in a river but it will not become a crocodile." (Willard Jenkins, "Wynton Bites Back: Addresses His Critics," *National Jazz Service Organization Jazz Journal* 5, no. 1 [ca. April 1994])

Notice that Marsalis hedges on a few of his answers. To the question, "Why do Marsalis's own band members figure in almost all of his concerts?" his response was, "The three or four concerts we play at Lincoln Center"—the number has increased since then—"have negligible impact on our financial situation." He did not answer the question.

Marsalis is evidently angry and indignant, to say the least. After all, he clearly loves the music and has personally played a major role in the resurgence of jazz since the mid-1980s. And he is one of the great musicians of our century. One might well ask if that isn't enough to satisfy his critics. But the fiery debate continues.

On Marsalis's heels, more and more young players, such as the truly exciting saxophonist Joshua Redman, are recently getting record deals and exposure. Again, this trend appears advantageous for the musicians, yet within the field, many are concerned about the focus on younger players. Francis Davis has been a particularly thoughtful and astute observer of the jazz scene, and he helps explain the problems with this movement.

The deadening sameness of most of what I was hearing on records and in clubs began to get to me about five years ago—not coincidentally around the same time that *The New York Times Sunday Magazine* ran a long piece in which the writer Tom Piazza enthused about a flock of musicians under the age of thirty who had recently been signed by major labels eager to find the next Wynton Marsalis.

Piazza opened with a look at the trumpeter Roy Hargrove wowing his elders on an unnamed Charlie Parker tune at Bradley's, a club in Greenwich Village. "Ten years ago, you could have stopped into every jazz club between Bradley's and Yankee Stadium and not found any 'youngsters' playing this way," Piazza claimed. "For a long time, young musicians were taught to play a hybrid form that was jazz in name only, often heavily electronic, with large infusions of funk and rock in it."

This was published in 1990, so "ten years ago" was 1980, a blink before Wynton and Branford Marsalis, when the most talked-about young musicians in Manhattan were Anthony Davis, George Lewis, Craig Harris, David Murray, and the like—nominal avant-gardists busy collaborating with poets, choreographers, and painters in a game attempt to erase the line that has traditionally separated jazz from the other performing arts. They had more on their minds than a Columbia Records contract and a week at the Village Vanguard. You didn't hear them at Bradley's, but maybe that spoke badly about Bradley's, not about them.

A few months later in 1990, *Time* ran a cover story on Wynton Marsalis (they were only seven or eight years late in getting around to him), with sidebars on most of Piazza's tadboppers. The whole package was headlined "The New Jazz Age," and a spate of such articles has followed in the years since. And they're still coming.

The problem with such "trend" pieces, quite apart from their refusal to consider that there might be young musicians shunned by major labels for not fitting the desired mold, is that they perpetuate the neocon myth that jazz evolved from bebop to aberrant fusion to bop again, with thirty-plus years of free and its offshoots not even counting as jazz. They also foster the illusion that nothing much was happening in jazz until the arrival of these neophobic youth, proof of which is that you hardly read a word about jazz in these magazines since the *last* time they published trend pieces on "the swing back to tradition" or whatever. (Francis Davis, "Introduction" in *Bebop and Nothingness* [New York: Schirmer Books, 1995])

Davis had more to say on the current jazz scene's youth craze in the *Atlantic Monthly.*

Youth has become the most frequent topic of conversation in jazz. The talk concerns a crop of instrumentalists in their twenties and very early thirties, including the tenor saxophonists Joshua Redman and James Carter, the trumpeters Roy Hargrove and Nicholas Payton, the pianists Cyrus Chestnut and Jacky Terrasson, and the bassist Christian McBride, who are supposedly luring audiences their own age and younger to jazz. . . .

You could call it the Wynton Marsalis factor. Every ten years or so, for a different set of reasons each time, cultural trendsetters rally behind one musician with whom they sense a bond and who then comes to symbolize jazz to the mass media. Before Marsalis it happened in turn to Dave Brubeck, Miles Davis, John Coltrane, and Keith Jarrett. Marsalis improbably combined youthful arrogance with an obeisance to tradition that bordered on ancestor worship: Columbia's success in marketing him persuaded the other majors that the trick to selling jazz was to play up its genealogy and long history of esoteric appeal even while attempting to demystify it by means of trim young figures in designer suits. Though unprecedented in recent memory, the election of a *type* of musician to carry the banner for jazz was probably inevitable, given the difficulty of finding another performer as charismatic as Marsalis and given the long-standing preference of magazine editors for pieces on jazz "trends," as opposed to on individual musicians. . . .

The animosity with which a lot of jazz critics regard Marsalis owes something to his having usurped their authority. His pronouncements on jazz in interviews and in occasional byline articles carry more weight with readers than do those of any of us who write regularly about jazz (including even Albert Murray and Stanley Crouch, Marsalis's associates at Lincoln Center). And in turning thumbs down on most of the innovations in jazz since 1960—in vehemently insisting that it can't be jazz if it doesn't swing from beginning to end and explicitly refer to the blues—Marsalis has been telling disgruntled longtime listeners exactly what they were waiting to hear. . . .

Longtime jazz listeners, for their part, want jazz to be as it was in the fifties and early sixties, when a devotion to jazz was still a sign of being hip. (Francis Davis, "Like Young," *Atlantic Monthly*, July 1996)

As for new listeners, Davis notes wryly, "People who have never really listened to jazz want it to go on sounding the way they've been led to believe it should, so that they'll be able to recognize it in case they ever chance to hear any"!

Tom Masland has observed that this youth orientation is simply a marketing strategy to attract young listeners.

Most fans are men in their 30s, 40s and 50s. But record companies want to pry college-age consumers, proven record buyers, away from mainstream popular music. So many have tried a tactic pioneered in rock and roll: creating stars. "I thought if I went after young artists at least that would pique the interest of the kids," says George Butler, a Columbia Records executive who takes credit for Marsalis's sudden rise. (Tom Masland, "Between Lions and Legends," *Newsweek*, February 24, 1992)

On the contrary, Francis Davis feels the industry's preoccupation with youth, aside from the artistic problems it presents, is not an effective way to bring in new listeners anyway.

There have always been young jazz musicians, but only lately has anyone made a fuss over them just for *being* young—instead of for auguring change. . . .

Are more young people listening to jazz because they can identify with [Joshua] Redman and the others? From what I've noticed, the answer is yes only if you count as "young" dating couples in their late twenties and early thirties. I've been to shows where the youngest people in the house were on the bandstand. In allowing itself to become so strongly identified with its past, jazz may be bargaining away its future. Positioning jazz as a sane acoustic alternative to raucous, mechanized pop might be an effective short-term sales strategy, but doesn't all this sanctimony about "tradition" and the emphasis on boilerplate bebop send a message to teenagers and college students that jazz offers absolutely nothing of interest to them? (Francis Davis, "Like Young")

Another problem raised by this "youth-ism" is that fine musicians who are not so young any more are often ignored.

[There are] dozens of fabulously gifted jazz artists who have paid for the fact that they are dead center in their careers. They served their apprenticeships long ago. Without pandering to popular tastes, they have survived. And while the latest young lions work to master the earlier idioms of acoustic, straight-ahead jazz, these older players stand at the cutting edge of its evolution. This should be *their* time, and they know it. Says bass player Ray Drummond, 45, "There are some guys my age who feel not just cheated, but betrayed." (Tom Masland, "Between Lions and Legends")

As Masland points out, these middle-aged artists are making an acceptable living, but it seems highly unfair that they are making less than people with fewer credentials. Another problem has developed that affects musicians of all ages: most jazz musicians freelance with a variety of bands, because very few bands can offer their members full-time work. According to Roxane Orgill, this situation is economically sound, but she fears it may not be musically productive.

Opportunities for live performance are so limited that only a handful of the so-called young lions—including Mr. Hargrove, Joshua Redman, Jacky Terrasson and, of course, Wynton Marsalis—can provide enough work to keep a band together. For musicians who don't have major recording contracts, the struggle is even greater.

The effect on jazz could be disastrous, because without working bands, the music can't develop. Whereas a classical score sits on a shelf until a conductor takes it down and leads an orchestra through a performance, jazz comes out of an oral tradition. The music has to be played, and by people who are familiar enough with one another to go out on a limb, to experiment as Joe Oliver did with Louis Armstrong in the Creole Jazz Band and as Duke Ellington did with his orchestra,

John Lewis with the Modern Jazz Quartet and Miles Davis with his various quintets and sextets. (Roxane Orgill, "Fewer Gigs Means Fewer Jazz Bands," *New York Times,* August 6, 1995)

Down Beat, which debuted in 1934 and is the most widely read periodical on jazz internationally, has joined the chorus of concern about the scarcity of full-time bands. In the issues of March and May 1997, John Corbett published the first two installments of an ongoing series about this problem. It is entitled "Fanfare For the Working Band."

12

Crossing Boundaries, 1980 to the Present

Nobody can really say what the future of jazz is, but one thing is clear: jazz will continue to interact with all other types of music, to draw from them, and to influence them in return. This give-and-take continues, as it has since the earliest days of the music, to lead towards classical music and toward popular styles.

Jazz musicians have always been interested in classical music. Classical music is an amazing tradition, and what musician could not have some interest in it? The new trend, however, is that the classical folks are now interested in jazz, creating an openness and a mutual respect that has long been wanting. Remember the articles about jazz from the 1920s? In 1989, Mark Tucker, a jazz scholar and professor then at Columbia University who has published highly regarded books on Duke Ellington, offered a review of some early meetings between jazz and classical composers and then provided more recent examples.

Jazz Just Keeps Knocking at the Concert Hall Door
MARK TUCKER

Jazz has been a familiar guest in the concert hall over the years, dropping in from time to time, stirring things up, then moving on to let musical life resume its more sedate patterns. Recently, though, the guest shows signs of moving in for good. Today's concertgoers pick up programs to find Ellington and Monk in spots previously reserved for Mozart and Brahms. Repertory ensembles like the American Jazz Orchestra help keep alive past jazz masterpieces. Conductors like Gunther Schuller, Maurice Peress and Marin Alsop champion jazz works as concert fare.

Classical soloists also are taking a keener interest in jazz. The cellist Yo Yo Ma has been studying the art of improvisation, while others— the clarinetist Richard Stoltzman, the pianist Steven Mayer and the violinist Nigel Kennedy—have built jazz into their programs. And as symphony orchestras face dwindling audiences, mounting financial problems and a standard repertory exhausted through overplaying, they, too, have turned to jazz for revitalization, as the New York Philharmonic will be doing this week and next month.

What we're seeing is an acceleration of musical fusion experiments that began in the 1920's. That decade produced a number of concert works liberally spiced with jazz ingredients, among them Darius Milhaud's "Création du Monde," George Antheil's Jazz Symphony and piano concertos by Maurice Ravel and Aaron Copland. Approaching the problem from a different angle, the band leader Paul Whiteman promoted the heavily arranged and richly textured music that became known as "symphonic jazz." The most enduring result of Whiteman's advocacy, of course, is "Rhapsody in Blue," the piece he commissioned from the young songwriter George Gershwin.

Even more adventurous were the Third Stream experiments of the 1950's. As the label implies, this music joined together the European classical and American jazz traditions. Third-stream compositions by Gunther Schuller, George Russell and John Lewis could be confrontational, boldly juxtaposing written sections with improvised ones and exploiting tensions between classical and jazz practice. Like some of the earlier efforts, however, these musical hybrids never quite took root, and are rarely heard in the concert hall today.

In the last few decades, many more jazz musicians have been busy breaking down barriers. In 1972 Ornette Coleman wrote "Skies of America," a symphonic suite in 21 movements. Dave Brubeck has focused on large-scale forms, including an oratorio, four cantatas and a piece for jazz combo and orchestra. Chick Corea, Carla Bley and Keith Jarrett have all composed works for the Chamber Music Society of Lincoln Center. The clarinetist Eddie Daniels has expanded the jazz concerto repertory. And the pianist Anthony Davis has turned to opera, evolving a multicultural musical vocabulary that freely blends elements of jazz, blues, Balinese gamelan and 20th-century European modernism. The New York Philharmonic's current season features two noteworthy collaborations between jazz and symphonic players.

On Friday . . . Zubin Mehta will conduct the premiere of Roger Kellaway's "Songs of Ascent for Tuba and Orchestra," with Warren Deck as soloist. On Dec. 14, 15, 16 and 19, the baritone saxophonist Gerry Mulligan will perform two of his compositions with the Philharmonic: "Entente," a customized solo vehicle for saxophone with orchestra; and "K-4 Pacific," in which Mr. Mulligan's jazz quartet will join the Philharmonic for a collective jam. While these works have fundamental differences, all three seek a reconciliation of symphonic and jazz forces, attempting to turn a potentially hazardous partnership into a harmonious coalition. If anyone is qualified for such a job, it's the pianist Roger Kellaway. An unabashed eclectic, he is adept at juggling various musical activities: playing jazz piano, writing music for film and television, composing chamber and symphonic works. In a sense his new piece grew organically from his multi-tracked career. As he says, "I've always loved classical music and jazz. 'Songs of Ascent' represents a culmination of a long path in experiencing both types of music simultaneously. The point was to use jazz colors and rhythmic momentum in a symphonic shape."

For "Songs of Ascent," Mr. Kellaway turned to a form shared by both classical and jazz musicians: theme and variations. "The introduction," he said in an interview, "presents the main material. The variations start with a bass line, harmonic progression and rhythmic cycles. It's almost like figured bass. What I've written on top of this feels like an improvisation—so it's more like an introduction and nine improvisations."

Basing a piece on a series of repeating chord cycles is second nature to a jazz musician. But Mr. Kellaway acknowledges that it may go against the grain of conventional composerly wisdom: "I have a 900-page dissertation on redundancy and repetition in composition and how to avoid it. As a jazz musician, my whole life has been repetition."

Certain sonorities in "Songs of Ascent" also come from jazz—conga in the percussion section and plunger-muted brass à la Ellington. The composer has also devised something he calls a "jazz color ensemble," made up of English horn, bass clarinet, bassoon, French horn and two flugelhorns.

On first glance these instruments hardly seem characteristic of jazz. But to Mr. Kellaway they evoke the palette of the late Gil Evans, one of jazz's great composers: "The 'jazz color ensemble' caused me to feel a harmonic and textural legacy with Gil. With it, if I'm dealing with a seven-part chord, each instrument can play an individual note and the tuba takes the seventh." Both the instruments and scoring techniques harken back to Evans's innovative arrangements for Claude Thornhill's orchestra and Miles Davis's nonet in the 1940's.

Gerry Mulligan was part of that scene, too, arranging for the bands of Thornhill, Gene Krupa and Elliott Lawrence, and playing on the famous "Birth of the Cool" recording sessions with Miles Davis. But in writing "Entente" he drew more directly on the European orchestral tradition: "As a listener I've worked my way backward, discovering more composers from before this century. I scored "Entente" for the Brahms orchestra, with woodwinds in threes. It's big enough to have plenty of guts, but can still play lightly."

. . . In mixing classical and jazz practice, one of the most problematic areas is rhythm. Many conservatory-trained players have difficulty achieving the relaxed yet precisely timed phrasing characteristic of jazz. They might effortlessly toss off the most complex rhythmic combinations imaginable, but ask them to swing straight eighth notes and many will draw a blank.

Marin Alsop, conductor of the jazz-friendly Concordia orchestra (who was recently named music director of the Long Island Philharmonic, as well), believes that the problem can be overcome: "A conductor verbalizes to the orchestra a lot. If it's a piece that really has to swing, you have to work on the eighth notes. Once you get the rhythmic feeling it's simply a matter of practice. As a fiddler, it took me six months to play Bach with the metronome going on beats two and four."

In "Entente," Mr. Mulligan attempted to steer around this problem: "I wrote rhythms that symphonic players are used to. The orchestra has its own language for swing. In every era composers used various devices to achieve that rhythmic momentum—that's what I tapped into." As it turns out, much of "Entente" is based on gentle, undulating bass patterns more characteristic of Latin jazz—even Ravel's "Bolero"—than straight-ahead swing. The orchestra's rhythms remain minimally syncopated, only occasionally breaking out into figures reminiscent of the big bands Mr. Mulligan arranged for in the 40's.

Mr. Kellaway, on the other hand, sought to incorporate the idea of a jazz rhythm section within the orchestra: "In jazz, it's the rhythm section's responsibility to maintain oneness. With an orchestra, there are three percussionists, piano and a conductor to bring together." Asked if this could be a problem, Mr. Kellaway exclaims, laughing, "Yes!" Still, he does not anticipate a fundamentally different rhythmic conception to get in the way of a good performance. "If the Philharmonic players perform the figures the way they're written, they'll sound fine," he says. "If they play them wider and with more depth—as a jazz person would—it'll sound fantastic."

In a sense, both Mr. Kellaway's and Mr. Mulligan's works are symptomatic of the increasing fluidity in late-20th-century American musical life. It seems as if everyone is crossing over these days: Itzhak Perlman plays Hoagy Carmichael, the Kronos Quartet programs Monk and Jimi Hendrix, Linda Ronstadt sings Puccini, Keith Jarrett interprets Bach and Mozart, and the rock drummer Stewart Copeland writes grand opera. One result of this activity is a kind of ventilation of the concert hall; rather than a dusty museum devoted to past relics, it is slowly opening its doors to more contemporary currents.

According to Mr. Mulligan, not just audiences but classical musicians appreciate the change. "There's a lot of enthusiasm on the part of orchestras to play music that relates to jazz," he says. "Many of the younger players have had experience in dance and jazz bands. This familiarity with their own music has changed their attitude."

While things seem to be loosening up in the concert halls, other institutions—predictably—lag behind. But perhaps one day there will arise an age of real musical "entente," when music students will be generally required to learn 12-bar blues form and improvising techniques; when pianists will win competitions playing Jelly Roll Morton and Art Tatum; when opera singers will study Sarah Vaughan as part of their basic training. For now, the appearance of jazz on symphony programs suggests greater upheaval ahead. (Mark Tucker, "Jazz Just Keeps Knocking at the Concert Hall Door," *New York Times,* November 19, 1989)

I have noticed, with some pleasure, that established classical artists are now more willing to take chances playing jazz in public. The phenomenal success of Jean-Pierre Rampal's recording of Claude Bolling's "Suite for Flute and Jazz Piano" back in 1975 helped set the stage for this encounter. While Rampal's part was written by French jazz pianist Bolling, other classical musicians, well into their careers, are taking the time to learn how to improvise. Clarinetist Richard Stoltzman has a wonderful attitude and has been perhaps the most successful. Violinist Itzhak Perlman, one of the world's greatest at the classics, is merely a good jazz player, reminding us that technique is not all. If he continues to work at learning jazz style, it will be exciting to follow him. Cellist Yo Yo Ma is working with vocalist Bobby McFerrin, who started in jazz, on jazz and other types of music.

At the same time, jazz crosses boundaries in the other direction, into the pop world. In the mid-1990s, rappers take jazz records of the 1960s that have a danceable beat and combine them with new sounds. (See Mark Gridley's discussion in chapter 2.) Guy Garcia provides some background to this so-called acid jazz movement, and notes that the label is constantly changing.

Since it emerged from London's dance club underground five years ago, acid jazz has grown from a cult into a global phenomenon. A fertile fusion of traditional jazz, 70's soul and funk, Latin percussion and hip-hop rhythms, it has spread from England to America via acid jazz parties staged at clubs like the Cooler and the Supper Club in New York, Brass in Los Angeles and Soul Sauce in Philadelphia.

Acid jazz has also taken root in Germany, Brazil and Japan, where local musicians are concocting their own derivations. As a result, some originators of acid jazz have begun to shy away from the term, which they feel no longer describes the diversity of the new hybrid. They prefer names like street soul, eclectro, jazz not jazz, hip-bop and alternative rhythm-and-blues.

With its upbeat vibe, underground allure and funky beat, acid jazz by whatever name bridges the musical gap between neo-beatniks in their 20's and middle-aged baby boomers. And by tapping the black roots of modern pop, it has introduced a new generation of listeners to vintage jazz and soul. . . .

Now acid jazz may be poised to enter the American mainstream. Its increasing influence has been noted in recent months by both *Rolling Stone* and *Billboard* magazines; *Billboard* devoted most of the cover of its Dec. 17 issue to acid jazz. The commercial and critical success of groups like Digable Planets, the Brand-New Heavies and Us3, whose album, "Hand on the Torch," has sold more than 700,000 copies in America alone, has piqued the interest of major record companies. . . .

Acid jazz is also inspiring creative collaborations between jazz veterans and younger stars. "Stolen Moments: Red Hot and Cool" pairs traditional jazz masters like Mr. Hancock and Donald Byrd with up-and-coming artists like the rapper and producer Guru and the singer Me'Shell Ndege'Ocello. . . .

Gilles Peterson, of Talkin' Loud and the London disk jockey credited with coining the term "acid jazz," now rejects it as too outdated to be meaningful. What started as a lark when he mixed classic jazz numbers with Brazilian percussion tracks and electronic "acid house" dance beats in the late 1980's has evolved into an array of styles that ranges from the electronically sampled jazz groove of Us3 to the eclectic hip-hop of Urban Species to the soulful pop of the Brand-New Heavies. . . .

. . . [I]t will no doubt continue to evolve as it seeps into the mainstream, spawning exotic new blends like "jazz con bossa," a combination of jazz and Brazilian bossa nova; "trip-hop," a blend of jazz and ambient techno; and, looming on the horizon, "jungle jazz," a raucous mix of reggae, techno and jazz already hip in England. (Guy Garcia, "For Hipsters of the 90's, Acid Jazz Defines Cool," *New York Times,* January 8, 1995)

Clearly, jazz will also continue to cross national boundaries. International audiences have enjoyed the music ever since the first Original Dixieland "Jass" Band records of 1917. By 1918 and 1919 recordings from Europe of bands playing their repertory, though not necessarily in the same style, were released. Today the music is more fully international in that the members of a single band often come from several countries.

Jazz is also more open to women than ever before. In the early days it was a kind of "boys' club," with the exception of singers and a few instrumentalists, primarily pianists. By the 1930s and 1940s, participation in all-women groups was one way for women instrumentalists to get gigs. In the 1960s a woman in the band would often provoke comment among audiences and reviewers. In the mid-1990s, the pianist, bassist, or whatever, man or woman, is usually introduced by name and that is that. Much has been written about women jazz artists, including my article "She Wiped All The Men Out: A Re-Evaluation of Women Instrumentalists and Composers In Jazz," in *Music Educators Journal* (September and October 1984), and several books, among them *American Women in Jazz* by Sally Placksin (Wideview Books, 1982), *Madame Jazz: Contemporary Women Instrumentalists* by Leslie Gourse (New York: Oxford University Press, 1995), and *Stormy Weather* by Linda Dahl (New York: Pantheon Books, 1984). Dahl is working on a biography of the celebrated pianist and composer Mary Lou Williams, who was active from the late 1920s through her death in 1981.

Finally, jazz is more accepted—by universities, by governments, by foundations, by concert presenters—than ever before. And that can only be good news.

Bibliography

Armstrong, Louis. "Jazz Is a Language." *Music Journal*, 1961.

Austin, Cecil. "Jazz." *Music and Letters*, July 1925.

Bauer, Marion. "L'Influence du 'Jazz-Band.'" *La Revue Musicale*, April 1924.

Bennett, Richard Rodney. "The Technique of the Jazz Singer." *Music and Musicians*, February 1972.

Berger, Francesco. "A Jazz Band Concert." *Monthly Musical Record*, 1919.

Berliner, Paul. *Thinking in Jazz*. Chicago: University of Chicago Press, 1994.

Berrett, Joshua. "Louis Armstrong and Opera." *Musical Quarterly*, summer 1992.

Booker, Guy. "Colored Historians Too Lazy to Write Own History of Jazz; Let Whites Do It." *Philadelphia Tribune*, weekly magazine section, August 13, 1955.

C. B. "Bebop Called Music in Tune With the Times." *Philadelphia Afro-American*, July 3, 1948.

Carter, Elmer Anderson. "Swing" (editorial). *Opportunity*, July 1938.

Coeuroy, André, and André Schaffner. *Le Jazz*. 1926.

Collier, James Lincoln. *The Reception of Jazz in America: A New View*. Brooklyn, N.Y.: Institute for Studies in American Music, 1988.

Count Basie. "The Story of Jazz." *Music Journal*, ca. 1955–61.

Dahl, Linda. *Stormy Weather*. New York: Pantheon Books, 1984.

Davis, Francis. "Introduction." In *Bebop and Nothingness*. New York: Schirmer Books, 1995.

———. "Like Young." *Atlantic Monthly*, July 1996.

"The Decline of Jazz" (editorial). *The Musician*, May 1922.

Engel, Carl. "Jazz: A Musical Discussion." *Atlantic Monthly*, August 1922.

Ephland, John. Editorial. *Down Beat*, November 1996.

Europe, James Reese. "A Negro Explains 'Jazz.'" *Literary Digest*, 1919.

Evangelist. "Songs of the Blacks." *Dwight's Journal of Music*, November 15, 1856.

Feather, Leonard. "The Decade of 'What is Jazz?'" *Boston Globe*, January 1, 1980. Reprinted from the *Los Angeles Times*.

———. *Inside Jazz*. New York: Da Capo Press, 1949.

———. "A Plea for Less Critical Infighting, More Attention to the Music Itself." *Down Beat*, December 16, 1965.

Gabbard, Krin. "Louis Armstrong and His Audiences." Published in this version for the first time. For a more detailed treatment of Gabbard's argument, see his *Jammin' at the Margins: Jazz and the American Cinema*. Chicago: University of Chicago Press, 1996.

Gade, Svend. *Jazz Mad.* New York: Jacobsen-Hodgkinson Corporation, 1927.

Garcia, Guy. "For Hipsters of the 90's, Acid Jazz Defines Cool." *New York Times,* January 8, 1995.

Gilbert, Henry F. "Concerning Jazz." *New Music Review,* December 1922.

Gillespie, Dizzy, and Tex Beneke. "To Bop or Not to Bop." *Record Review,* September 1949.

Gitler, Ira. Review of *Straight Ahead,* by Abbey Lincoln. *Down Beat,* November 9, 1961.

Gleeson, E. T. "Scoop." "I Remember: The Birth of Jazz." *San Francisco Call-Bulletin,* September 3, 1938.

Gold, Robert S. *Jazz Talk.* New York: Bobbs-Merrill, 1975.

Goodman, Benny, and Irving Kolodin. *The Kingdom of Swing.* New York: Frederick Ungar, 1939.

Gottlieb, Bill. "The Anatomy of Bebop." *New York Herald Tribune,* September 26, 1947.

Gourse, Leslie. *Madame Jazz: Contemporary Women Instrumentalists.* New York: Oxford University Press, 1995.

Gridley, Mark. *Concise Guide to Jazz.* 2nd edition. Upper Saddle River, N.J.: Prentice-Hall, 1997.

————. *Jazz Styles: History and Analysis.* 6th edition. Upper Saddle River, N.J.: Prentice-Hall, 1997.

Gridley, Mark, Robert Maxham, and Robert Hoff. "Three Approaches to Defining Jazz." *The Musical Quarterly* 73, no. 4 (1989).

Gushee, Lawrence. "Lester Young's 'Shoe Shine Boy.'" In International Musicological Society, *Report of the Twelfth Congress, Berkeley, 1977.* Edited by Daniel Heartz and Bonnie Wade. Kassell: Barenreiter, 1981. (Originally presented as a lecture given in 1977.)

————. "The Nineteenth-Century Origins of Jazz." Reprinted from *Black Music Research Journal* 14, no. 1 (spring 1994).

Handy, W. C. *Blues: An Anthology.* New York: Albert and Charles Boni, 1926.

————. *Father of the Blues.* New York: Macmillan, 1941.

Henderson, Harry, and Sam Shaw. "And Now We Go Bebop!" *Collier's,* March 20, 1948.

Holbrook, Dick. "Our Word JAZZ." *Storyville* 50 (December 1973–January 1974).

Hopkins, Ernest J. "In Praise of 'Jazz,' a Futurist Word Which Has Just Joined the Language." *San Francisco Bulletin,* April 5, 1913.

Hourwich, Rebecca. "Where the Jazz Begins." *Collier's,* January 23, 1926.

Jenkins, Willard. "Wynton Bites Back: Addresses His Critics." *National Jazz Service Organization Jazz Journal* 5, no. 1 (ca. April 1994).

Johnson, Charles S. "Jazz" (editorial). *Opportunity, Journal of Negro Life,* April 1928.

————. "The Origin of Jazz" (editorial). *Opportunity, Journal of Negro Life,* January 1923.

Jones, LeRoi (Imamu Amiri Baraka). *Blues People.* New York: William Morrow, 1963.

————. "The Jazz Avant-Garde." *Metronome,* September 1961.

Korngold, Julius. "Jazz." *Detroit Symphony Program Booklet,* 1928.

Lambert, Constant. "The Spirit of Jazz." In *Music Ho!* New York: Faber & Faber, 1934.

Leonard, Neil. *Jazz and the White Americans.* Chicago: University of Chicago Press, 1962.

Levin, Michael, and John S. Wilson. "No Bop Roots in Jazz: Parker." *Down Beat,* September 4, 1949.

Locke, Alain. "Negro Music Goes to Par." *Opportunity,* July 1939.

————, ed. *The New Negro.* New York: Albert and Charles Boni, 1925.

Lomax, Alan. *Mister Jelly Roll.* Berkeley and Los Angeles: University of California Press, 1950.

"Louis Armstrong on 'Re Bop.'" *Esquire's 1947 Jazz Book.*

Major, Clarence. *Juba To Jive: A Dictionary of African-American Slang.* New York: Viking, 1994.

Marshall, Marilyn. "Are Blacks Giving Away Jazz?" *Ebony,* February 1988.

Masland, Tom. "Between Lions and Legends." *Newsweek,* February 24, 1992.

Matthews, Ralph. "Anything for a Thrill." *Philadelphia Afro-American,* February 22, 1947.

Moore, Phil. "Jim Crow on the Bandstand." *Negro Digest,* September 1946.

Morgenstern, Dan (moderator). "Point of Contact: A Discussion." *Down Beat Music '66,* 1966.

Morton, Jelly Roll. "A Discourse on Jazz." Transcribed by Peter Pullman. Published here for the first time.

Niles, Abbe. "Ballads, Songs, and Snatches." *The Bookman,* January 1929.

Orgill, Roxane. "Fewer Gigs Means Fewer Jazz Bands." *New York Times,* August 6, 1995.

Osgood, Henry O. *So This Is Jazz*. Boston: Little, Brown and Company, 1926.

Panassié, Hugues. *Hot Jazz*. New York: M. Witmark and Sons, 1936.

———. *The Real Jazz*. Published in French, 1940. First English edition, New York: Smith and Durrell, 1942. Revised and corrected edition, New York: A. S. Barnes and Co., 1960.

Pareles, Jon. "Jazz Swings Back to Tradition." *New York Times Magazine*, June 17, 1984.

Placksin, Sally. *American Women in Jazz*. Wideview Books, 1982.

Porter, Lewis, ed. *A Lester Young Reader*. Washington, D.C.: Smithsonian Institution Press, 1991.

———. "She Wiped All The Men Out: A Re-Evaluation of Women Instrumentalists and Composers In Jazz." *Music Educators Journal* (September–October 1984).

"Racial Prejudice in Jazz." Panel discussion, *Down Beat*, March 15, 1962.

Rockwell, John. "Can Jazz Survive 'Classical' Treatment?" *New York Times*, September 14, 1986.

Rockwell, John, ed. *A Virgil Thomson Reader*. New York: Dutton, 1981.

Rogers, James A. "Jazz at Home." In Alain Locke, ed. *The New Negro*. New York: Albert and Charles Boni, 1925.

Rose, Al. "Critic Raps False Interpretation of Music, Lauds Jazz as Only True Negro Music Form." *Philadelphia Tribune*, ca. March 16, 1948.

Safire, William. "On Language." *New York Times Magazine*, April 1981.

Sargant, Norman, and Tom Sargant. "Negro-American Music or The Origin of Jazz." *Musical Times*, September 1, 1931.

Sargeant, Winthrop. "Is Jazz Music?" *American Mercury Magazine*, October 1943.

———. *Jazz: Hot and Hybrid*. New York: Arrow Editions, 1938. Revised, 1946 and 1964. Third edition, enlarged, New York: Da Capo Press, 1975.

Seldes, Gilbert. "Toujours Jazz." In *The Seven Lively Arts*. New York: Harper & Brothers, 1924.

Shepp, Archie. "An Artist Speaks Bluntly." *Down Beat*, December 16, 1965.

Simon, George. "Bebop's the Easy Out, Claims Louis." *Metronome*, March 1948, pp. 14–15.

Stephens, Roy W. "Writer Raps Armstrong for Criticism of Trend." *Philadelphia Afro-American*, November 15, 1947.

Stoddard, Tom. *Jazz On the Barbary Coast*. Chigwell, U.K.: Storyville Publications, 1982.

"Straton Says Jazz Is 'Agency of Devil.'" *New York Times*, May 7, 1926.

Stringham, Edwin. "'Jazz'—An Educational Problem." *Musical Quarterly*, April 1926.

Taylor, Billy. "Negroes Don't know Anything about Jazz." *Duke Magazine*, August 1957.

Thomson, Virgil. "Swing Again." *Modern Music* 15, no. 3 (March–April 1938).

———. "Swing Music." *Modern Music* 13, no. 4, (May–June 1936). Reprinted in *A Virgil Thomson Reader*. Edited by John Rockwell. New York: Dutton, 1981.

Tucker, Mark. "Jazz Just Keeps Knocking at the Concert Hall Door." *New York Times*, November 19, 1989.

"War Rages Over 'Bebop' Music Style." *Philadelphia Afro-American*, November 15, 1947.

Waterman, Glenn. *Piano Jazz*. Los Angeles: self-published, 1917, 1924.

Watrous, Peter. "A Jazz Generation and the Miles Davis Curse." *New York Times*, October 15, 1995.

———. "Jazz Moves Fast Forward into Its Past." *New York Times*, September 18, 1988.

Wilson, John S. "The Old Black Jazzmen: Where Are They Now?" *New York Times*, July 21, 1969.

Winick, Charles. "The Use of Drugs by Jazz Musicians." *Social Problems* 7, no. 3 (winter 1959–60).

Woideck, Carl. *Charlie Parker: His Music and Life*. Ann Arbor: University of Michigan Press, 1996.

Permissions

"A Discourse on Jazz," by Jelly Roll Morton. Transcription copyright ©1996 Peter Pullman. From a forthcoming Jelly Roll Morton anthology. Used by permission. All rights reserved.

"Three Approaches to Defining Jazz," by Mark Gridley, Robert Maxham, and Robert Hoff. Copyright © Oxford University Press. Used by permission.

Virgil Thomson, "Swing Again." Reprinted from *Modern Music* 15, no. 3 (March–April 1938). Copyright © League of Composers/International Society for Contemporary Music. Used by permission.

"The Technique of the Jazz Singer." Originally in *Music and Musicians,* February 1972. Copyright © Richard Rodney Bennett. Used by permission.

Excerpts on analysis from "Lester Young's 'Shoe Shine Boy,'" by Lawrence Gushee. Copyright © 1981 Lawrence Gushee. Used by permission.

Editorials from *Opportunity, Journal of Negro Life,* 1920s. Copyright © 1923, 1928 National Urban League, Inc. Used by permission.

"The Nineteenth-Century Origins of Jazz," by Lawrence Gushee. Originally published in *Black Music Research Journal* 14, no. 1 (spring 1994). Reprinted by permission.

"Jazz" (editorial), by Charles S. Johnson. Copyright © 1925 National Urban League, Inc. Used by permission.

Excerpts from Gilbert Seldes, "Toujours Jazz," in *The Seven Lively Arts,* Harper & Brothers, 1924. Copyright © Estate of Gilbert Seldes. Used by permission.

Excerpts from "The Spirit of Jazz," by Constant Lambert, from *Music Ho!,* Faber & Faber, 1934. Copyright © Faber and Faber Ltd. Used by permission.

"Swing" (editorial), by Elmer Anderson Carter. Copyright © 1938 National Urban League, Inc. Used by permission.

Excerpt from "Negro Music Goes to Par," by Alain Locke. Copyright © 1939 National Urban League, Inc. Used by permission.

"Louis Armstrong and His Audiences," by Krin Gabbard. Copyright © 1997 Krin Gabbard. Used by permission of the author.

"The Anatomy of Bebop," by Bill Gottlieb. Originally printed in the *New York Herald-Tribune,* September 26, 1947. Copyright © William Gottlieb. Reprinted by permission.

"Writer Raps Armstrong for Criticism of Trend," by Roy Stephens. *Philadelphia Afro-American,* November 15, 1947. Copyright © Afro-American Newspapers Archives and Research Center. Used by permission.

Index

Page numbers cited in *italic* indicate readings, listed here under the author's name. An *n* placed directly following a page citation indicates a footnote.

A

Abercrombie, John, 234
acid jazz, 37
acoustic music, 242
Adderley, Cannonball, 223, 229, 231–32, 248
Adderley, Nat, 248
Adorno, Theodor, 167
African American jazz scholarship, 199–207
African American names, 85n
African American stereotypes, 203–4
Afro-Spanish music, 89, 103–5, 111, 259
All Music Guide to Jazz (Gridley), 37
Allen, Dick, 108
Alpert, Herb, 22, 234
Alsop, Marin, 276, 278
Altshul, Barry, 233
American Jazz Orchestra, 246–47, 276
American Women in Jazz (Placksin), 282
Americanisms (Bartlett), 3
Ammons, Gene, 224
Amsterdam News (periodical), 90
Antheil, George, 19, 276
"Anything for a Thrill." *See* Matthews, Ralph
Apollo Theatre, 206
"Are Blacks Giving Away Jazz?" *See* Marshall, Marilyn
Armstrong, Louis, 10, 101n, 155, 164–70, *185–87*, 187
    and African American tradition, 166
    and bebop, 173
    and Bessie Smith, 58
    and drugs, 189
    in films, 166–67, 169
    and George Moret, 109
    greatness of, 181
    and improvisation, 36
    innovations of, 219, 272
    on jazz, 185–87
    and Michael Jackson, 170
    musical style of, 75n
    and New Orleans jazz, 166
    and popular songs, 177
    popularity of, 250
    and racial integration, 168
    record sales of, 35
    and Wynton Marsalis, 248
Artists & Models (film), 169
Association for the Advancement of Creative Music (AACM), 234, 235
Austin, Cecil, *146–47*
Avakian, George, 216
Ayler, Albert, 36

B

Bach, Johann Sebastian, 45–46, 48, 52
Baldwin, James, 166, 169
Balliett, Whitney, ix, 205
banjo, in jazz, 49, 128, 129
Baquet, Achille, 109–110
Baquet, George, 109–110
Baraka, Imamu Amiri (LeRoi Jones), 87, 166, *220–29*
Barés, Basile, 100

Bartók, Béla, 179, 221
Bartz, Gary, 242
Basie, William "Count," 27, 33, 34, 53, 161, 187–88, 252
bass, string, 17, 70, 109, 225, 226
Bassey, Shirley, 59
Bauer, Marion, 130–31
bebop, 19, 36, 164, 173–88, 202, 215, 220, 223–26, 250
    Armstrong on, 182–84
    as basic jazz, 254
    and blues, 180
    and classical music, 180
    and dancing, 173, 177, 179
    dissonance in, 174, 176, 179
    Gillespie on, 178
    hard, 226
    as improvised jazz, 187
    and melody, 182
    negative reactions to, 173, 180
    revival of, 247, 269
    rhythm in, 225
Bebop and Nothingness. See Davis, Francis
"Bebop's the Easy Out, Claims Louis." *See* Simon, George
Beethoven, Ludwig van, 40, 222, 254
Beiderbecke, Bix, 72, 166
Bell, Clive, 122, *138–39*
Beneke, Tex, 177, *179*
Bennett, Richard Rodney, *57–67*
Berendt, Joachim, 19
Berger, Francesco, 128, *127–31*
Berigan, Bunny, 177, 190
Berlin, Irving, 10, 81, 82–83, 132, 137
Berliner, Paul, 39, 55
Bernstein, Leonard, 19
Berrett, Joshua, 185
big band music. *See* swing
Big Broadcast, The (film), 190
Billboard (periodical), 281
Blake, Eubie, 236
Blakey, Art, 37, 195, 235, 248, 253
Blesh, Rudi, 205
Bley, Carla, 277
blues, 19, 30, 32, 34, 36, 56, 58, 100–101, 109, 132, 135, 153, 156, 221, 228, 229
Blues: An Anthology (Handy), 157
Blues People (Baraka), 87, 166, 229
Bofill, Angela, 234
Bolden, Buddy, 94, 108n, 115, 200, 263
Bolling, Claude, 280
boogie woogie, 19, 56, 57
Booker, Guy, *199–201*
Bowie, Lester, 266
Braff, Ruby, 221

Brand-New Heavies (group), 281
Braxton, Anthony, 233, 235, 250, 261
break routines, 93
Brillant, Maurice, 131
Brown, James, 233
Brown, Jasbo, 1
Brown, Tom, 10
Brubeck, Dave, 203, 226, 236, 270, 276–77
Burchfield, Robert, 8
Burleigh, Harry, 126
Butler, George, 271
Byrd, Donald, 281

C
cakewalks, 101
Calloway, Cab, 159, 189–90, 193, 195
Carmichael, Hoagy, 279
Carnegie Hall Corporation, 206, 257
Carrington, Terri Lyne, 245
Carroll, Joe, 65
Carter, Benny, 188
Carter, Betty, 65, 220
Carter, Elmer Anderson, *159–61*
Carter, James, 270
Castle, Vernon and Irene, 125
Charleston (dance), 82, 83
Charlie Parker: His Music and Life (Woideck), 195
Cherry, Don, 228
Chestnut, Cyrus, 270
Chicago, jazz in, 116, 211, 214
Christian, Charlie, 198
Christy, June, 64
cigarettes, and drug addiction, 193–94
Coeuroy, André, 90–91, 131
Coleman, Ornette, 27, 219, 221, 224, 225, 227, 238, 239, 240, 241, 247, 250, 261, 263, 276
Collier, James Lincoln, 158
Collier's (periodical), 173
"Colored Historians Too Lazy to Write Own History of Jazz." *See* Booker, Guy
Coltrane, John, 28, 39, 170, 212, 219, 226, 227, 228, 229, 247, 250, 264, 270
"Concerning Jazz." *See* Gilbert, Henry F.
Concise Guide to Jazz (Gridley), 37
Coniff, Ray, 22
Connor, Chris, 60, 63, 64
Cook, Will Marion, 107–8, 126
Copeland, Stewart, 279
Copland, Aaron, 150, 155, 276
Corbett, John, 273
Corea, Chick, 233, 238, 241, 242, 244, 277
Coss, Bill, 209–11
Coustaut, Sylvester, 111
Cox, Ida, 200

Creole Jazz Band, 272
Creole music, 96–97
Creole patois, 2
"Critic Raps False Interpretation." *See* Rose, Al
Crosby, Stills, Nash and Young, 240
Crouch, Stanley, 170, 259, 270

D
Dahl, Linda, 282
d'Alvarez, Marguerite, 143
Dameron, Tadd, 175
dance, African influence on, 88
Daniels, Eddie, 277
Davis, Anthony, 248, 255–56, 257, 269, 277
Davis, Eddie "Lockjaw," 187
Davis, Francis, *268–69, 270–71, 271–72*
Davis, Miles, 35, 167, 177, 195, 233, 238, 240,
    244, 270, 273, 278
Davis, Richard, 253
Dawson, Eddie, 103
Dearie, Blossom, 63
"Decade of 'What is Jazz?'" *See* Feather,
    Leonard
"Decline of Jazz, The" *141–43*
DeFranco, Buddy, 180
DeMicheal, Don, 209–11, 212
Desdunes, Daniel, 111, 112
Digable Planets (group), 281
"Discourse on Jazz, A." *See* Morton, Jelly Roll
Dixieland jazz, 8, 92, 93, 116, 173
Dixieland Jazz Band. *See* Original Dixieland
    Jazz Band
D'Lugoff, Art, 229, 232
Dolphy, Eric, 224, 227
Donaldson, Lou, 37
Dorham, Kenny, 177, 230
Doublet, Charles, 111–12, 113
Down Beat (periodical), 208, 209, 212–17, 229,
    242, 262, 273
Down Beat Music, 29
Drummond, Ray, 272
drums, role of, 18, 26, 32, 49, 51, 128, 187, 225,
    226
Dubuclet, Lawrence, 100
Dukas, Paul, 131

E
Early, Gerald, 168
Ebony (periodical), 207, 220
Ellington, Duke, 10, 19, 22–23, 157–58, 159,
    187, 205, 212, 244, 246
        as composer, 154–55
        in concert halls, 276
        durability of, 254
        and improvisation, 25

innovations of, 272
and jazz as a word, 11
and popular music, 239
popularity of, 250
and swing, 29, 34
on Winthrop Sargeant, 57
Ellis, Don, 209
Ellison, Lorraine, 65
Ellison, Ralph, 168–69
Emmett, Dan, 96
Encyclopedia of Jazz (Feather), 212
Engel, Carl, 132–33
"Entente" (Mulligan), 278, 279
Equal Opportunity Journal. See Opportunity
Esquire's Jazz Book, 182
Europe, James Reese, 1, 125, *126–27*
Evangelist (pseud.), *77–81*
Evans, Bill, 27, 237
Evans, Gil, 278

F
Faddis, Jon, 235
Faith, Percy, 22
family resemblances theory, 29–32. *See also*
    Wittgenstein, Ludwig
Father of the Blues (Handy), 157
Feather, Leonard, 188, 205, 212, *215–17,* 233,
    234–37
"Fewer Gigs Means Fewer Jazz Bands." *See*
    Orgill, Roxane
Filhe, George, 110–11, 112
Finck, Henry T., 82
Finckel, Eddie, 180
Finkelstein, Sidney, 205
Fischer, David, 96
Fitzgerald, Ella, 60, 61
Fitzgerald, F. Scott, 30
folk music. *See also* jazz, and folk music
        African American, 54
        defined, 54
"For Hipsters of the 90's." *See* Garcia, Guy
Ford, Richie, 236
Foster, Frank, 108, 187
Foster, Stephen, 82
Foster, Will, 106
Francis, W. T., 104, 108, 117
Franklin, Aretha, 65
funk, 280
fusion, 207–8, 233, 234, 235, 237–40, 241,
    243–44, 250, 269

G
Gabbard, Krin, *164–70*
Gade, Svend, *149–50*
Garcia, Guy, *280–81*

Gates, Henry Louis Jr., 169
Gershwin, George, 10, 143, 153, 276
Getz, Stan, 195
Giddins, Gary, 167, 264
Gilbert, Henry F., 144, *144–45*
Gillespie, Dizzy, 177, *178*, 187, 202, 216
 Armstrong on, 182
 and bebop, 250
 at Carnegie Hall, 174
 greatness of, 216
 as innovator, 179
 musical style of, 175
 negative criticism of, 180–81
 relevance today, 235
Gitler, Ira, 208–11, 214, 215
Gleason, Ralph, 14, 216
Gleeson, E. T. "Scoop," 5, 10
Goffin, Robert, 110, 111, 205
Golden Rule (group), 95
Goldstein, Walter, 1–8, 105–6
Goodman, Benny, 175, 199
 and black musicians, 198
 in Carnegie Hall, 47
 as "King of Swing," 159, 160
 record sales of, 35
 and swing beginnings, 178
 as teacher, 162
 Virgil Thomson on, 46
Gordon, Dexter, 195, 235
Gordon, Max, 231
Gorelik, Kenny G., 37, 240, 243, 244, 261
Gottlieb, Bill, 174, *175–76*
Gottschalk, Louis Moreau, 96, 100
Gould, Jack, 160–61
Gourse, Leslie, 282
Graettinger, Robert, 33
Granz, Norman, 174
Gridley, Mark, 18–20, 26, 28, 35n, 36, 37, 45, 280
Griffin, Johnny, 235
Griffith, Earl, 228
Guilcher, Jean-Michel, 97
guitar, jazz, 49, 70, 103, 109, 176, 206
Gushee, Lawrence, 3, 8, 13, 67, *68–75*, 91, *92–117*, 99n, 121

H
Hakim, Sadik (Argonne Thornton), 177
Hamilton, Scott, 236
Hammond, John, 198
Hampton, Lionel, 188, 198
Hancock, Herbie, 233, 237, 241, 242, 244, 248, 253
Handy, W. C., 157, 200
Hargrove, Roy, 269, 270, 272

Harlem Renaissance, 90
Harrell, Tom, 235–36
Harris, Craig, 269
Harrison, Donald, 245
Harrison, Max, 20
Hawkins, Coleman, 188, 190, 228, 461
Hearn, Lafcadio, 101–2, 104, 108
Heath, Jimmy, 179, 181
Henderson, Fletcher, 184, 198
Henderson, Harry, 174
Henderson, Horace, 184
Henderson, Joe, 241–42
Hendrix, Jimi, 279
Hentoff, Nat, 205, 209–11, 216
Herman, Woody, 30, 31, 180, 183, 199
Heywood, Eddie, 195
High Society (film), 166
Hill, Calvin, 242
Hines, Earl, 263
hip-hop, 280, 281
Hobson, Wilder, 19
Hodeir, André, 26
Hodges, Johnny, 22–23
Hoff, Robert, *18–20*, 36
Hogan, Ernest, 115, 116n
Hogan Jazz Archive, 108
Holbrook, Dick, 2–6, 8, 9–10
Holiday, Billie, 58–61, 180, 190, 195, 200, 223, 246
Holland, Dave, 233
Hopkins, Ernest J., *6–7*, 8
Horn, Shirley, 63
hot, as word, 48
Hot Jazz (Panassié), 11
Hourwich, Rebecca, *87–117*
Hubbard, Freddie, 243–44
Hughes, Langston, 201, 204
Hunter, Alberta, 236

I
improvisation. *See* jazz, and improvisation
"In Praise of Jazz, a Futurist Word." *See* Hopkins, Ernest J.
Inside Bebop (Feather), 188
Institute of Jazz Studies (Rutgers), 229
International House (film), 189–90
"Is Jazz Music?" *See* Sargeant, Winthrop
Isle of Wight Pop Festival, 240

J
Jackson, Michael, 170, 252
Jackson, Milt, 228
James, Bob, 234
jamming, 45, 48
Jarrett, Keith, 36, 234, 270, 279

jazz, 34–35
  and African American churches, 205
  African American roots of, 20, 57,
    77–81, 81, 82, 126, 130, 135–36,
    150–53, 197, 198
  African American writers on, x, 199–207
  and African music, 70, 88–91, 151, 198,
    227, 228
  as American music, 123, 134, 144
  analysis of, 39–76
  as art, 34–35, 206
  audiences for, 251
  avant-garde, 219–44, 245, 247, 249, 251,
    259
  black-white issue in, 136, 159–62,
    199–201, 251
  and blues, 221
  and classical music, 45, 55, 56, 130, 132,
    135, 152, 154, 155, 167, 179–81,
    221–22, 226, 251, 255, 275, 278
  in concert halls, 275–76
  courses on, 204–5, 207
  and dancing, 45, 70, 92, 97–98, 101n,
    148, 239
  decline predicted for, 140–42, 148
  defined, 10–11, 13–38, 122
  dissonance in, 147
  Dixieland, 230
  early, 121–58
  in England, 127–30, 146–47, 151
  in Europe, 16, 65–66, 122, 125, 126, 158,
    174, 280, 282
  evolution of, 55–56
  and folk music, 54–56, 58, 123, 163
  and gospel music, 65
  Harvard Dictionary of Music on, 19
  improvisation in, 17, 19–24, 22, 23, 25,
    30, 33, 35, 36, 39–40, 45, 55, 132–33,
    154, 241, 246–47, 250, 254
  Jews and, 151, 153–54
  as joyful, 125, 131
  jungle, 281
  meter in, 46
  negative reactions to, 11–12, 122–23,
    131, 134, 137, 145–50
  in the 1920s, x, 10, 11, 30, 72, 82, 122,
    134–35, 157, 176, 187, 275
  in the 1930s, 27, 34, 53, 72, 176, 187,
    250, 282
  in the 1940s, 215, 226, 250, 261, 279, 282
  in the 1950s, 220, 226, 229, 276
  in the 1960s, x, 34, 189, 196, 220, 226,
    233, 234, 242, 247, 250, 254, 258,
    261, 282
  in the 1970s, 233, 239, 242–43, 247, 250,
    254, 269, 280
  in the 1980s, 242, 245–74, 254, 268, 281
  in the 1990s, 275–82
  origins of, 77–120
  and politics, 251
  and popular music, 69, 132, 141, 144,
    156, 167, 170, 208
  and race, 197–217
  and ragtime, 90, 91, 116, 133, 136
  and rap, 37–38
  revival of traditional, 245–74
  rhythm and, 46
  and Russian music, 126
  and sexuality, 3, 153, 169, 170
  and swing, 27, 31, 35, 163, 228–29
  syncopation in, 18, 30, 135, 138
  tempo in, 28
  Third Stream, 276
  and timbre, 32
  and vaudeville, 164
  written, 132–33
"Jazz." *See* Austin, Cecil; Korngold, Julius
"Jazz: a Musical Discussion" (Engel), 131–33
"'Jazz'—an Educational Problem" (Stringham),
  133–34
jazz, as a word, 1–12, 92, 102–3, 122, 133
  and Creole patois, 2
  and dancing, 19
  first printed use of, 9–10
  first use in music, 10
  nonmusical uses of, 123
  Oxford English Dictionary on, 3, 9
  in sports, 1, 4, 7
Jazz: From Its Origins to the Present (Porter
  and Ullman), xi
Jazz: Hot and Hybrid (Sargeant), 53
Jazz, Le (Schaeffner and Coeuroy), 90–91, 132
"Jazz, the Word" (Tamony), 3
Jazz Age, 1920s as, 11, 30
jazz albums
  Birdland (Zawinul), 33
  Birth of the Cool (Davis), 278
  Bitches Brew (Davis), 233, 239
  Black, Brown & Beige (Ellington),
    22–23, 29, 30
  In the Box (Adderley), 248
  Dancing in Your Head (Coleman), 241
  Filles de Kilimanjaro (Davis), 238–39
  Hand on the Torch (Us3), 281
  Headhunters (Hancock), 233, 241
  High Life (Shorter), 238, 242
  Interstellar Space (Coltrane), 28
  Koko (Parker), 33
  Live at the Plugged Nickel (Davis), 239
  Lush Life (Strayhorn), 242

Miles in the Sky (Davis), 233
Olé Coltrane (Coltrane), 46
One O'Clock Jump (Basie), 33
Return to Forever (Corea), 233
Sorcerer (Davis), 233
Soul Experiment, A (Hubbard), 243–44
Think of One (Marsalis), 252
Uncle Josh in Society, 9
Jazz and the White Americans (Leonard), 143
"Jazz at Home." *See* Rogers, James A.
Jazz at Kennedy Center, 12
Jazz at Lincoln Center, 12, 219, 246, 259, 260, 261–62, 264, 265
"Jazz Avant Garde, The." *See* Baraka, Imamu Amiri
"Jazz Band Concert, A." *See* Berger, Francesco
jazz fans, 205
"Jazz Just Keeps Knocking at the Concert Hall Door." *See* Tucker, Mark
Jazz Mad. See Gade, Svend
Jazz Messengers (group), 228, 235, 253
"Jazz Moves Fast Forward into its Past." *See* Watrous, Peter
jazz musicians, 203
    as alcoholics, 190, 192
    artistic freedom of, 236
    budgets of, 237
    conservative, 247–48
    drugs and, 189–96
    fusion and, 244
    ideas for, 223
    and popular culture, 239
    women, 282
    young, 206, 268–71
Jazz on the Barbary Coast (Stoddard), 131–32
Jazz (periodical), 215
jazz pieces
    "Beale Street Blues" (Handy), 136
    "Bird in Igor's Yard, A" (Russell), 180
    "Birdland" (Zawinul), 33
    "Boo Boo's Birthday" (Monk), 244
    "Boyd Meets Stravinsky" (Finckel), 180
    "Buddy Bolden Blues" (Morton), 94
    "Chameleon" (Hancock), 233
    "Chant of the Weed" (Redman), 189, 193
    "Cheryl" (Bird), 225
    "Come Along, I'm Through With Worrying" (Creamer and Layton), 135, 136
    "Condition Blue" (McLean), 225
    "Confirmation" (Bird), 225
    "Coon Jine, Baby, Coon Jine," 107
    "Criss Cross" (Monk), 244
    "Darktown Strutters' Ball" (Brooks), 14
    "Dr. Jackle" (McLean), 225
    "Emanon" (Gillespie), 180
    "Fables of Faubus" (Mingus), 168
    "Fine Romance, A" (Kern), 59–60
    "Four in One" (Monk), 225
    "Hot and Bothered" (Ellington), 156
    "How High the Moon" (Hamilton and Lewis), 176
    "Minnie the Moocher" (Calloway), 193
    "In the Mood" (Garland and Razaf), 177
    "Mood Indigo" (Ellington), 156
    "Muggles" (Armstrong), 189
    "My Favorite Things" (Coltrane), 46
    "One O'Clock Jump" (Basie), 33
    "Ramblin'" (Coleman), 225
    "Rhapsody in Blue" (Gershwin), 28, 30, 33, 276
    "Shuffle Along" (Sissle and Blake), 135
    "Song is You, The" (Adderley), 231
    "St. Louis Tickle" (Barney and Seymore), 94
    "Sweet Sue" (Armstrong), 189
    "Tea for Two" (Caesar and Youmans), 62
    "Things to Come" (Gillespie), 175
    "Tiger Rag" (Edwards, LaRocca, Spargo, Shields, and De Costa), 176
    "West End Blues" (Armstrong), 181
    "Whispering (Groovin' High)," 176
    "Willow, Weep for Me" (Adderley), 231
Jazz Singer, The (film), 20, 30, 34
jazz singers, 57–67
    gospel music and, 65
    improvisation and, 60–62, 63, 66
Jazz Styles: History and Analysis (Gridley), 17, 37ww
"Jazz Swings Back to Tradition." *See* Pareles, Jon
Jazz Talk (Gold), 4
Jazzmen (Ramsey and Smith), 115
Jenkins, Willard, *260–68*
"Jim Crow on the Band Stand." *See* Moore, Phil
Johnson, Budd, 189
Johnson, Bunk, 216
Johnson, Charles S., *82–83*, 84, 121, *122–25*
Johnson, James Weldon, 201, 204
Jolson, Al, 20, 30, 34, 153
Jones, Elvin, 226
Jones, Jo, 53
Jones, LeRoi. *See* Baraka, Imamu Amiri
Jones, Quincy, 203
Jones, Thad, 187
Joplin, Scott, 94, 256
Jordan, Sheila, 65
Joseph Papp Public Theater, 257

K

Kart, Larry, 243
Keepnews, Orrin, 205
Kellaway, Roger, 277–78, 279
Kennedy, Nigel, 276
Kenny G. *See* Gorelik, Kenny G.
Kenton, Stan, 22, 33, 64, 174
Kern, Jerome, 132
Kingdom of Swing (Goodman), 198
Kingsley, Walter, 2–3, 93, 102
Kirk, Roland, 229
Kirkland, Kenny, 245
Klugh, Earl, 234
Kmen, Henry, 95–96, 97, 117
Kofsky, Frank, 215
Kool Jazz Festival, 250
Korngold, Julius, *147–49*
Kostelanetz, André, 22
Krehbiel, Henry, 101–4
Krog, Karin, 66
Krupa, Gene, 195, 278

L

Laine, Cleo, 60, 66
Lambert, Constant, 150, *151–54, 154–57*
Lamothe, Ferdinand Joseph. *See* Morton, Jelly
    Roll
Lange, Horst, 92–94
Lash, Irving, 175
Lawrence, Elliott, 278
Lawson, John Howard, 123
Ledbetter, Huddie "Leadbelly," 13
Leonard, Neil, 144
Lester Young Anthology, A (Porter, ed.), 67
"Lester Young's 'Shoe Shine Boy.'" *See*
    Gushee, Lawrence
Lewis, George, 269
Lewis, John, 203, 226, 272–73, 276
Lewis, Ted, 34, 139
Lifetime (group), 240
"Like Young." *See* Davis, Francis
Lincoln, Abbey, 208–11
Locke, Alain, 53–54, 89–90, *162–64*
Lomax, Alan, 13, 200, 205

M

Ma, Yo Yo, 276, 280
Madame Jazz (Gourse), 282
Major, Clarence, 2
Malcolm X, 216
Malson, Lucien, 90–91
Man Called Adam, A (film), 167
Man with the Golden Arm, The (film), 195
Mangione, Chuck, 22
Manhattan Transfer (group), 24, 29, 30, 35

Manuel, Peter, 26
Marsalis, Branford, 245, 248, 269
Marsalis, Ellis, 253
Marsalis, Wynton, 245, 248, 249, 252–54, 257,
    259, 260–68, 269, 272
Marshall, Marilyn, *207*, 245
Martin, Henry, 20
Masland, Tom, 271, 272
Matas, Rudolph, 104
Matthews, Ralph, *191–94*
Maxham, Robert, *18–20*, 36
Mayer, Steven, 276
McBride, Christian, 270
McFerrin, Bobby, 280
McGhee, Howard, 195
McIntyre, Ken, 224
McLean, Jackie, 8, 225, 253
McRae, Carmen, 60, 63
Meldhau, Brad, 196
Messenger, The (periodical), 90
Metheny, Pat, 234
Metronome (periodical), 99, 216, 229
Milhaud, Darius, 276
Miller, Glenn, 20, 30, 35, 177
Miller, Mulgrew, 245
Mills, Florence, 137
Mills Brothers, 165
Mingus, Charles, 168, 237, 246
Mister Jelly Roll (Lomax), 14
Mitchell, Joni, 237
Mo' Better Blues (film), 167
Modern Jazz Quartet (group), 31, 273
Monk, Thelonious, 167, 175, 182, 200, 222, 244,
    261, 279
Moore, Phil, *161–62*
Morgenstern, Dan, 212, *230–32*
Morton, Jelly Roll (Ferdinand Joseph
    Lamothe), 13, *14–16*, 36, 200, 256
Muhammed, Elijah, 209, 210
Mulligan, Gerry, 226, 236, 277, 278
Murphy, Mark, 65
Murray, Albert, 168, 267, 270
Murray, David, 248, 249, 251–52, 255, 257–59,
    269
Murray, Sonny, 229
Music Ho! (Lambert), 150–53
musicals, Broadway, 22
Musician, The (periodical), 140–42

N

Nash, Ted, 236
National Endowment for the Arts, 208, 256
Native Americans, 198
Navarro, Fats, 195
Needle, The (periodical), 57

"Negro-American Music or the Origin of Jazz." *See* Sargant, Norman and Tom
"Negro Explains Jazz, A." *See* Europe, James Reese
"Negro Music" (Cook), 107
"Negro Music Goes to Par." *See* Locke, Alain
"Negroes Don't Know Anything About Jazz." *See* Taylor, Billy
Nelson, Louis Delille "Big Eye," 109–10, 227
Nelson, Oliver, 228
New Negro, The (Locke), 89–90, 162
New Orleans (film), 167
New Orleans jazz, 17, 47, 94, 180, 187, 216
    African Americans and, 98–99
    and Afro-Spanish music, 103–5, 111
    and dance halls, 115
    Henry Kmen on, 95
    and jazz as a word, 8, 9, 92, 102
    in the nineteenth century, 98–100
    and ragtime, 107–8
Nickerson, William, 112
Niles, Edward, 157, *157–58*
Nunez, Alcide "Yellow," 93
Nyro, Laura, 61, 240

O

O'Day, Anita, 61, 64
Oliver, Joe, 223, 272
Opportunity (periodical), 81–82, 121, 159
"Or not to Bop." *See* Beneke, Tex
Oregon (group), 234
Orgill, Roxane, 272–73
"Origin of Jazz." *See* Johnson, Charles S.
Original Dixieland "Jass" Band, 8, 92, 93, 116, 198, 282
Osgood, Henry, 18
Ottley, Roi, 201
Owens, Thomas, 68

P

Panassié, Hughes, 205
Pareles, Jon, *149–259*, 248
Paris Blues (film), 167, 185
Parker, Charlie, 68, 166, 177, 187, 202, 221, 264
    and bebop, 250
    on Calloway, 195
    and classical music, 179–80
    and drugs, 190
    greatness of, 174, 175, 216
    and the human voice, 228
    imitators of, 223–24
    and improvisation, 69n
    innovations of, 72, 73, 216, 219
    negative criticism of, 182
    solos of, 39

Thomas Owens on, 68
Parker, Horatio, 122
Parton, Dolly, 237
Payton, Nicholas, 270
Pekar, Harvey, 26, 27–28
Peress, Maurice, 276
Perez, Manuel, 111–12, 113
Perlman, Itzhak, 279, 280
Peter, Paul, and Mary, 20, 34, 37
Peterson, Gilles, 281
Peterson, Oscar, 222
Piaf, Edith, 61, 63
Piano Jazz. See Waterman, Glenn
Piazza, Tom, 268–69
Picou, Alphonse, 109–10
Placksin, Sally, 282
Playboy (periodical), 20, 34, 37
"Plea for Less Critical Infighting, A." *See* Feather, Leonard
"Plus de Jazz." *See* Bell, Clive
"Point of Contact: a Discussion." *See* Morgenstern, Dan, ed.
popular music, defined, 54–55
Porter, Cole, 137
Porter, Lewis, 282
Powell, Bud, 177, 221
Primer of Jazz (Hughes), 201, 204
"Processional" (Lawson), 123
Pullman, Peter, 14

R

radio, African American, 207
Raeburn, Boyd, 175, 180, 216
ragtime, 90, 91, 94, 96, 99, 101, 106–17, 108, 113–15, 122, 123, 125, 137–42
Rampal, Jean-Pierre, 280
rap, 37–38
Ravel, Maurice, 276
Rawls, Lou, 65
Real Jazz, The (Panassié), 11
Reception of Jazz in America (Collier), 158
Record Review (periodical), 179
Redman, Don, 189, 193
Redman, Joshua, 268, 270, 271, 272
Reys, Rita, 66
rhythm and blues, 214, 228
rhythm and blues, alternative, 281
Rich, Buddy, 246
ride rhythm, 26
Ridley, Jasper, 8
riffs, 15, 16
Roach, Max, 207, 209–11, 253
Robinson, J. Russell, 93
rock 'n' roll, 65, 190, 199, 238, 239, 242, 250
Rockwell, John, 246–47

Rogers, James A., 89, *90*, *125–26*
Rogers, Shorty, 203, 226
Rolling Stone (periodical), 281
Rollins, Sonny, 224, 228, 236, 238
Ronstadt, Linda, 279
Rose, Al, *180–81*
Rouse, Charlie, 264
Roussel, Albert, 131
Ruff, Willie, 19
Russell, Bill, 108, 110, 115
Russell, George, 180, 212, 276
Rust, Brian, 20, 35

S
Safire, William, 8–9
Samuels, O. M., 114–16
Sanders, Pharoah, 251
Sargant, Norman and Tom, *83–84*, *154*
Sargeant, Winthrop, 53, 55, *56–57*
scatting, 225
Schaeffner, André, 90–91, 131
Schifrin, Lalo, 209
Schirmer, G., Inc., 132
Schnitter, Dave, 236
Schoenberg, Arnold, 221
Schuller, Gunther, 63, 68, 70, 276
Schumann, Robert, 50
Scott, Jimmy, 65
Seldes, Gilbert, 122, 124, *134–40*
Seven Lively Arts, The (Seldes), 133–40
Shaw, Sam, 174
Shepp, Archie, 211, *212–15*, 224, 227, 228, 229, 230–32, 251, 253
Shorter, Wayne, 224, 227, 228, 238, 240–242, 244
Simmons, John, 195
Simon, George, *185*
Sinatra, Frank, 61, 195
Since Cézanne (Bell), 137–38
"Skies of America" (Coleman), 276
Slattery, William "Spike," 10
slavery, African American, 80, 84–87, 86–87, 89
Smith, Bessie, 58, 180, 200
Smith, Charles E., 205
Smith, Leroy "Stuff," 191–92, 202
So This Is Jazz (Osgood), 11
Société des Jeunes Amis, 112
"Songs of Ascent" (Kellaway), 277
"Songs of the Blacks." *See* Evangelist
"Sonny's Dream" (Baldwin), 166, 169
Southern, Jeri, 63
Spaeth, Sigmund, 18
speakeasies, 191, 192
"Spirit of Jazz, The." *See* Lambert, Constant
spirituals, African American, 79, 135

Spriccio, Tutor, 93
Spriggins, E. Belfield, 94
St. Cyr, Johnny, 94–95
Stephens, Roy W., *182–84*
Stewart, Buddy, 178
Sting, 248
Stitt, Sonny, 27
Stoddard, Tom, 132
Stoltzman, Richard, 276, 280
Stone, Sly, 233
Stormy Weather (Dahl), 282
"Story of Jazz, The." *See* Basie, William "Count"
Storyville (periodical), 3
Straton, John Roach, 143, 147
Straus, Nick, 11, 37
Stravinsky, Igor, 137, 142, 150, 179, 221
Strayhorn, Billy, 242, 244
Stringham, Edwin, 133–34, 150
Sullivan, Ira, 211
Sullivan, Lester, 112
Supersax (group), 24
swing, 28, 30, 34, 228–29
    and African Americans, 159–72
    and bebop, 182
    contemporary, 249
    and dance music, 27, 48
    decline of, 175
    defined, 21, 36, 45, 53
    early, 110–11
    quantitative music and, 47–49
    and speakeasies, 191
    syncopation in, 25, 26
    tempo in, 26
    as two-step, 447
"Swing." *See* Carter, Elmer Anderson
"Swing Again." *See* Thomson, Virgil
swing bands, 49–52. *See also* individual performers
Swing Wedding (film), 169

T
Tabackin, Lew, 236
Tamony, Peter, 3, 4, 9, 10
Taylor, Billy, 133, 201, *202–7*, 220
Taylor, Cecil, 23, 26, 29, 31, 219, 227, 229, 230, 231–32, 232, 261
"Technique of the Jazz Singer." *See* Bennett, Richard Rodney
Termini, Joe, 231
Terrasson, Jacky, 270, 272
They All Played Ragtime (Janis and Blesh), 110
Thinking in Jazz (Berliner), 39, 55
Thomas, David Clayton, 61

Thomson, Virgil, 18, 45–46, 47–53, 167
Thornhill, Claude, 278
Thornton, Argonne. *See* Hakim, Sadik
"Three Approaches to Jazz." *See* Gridley
Time (periodical), 269
Tio, Lorenzo Sr., 109, 111–12, 113
Tio, Luis, 109
To Be or Not to Bop (Gillespie), 174
"To Bop . . . ." *See* Gillespie, Dizzy
"Toujours Jazz." *See* Seldes, Gilbert
trade unions, musicians', 160–62
tribalism, and jazz, 197–98
Tucker, Mark, 275–80
Tupper, Martin, 153
Turkey Trot (dance), 114–16
Twelve Monkeys (film), 164
twelve-tone technique, 188
two-step, 113–15, 447
Tyers, William, 126
Tyner, McCoy, 242

U
Urban Species (group), 281

V
Vallee, Rudy, 19, 34
Van Dyck, Henry, 122
Van Vechten, Carl, 123
Variety (periodical), 114, 116
Vaughan, Sarah, 59, 60, 63, 180, 236
Ventura, Charlie, 178
Victrola, 93, 124
Village Voice (periodical), 262, 263
Vinson, Eddie "Cleanhead," 181
Virgil Thomson Reader, 46
voice, human, 227

W
Waits, Freddie, 242
Wallace, Michele, 169–70
Waller, Fats, 31, 236
Walmsley, Buck, 212, 214
Ware, Wilbur, 224, 226
Waring, Fred, 178

Washington, Dinah, 188, 200
Waterman, Glenn, 40, 42–45
Watrous, Bill, 236
Watrous, Peter, 237, 238–42, 246, 247–48, 261
Weather Report (group), 33, 238, 240–41
Webern, Anton, 221
Welk, Lawrence, 215
Wenrich, Percy, 110, 111
West, George, 30
"Where Jazz Begins." *See* Hourwich, Rebecca
Whitehead, Kevin, 260–63
Whiteman, Paul, 34, 91, 132, 134, 137, 139,
    142, 145, 198, 199, 276
Whitney, Dwight, 182
William Ransom Hogan Jazz Archive (Tulane),
    103, 110
Williams, Cootie, 248
Williams, Joe, 243–44
Williams, Martin, 215
Williams, Mary Lou, 188, 282
Williams, Tony, 240
Wilson, Teddy, 162, 177, 198
Winick, Charles, 195–96
Winston, George, 34–35
Winstone, Norma, 66
Wittgenstein, Ludwig, 29, 30, 34, 37
Woideck, Carl, 195
Woodson, Carter G., 201
Workman, Reggie, 261
World's Columbia Exposition (Chicago), 107,
    108
Wright, Specs, 181
"Writer Raps Armstrong." *See* Stephens, Roy
    W.
"Wynton Bites Back." *See* Jenkins, Willard

Y
Yancey, Jimmy, 200
Youmans, Vincent, 19
Young, Lester, 67–75, 190, 228

Z
Zawinul, Joe, 33, 244
Ziegfeld, Florenz, 3